The Power of Assessment

Transforming Teaching and Learning

Margo L. Dichtelmiller

Foreword by Diane Trister Dodge

 **Teaching**Strategies® · Washington, D.C.

Editor: Toni Bickart
Design, layout, and production: Abner Nieves
Selected illustrations: Anthony LeTourneau
Cover design: Martha Leone, Jeff Cross

Teaching Strategies, Inc.
P.O. Box 42243
Washington, DC 20015

www.TeachingStrategies.com

Teaching Strategies, The Creative Curriculum, and Teaching Strategies GOLD names and logos are registered trademarks of Teaching Strategies, Inc.
The Work Sampling System is a registered trademark of Pearson Education, Inc.
HighScope is a registered trademark of the HighScope Educational Research Foundation.
Teaching Strategies Assessment Opportunity Cards is a trademark of Teaching Strategies, Inc.
The Ounce Scale is a trademark of Pearson Education, Inc.
Focused Portfolios is a trademark of Redleaf Press.

ISBN: 978-1-60617-392-3

Library of Congress Cataloging-in-Publication Data

Dichtelmiller, Margo L. (Margo Lizabeth), 1954-
  The power of assessment : transforming teaching and learning / Margo L. Dichtelmiller ; foreword by Diane Trister Dodge.
      p. cm.
  Includes bibliographical references.
  ISBN 978-1-60617-392-3
  1. Educational tests and measurements--United States. 2. Early childhood education--United States--Evaluation. I. Title.
  LB3051.D533 2011
  371.260973--dc23
                    2011022397

1 2 3 4 5 6 7 8 9 10   17 16 15 14 13 12 11
         Printing   Year Printed

Printed and bound in United States of America.

Dedicated to

Dorothea (Dot) Marsden, for her deep understanding of young children, steadfast commitment to their development, and enthusiastic support of all my endeavors.

Acknowledgments

The Power of Assessment is based on my own experiences as an early childhood teacher, a consultant, and a professor teaching undergraduates and teachers about assessment. However, it was not created in isolation. I relied on the stories and experiences of colleagues, teachers, and students to help me illustrate the benefits and rewards of assessment. In particular, a group of teachers and pre-service teachers were my regular consultants on the book. They included Laura Brown, Centennial Lane Elementary, Howard County, Maryland; Becky Forsyth, Children's Institute, Eastern Michigan University, Ypsilanti, MI; Julie E. Glowski, EMU student, Livonia, MI; Elaine Greer, family child care provider, Eagan, MN; Erin Hampton, Oregon Child Development Coalition, Klamath Falls, OR; Patricia Lakos, Eastern Michigan University student, Howell, MI; Sally Mowers, Great Start School Readiness Program, Howell, MI; Robin Psenka, Gretchen's House at Little Oaks, Pontiac, MI; Louis Romei, Garfield Early Childhood Learning Center, Garfield, NJ; Katie Rosander, University of Michigan Towsley Children's House, Ann Arbor, MI; Angelique Rudolph, University of Michigan Towsley Children's House, Ann Arbor, MI; Debra Stevens, Perry Child Development Center, Ypsilanti, MI; Lesley Straley, kindergarten teacher, Townshend, VT; and Krista Walton, Discovery Center, Ann Arbor, MI. (When their accounts are included in this book, names were changed.)

My thanks go to a group of colleagues who read chapters, answered questions about their work as consultants and educators, and otherwise helped in a variety of ways: Dr. Martha Baiyee, Eastern Michigan University; Dr. Kim Browning, HighScope Educational Research Foundation; Dr. Julie Culhane, etc educational training and consulting, Northampton, MA; Sue Dieter, Tecumseh Public Schools; Dr. Aviva Dorfman, University of Michigan-Flint; Dr. Sylvia Jones, Eastern Michigan University; Melissa Kaden, etc educational training and consulting, Amherst, MA; Dot Marsden, early childhood consultant, Rock Hill, SC; Beth Marshall, HighScope Educational Research Foundation; Dr. Pat Pokay, Eastern Michigan University; and Charlotte Stetson, early childhood consultant, Hancock, ME.

Thanks go to Larry Bram, who was publisher at Teaching Strategies, Inc. when this project was conceptualized. Thanks also to the Teaching Strategies staff members who helped with editing, design, and production: Toni Bickart, Jeff Cross, Martha Leone, Francine Markowitz, Abner Nieves, Laurie Taub, and Margot Ziperman.

This book would not have been completed without Judy R. Jablon and Amy Laura Dombro, who were regular collaborators throughout the writing. Judy maintained the broad vision of the book, paid persistent attention to detail and continuity, discussed endless questions, and provided ongoing moral support. Amy Dombro brought an unrelenting focus on the story, the reader, and the teacher, and she kept the book user-friendly and grounded in classroom life. And finally, my love and thanks to my partner, Nancy Katz, for her love and support during all phases of the book: procrastinating and worrying about doing so, writing regularly, and wanting to write all the time to finish it.

I hope this book will help teachers realize that the purpose of classroom assessment reflects why they went into teaching: They love getting to know children and want to support their growth.

Margo Dichtelmiller
June 2011

Contents

Foreword

It gives me great pleasure to introduce *The Power of Assessment*. This wonderful book is Margo Dichtelmiller's important new contribution to the field of early childhood assessment. All of us who are concerned about positive child outcomes can learn from the book's focus on assessment to support learning. Because intentional teaching is essential to children's learning, we need to strengthen our understanding of how teachers can use information systematically to improve teaching and learning for all children.

The Power of Assessment honors the work teachers do to build supportive relationships with children and promote children's learning. Margo argues convincingly that the assessment process can be a powerful classroom tool. By explaining the assessment process as a cycle, *The Power of Assessment* shows why assessment information is essential to everything teachers do. It is a process to be understood and valued, rather than considered burdensome and constraining.

In my work with teachers, I am often asked, "What and how much information do I have to collect?" *The Power of Assessment* uses classroom scenarios to answer that question. Margo discusses when and how to use checklists and rating scales, how to record and organize observation notes, and how organizing careful selections of children's work in portfolios supports teachers' ability to analyze the information they gather.

A strong and unique emphasis of this book is how the assessment process can help children become active, self-directed learners. Margo also guides teachers' collaboration with family members, explaining the kinds of information family members need and want from teachers and the information families can offer to teachers.

Given the wide variety of assessment instruments, it is essential that potential users understand what each tool is designed to do. *The Power of Assessment* explains how to evaluate the quality of an assessment tool. By using classroom examples to explore the concepts of reliability, validity, and fairness, Margo makes these concepts meaningful and clear. She then provides detailed information and samples from three high-quality assessment systems, including our own *Teaching Strategies GOLD*®.

Diane Trister Dodge
President
Teaching Strategies, Inc.

CHAPTER 1

Introduction

Assessment can be a daunting word that conjures up memories of last-minute preparation and of tests covering unstudied material. The word may also stir feelings of anxiety or fear of being judged. For teachers, *assessment* may mean program mandates—difficult and detailed multistep tasks that create more paperwork and leave less time for teaching.

Nevertheless, assessment is something you do every day in your personal life. When you smell a melon to see whether or not it is ripe, test-drive cars before deciding which to buy, or take your child's temperature to determine whether or not to call the doctor, you are assessing. Each time you use a meat thermometer to check whether or not a roast is done, change a necklace after looking in the mirror, taste soup before adding salt, or try on five pairs of black pants in order to purchase one pair—you guessed it—you are assessing. When you collect information in order to make good decisions, you are using an assessment process.

You assess every day in your professional life as well, whether consciously or unconsciously. When you scan the classroom to make sure each child is engaged with an activity, observe a child working a puzzle and decide to offer help before he becomes frustrated, or review children's reading comprehension skills before planning ways to promote those skills during small-group time, you are assessing. In fact, research shows that teachers spend about a quarter to a third of their time in assessment-related activities (Stiggins, 2007).

Assessment is a powerful teaching tool. The gathered information contributes greatly to your work by

- reinforcing your knowledge of child development
- enriching your relationships with children
- strengthening communication with families
- providing the foundation for program decisions
- enhancing your sense of professionalism

Effective assessment requires that teachers have an attitude of *persistent curiosity* about children, teaching, and learning. Teachers actively search for information rather than wait passively to experience an insight about children. Cultivating the mindset of a researcher or investigator is necessary to being an effective assessor and, as a result, an effective teacher.

A Personal Look at Assessment

My interest in assessment began when I was an early childhood special education teacher. Full of energy and ideas—having just completed a master's program—I planned to assess my children's progress regularly and systematically. I wanted to get to know the children and find out about their knowledge and skills in order to create opportunities for them to take new developmental steps.

I loved getting to know the children in my classroom. I was curious about them and constantly asked,

- What do they like to do?
- What captures their minds? Their hearts?
- What do they know?
- What skills do they have?
- How do they learn?
- What are their unique qualities?

To find answers to my questions, I created a long, detailed assessment tool, compiling items from other early childhood assessment instruments. This predated computers, so I mimeographed a copy for each child.

Each page had one or two items, along with statements describing levels of each skill. Needless to say, I completed the entire checklist for each child *only once* before realizing that my checklist was unmanageable. It was impossible for me to use it frequently enough to assess the children, who grew and changed very quickly.

Beyond Paperwork: Intentional Assessment to Support Learning

Many teachers get so caught up in the paperwork, requirements, and "how-to" of assessment that they forget its main purpose, which is to figure out how best to support children's learning. You are incredibly busy every day, so, to be powerful, an assessment process must collect the right information, gather the right amount of information, and document it in an efficient and targeted way. Most importantly, you need efficient ways to translate what you learn about children into good decisions and teaching strategies.

Looking back, I had some basic questions about making the assessment process work for me. These questions continued to guide my thinking as I worked with colleagues to develop *The Work Sampling System*® (Dichtelmiller, Jablon, Dorfman, Marsden, & Meisels, 2001; Dichtelmiller, Jablon, Marsden, & Meisels, 2001). These questions still guide my thinking as I teach undergraduate and graduate students. You may have similar questions.

What information should I collect? I quickly realized that, before I could determine what to collect, I had to be clear about what I wanted to learn. What were my questions about children? I knew I had questions about children's physical, language, cognitive, and social–emotional development. I also knew that some information is easy to collect but that gathering other information is far more difficult. It is easy, for example, to find out whether a child can rote count, name shapes, or hop on one foot. Capturing children's motivation to learn, their enthusiasm, and their problem-solving skills is far more difficult. Although these skills and behaviors are harder to assess, they are vital to children's learning and their futures as competent adults.

How should I gather information? How much do I need? My lengthy checklist was certainly not realistic—or efficient! I had to figure out how to collect information systematically so that I could effectively answer my questions. I continually tried new assessment methods. I learned that my observations were more meaningful when I was not testing children.

You might be wondering, "Were you really testing preschoolers?" Yes, I confess: I was. Like many early childhood teachers, I worked one-to-one with children in a quiet corner of the classroom, asking them questions and having them perform tasks on demand. However, I soon realized that I learned more about them during play, routines, and other typical classroom activities than when I was busy testing for my checklist.

What am I learning about each child? After several weeks of collecting information about children, I frequently felt overwhelmed by my documentation. I knew that I had a great deal of information, but it was not very organized and therefore not easy to use. I had to organize the data and put the pieces of information together in order to understand each child in a new way. I realized that collecting assessment information was only useful when I regularly took the time to interpret it. The review process enabled me to draw some tentative conclusions about the children. I knew these conclusions might change as I gathered new information, but they summarized what I understood at that moment about each child.

How do I use what I learn? I was never sure I was incorporating what I was learning from my checklist in my weekly planning and interactions with children. For example, I once reviewed my checklist and wished that, before I put two balance beams in the obstacle course, I had remembered that Danny was afraid to walk on balance beams. One beam surely would have been enough! I wished that, when I counted bears with Rosa, I had recalled her mastery of rote counting through ten but that she needed help with understanding quantity—what *five* really means. I needed a routine to make sure that what I learned from assessment became part of my planning and teaching.

These questions motivated me to continue to learn about assessment and how different kinds of assessment information and processes could help me be a more effective teacher. As I thought about these questions, I realized that assessment is a cycle in which teachers ask questions, collect data, interpret the data, and take action.

What Lies Ahead

The Power of Assessment is for early childhood teachers—and aspiring early childhood teachers—who work daily to build supportive relationships with children and who strive to fine-tune their teaching. It shows how assessing young children in mindful, deliberate ways leads to more effective teaching and better outcomes.

Children's learning is at the heart of this book. The most important measure of successful teaching is its positive impact on children's learning. *The Power of Assessment* is about a particular type of assessment, which is known as *assessment for learning*. It is also called *formative assessment* (McMillan, 2007; Popham, 2008). The term refers to how teachers collect and use information in a systematic way to enhance children's learning (McMillan, 2007; Popham, 2008).

Teachers, children, and families are the important players in *The Power of Assessment*, with teachers assuming the primary responsibility for assessment. It is the teacher who answers the questions "What do I want children to learn today?" and "What do I want to learn about children today?" (C. Stetson, personal communication, January 22, 2008). This book's goal is to help you realize the power of assessing children by answering those questions.

The Power of Assessment begins in **Chapter 1** with an overview of assessment. **Chapter 2** defines assessment as a cycle and presents the purposes and types of early childhood assessment tools. **Chapter 3** further defines assessment for learning and describes in greater depth the interrelationships relationships among assessing, teaching, and learning.

Each part of the assessment cycle is discussed at length in chapters 4–11. **Chapter 4** addresses the questions that initiate the assessment cycle and considers two primary assessment challenges: what information to collect (the content of assessment) and how much information to collect.

Chapters 5–9 examine methods for collecting information and discussing assessment with children and families. **Chapter 5** explains how to observe. **Chapter 6** explores how teachers use checklists and rating scales to summarize information gained by observing. **Chapter 7** explains how to supplement observational assessment information by organizing children's work in portfolios and analyzing it.

Chapters 8 and 9 explore how teachers communicate with children and families about assessment. **Chapter 8** discusses strategies for helping children become active, self-directed learners. **Chapter 9** addresses the process of collaborating with families to gather assessment information. It also talks about using written reports and conducting family–teacher conferences.

An important part of the assessment cycle is analyzing information correctly and planning next steps. Toward this end, **Chapter 10** focuses on the process of interpreting the data you have collected. To be sure you understand the information and interpret it accurately, you need systems in place for reviewing and analyzing the data. **Chapter 11** highlights the many ways teachers can base their actions on their interpretations of assessment data.

Chapters 12–14 focus on broad early childhood assessment issues. Teachers are often consulted when tools are being selected, so these chapters enable you to gather data to inform your opinions. **Chapter 12** explores how to evaluate the quality of an assessment tool. Validity, reliability, and fairness are emphasized. **Chapter 13** includes an overview of several widely used, high-quality early childhood assessment tools. **Chapter 14** describes tests and the problems with using them to assess young children.

Chapter 15 once again focuses directly on you, the teacher. It summarizes the power of assessment for classroom teachers, offers strategies for realizing those powers, and proposes steps to take as you move forward to expand the role of assessment in your teaching.

As you integrate the assessment cycle and its processes into the daily routines of classroom life, your curiosity about children, learning, and teaching deepens. Most importantly, teaching becomes even more satisfying as you try new approaches and develop positive relationships with each and every child in your class. For me, assessment's greatest power is that it enables you to get to know children as learners—and as individuals. Once you have positive relationships with children and their families, you can more effectively foster children's development, learning, and curiosity about the world.

References

Dichtelmiller, M. L., Jablon, J. R., Dorfman, A. B., Marsden, D. B., & Meisels, S. J. (2001). *Work sampling in the classroom: A teacher's manual* (4th ed.). New York: Pearson.

Dichtelmiller, M. L., Jablon, J. R., Marsden, D. B., & Meisels, S. J. (2001). *The Work Sampling System omnibus guidelines: Preschool through third grade* (4th ed.). New York: Pearson PyschCorp™.

McMillan, J. H. (Ed.). (2007). *Formative classroom assessment: Theory and practice*. New York: Teachers College Press.

Popham, W. J. (2008). *Transformative assessment*. Alexandria, VA: ASCD.

Stiggins, R. J. (2007). Conquering the formative assessment frontier. In J. H. McMillan (Ed.), *Formative classroom assessment* (pp. 8–28). New York: Teachers College Press.

CHAPTER 2

Early Childhood Assessment: The Big Picture

Early childhood assessment is a broad term that can be used to describe each of these situations:

A preschool teacher analyzes a collection of observation notes she has recorded over the course of a week in order to make plans for the coming week's activities.

A school psychologist gives a battery of tests to a young child to determine the type and extent of the child's disabilities.

A program director compiles data about children's learning to show that her program is effective.

A group of teachers uses a standardized instrument to evaluate the literacy environment in their classrooms.

Federal officials monitor the quality and effectiveness of Head Start programs.

As you can see from these examples, educators use assessment information for many purposes. This chapter presents basic information about early childhood assessment. It discusses

- assessment as a cycle
- purposes of assessment
- types of assessment and assessment tools
- use of a variety of assessment tools

Defining Assessment as a Cycle

Assessment is defined in many different ways (McAfee & Leong, 2007; Mindes, 2007). *The Power of Assessment* defines it as a systematic process of collecting and interpreting information in order to answer questions about children's development and learning.

Assessment is a *cyclical process* involving several steps. It begins with a question—often something you want to learn—that arises because you must make a decision. Depending on the question, information is collected in a variety of ways. Once collected, this information is referred to as *data* or *evidence*. Next, you interpret the data. Then, on the basis of what you have learned, you decide how to support the child's development and learning. Here are the steps of the assessment cycle:

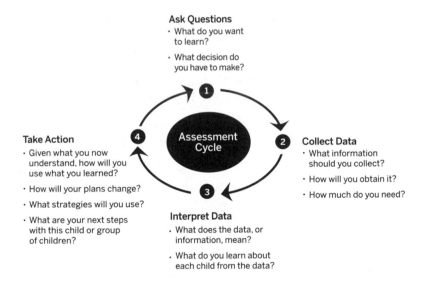

Assessment is called a *cycle* because the four steps continuously repeat. Each time you put your plan into action, you observe how the child responds. This in turn leads to new questions and decisions. They are the focus of your next assessment activities.

Effective teachers assess children throughout each day, whether they are aware of it or not. As you read the following example, notice how Mallory uses the assessment cycle of asking questions, collecting data, interpreting the evidence, and taking action to support children's learning.

> Mallory reads a story to the children at the beginning of the week. She chooses *Giraffes Can't Dance*, by Giles Andreae and Guy Parker-Rees, and plans how she will read it aloud. She wants children to enjoy story experiences and to develop good comprehension skills. As she reads, she observes their reactions and listens to their comments. She wonders whether or not the children can follow the plot and later recall the sequence of story events. She decides to use writing time to gather more information and invites children to retell the story by drawing and dictating. Their drawings confirm her concerns: Many children did not recall the sequence of events. She decides to reread the story, stopping more frequently to ask specific, planned questions. She also reads the book to small groups of children, encouraging more interaction as she reads. During the additional readings and discussions, she observes that children's comprehension of the story improves dramatically.

Effective assessment is systematic and not left to chance. Systematic assessment is integrated into everyday life in the classroom. Teachers plan assessment activities and prepare for spontaneous assessment opportunities in the same ways they plan instructional experiences and respond to teachable moments. When assessment is interwoven with teaching and learning and when it occurs in the context of regular classroom activities, it is called *curriculum-embedded assessment*.

Let's examine this example in terms of the steps of the assessment cycle:

· **Ask questions** Mallory has an initial question: "Did the children follow the plot and recall the sequence of events?"

· **Collect data** Mallory has children retell the story by drawing and dictating.

· **Interpret data** Mallory studies the children's work, and her initial concern is confirmed: The children do not seem to know the story sequence.

· **Take action** Mallory implements an instructional plan, rereading the story in small and large groups. She also asks carefully considered questions. Finally, she reassesses the children's comprehension through oral retellings.

Using the cycle of assessment, Mallory enhances both her teaching and children's learning.

Purposes of Assessment

Assessment is used for a variety of purposes (Neisworth & Bagnato, 2004; Shephard, Kagan & Wurtz, 1998). Early childhood educators assess for these reasons:

Promote children's learning and development. Early childhood teachers are interested primarily in using assessment to help children develop and learn. When the assessment process provides information about children's skills, abilities, knowledge, and interests, teachers can use that information to plan experiences that are finely tuned to children's needs. Teachers wonder, "What does this child know? What can this child do? What engages this child's curiosity? How will what I know about this child help me shape meaningful learning experiences?"

Identify children who may have special needs. Teachers need reliable ways to quickly identify children who may have difficulty learning and who would benefit from further evaluation by specialists. Teachers might want answers to questions such as these: Is this child developing as expected? Is this child at risk for school failure? Is this delay in development significant? Does this child need more thorough evaluation?

Determine whether a child has a disability and how that disability affects the child's development and learning. After working with a child for several weeks or months, you may suspect that he or she may have a disability. At that point, you can turn to a team of diagnosticians to help answer the following questions: What exactly is the disability? How does the disability affect the child's development and learning? How will I accommodate this child's special needs in my program?

Evaluate the effectiveness of programs for young children (accountability). More often than not, organizations that fund early childhood programs want to be sure that the money is being used effectively to support young children's learning. Program administrators and teachers need ways of showing the value and benefits of their efforts with young children. The assessment process may be used to answer questions such as these: How effective is the program? Are children learning?

Types of Assessment and Assessment Tools

As an early childhood teacher, you may have experience with various types of assessment and assessment tools. The purpose for assessing children should determine the type of tool used. Understanding the types of assessment tools empowers you to decide which will best answer your questions. There are five major types of assessment tools:

- learning and development
- screening
- readiness
- diagnostic evaluation
- program quality

Assessment tools should only be used for the purposes for which they were designed (Snow & Van Hemel, 2008). It is important to be able to distinguish one type of assessment tool from another so you can use each appropriately.

Learning and Development

Assessment is the process of discovering what children *know* and can *do*. It can reveal their strengths and weaknesses, and how you can help them. Typically, as a teacher of young children, you use informal methods: observation, portfolios, conversations, checklists, and rating scales. These tools are used instead of tests to assess children's learning. With older children, this type of assessment is referred to as *assessment of achievement.*

Formative assessment tools help you adjust your teaching to improve children's learning. For *formative assessment,* you want to answer these questions: How are children learning? What can I do to improve their learning? This is also known as assessment *for* learning (McMillan, 2007; Popham, 2008). For instance, you are using formative assessment when you notice a child leaning into the space of another to see the pictures in the book being read aloud. On the basis of your observation, you decide to seat her where she can see the book without distracting another child.

Formative assessment provides feedback to teachers about their teaching and to children about their learning strategies (Popham, 2008). Teachers might change their approach, the environment, materials, vocabulary, interactions, or plans in order to help children learn more effectively. In this book, formative assessment is referred to as *classroom assessment* because it is inextricably tied to the classroom curriculum.

Popham (2008) sees **summative assessment** as "a way to determine the effectiveness of already-completed instructional activities" (p. 4). Summative assessment information can be used for many purposes:

- demonstrate a program's effectiveness
- determine grades
- share children's accomplishments with family members

Summative assessment tools are used at the end of a period of time or a unit of learning. For *summative assessment,* you want to answer these questions: What did children learn? How much progress did they make? Sometimes referred to as assessment *of* learning, summative assessment presents information about what children know and the skills they have acquired. You are using summative assessment, for instance, when comparing a child's progress from one assessment period to another or when reporting a child's overall levels of achievement to his or her family at particular times throughout the year.

In reports to families, teachers relay information about children's *performance* and *progress. Performance* refers to a child's current status: Right now, what skills does a child have? Which concepts does he or she understand? In contrast, when teachers are assessing particular knowledge or skills over time, they are measuring *progress.* Summative assessment measures both performance and progress.

- How do you currently assess children's learning?
- When did you last complete summative assessment of children? How did you do this?
- How does formative assessment fit into your day-to-day activities?

Reflect on Your Practice

Screening

Screenings are brief assessment procedures conducted early in the year and given to each child. These assessments identify whether a child needs further evaluation. A common example is a quickly administered hearing screening. The examiner may say, "Drop the block when you hear a sound." The results of this type of screening are used to determine whether a child needs a follow-up examination with an ear, nose, and throat doctor (otolaryngologist) or a hearing specialist (audiologist).

Developmental screening tools identify children who may have developmental disabilities or learning problems. Developmental screening focuses on whether a child has the ability or potential to acquire skills (Meisels & Atkins-Burnett, 2005). Teachers and paraprofessionals may administer these tests, but they must be trained to use particular screening instruments.

Screening results usually lead to one of three conclusions about the child's development:

- The child is developing as expected, so no special action is necessary.

- The child will need to be screened again because the examiner (the person conducting the screening) had reason to believe that the assessment situation was not conducive to gathering accurate information. For example, the child may have been too fearful to participate, or the infant may have fallen asleep during the screening.

- The child may have a disability and needs additional, extensive evaluation to determine whether or not this is the case.

Follow-up is essential. In a joint position statement, *Early Childhood Curriculum, Assessment, and Program Evaluation*, the National Association for the Education of Young Children (NAEYC) and the National Association of Early Childhood Specialists in State Departments of Education (NAECS/SDE) (2003) recommend that screenings always include follow-up. Whenever screening results indicate that the child needs to be screened again or receive further evaluation, a professional must be identified who will make sure the rescreening or evaluation occurs.

Misuse may be a problem. Assessment tools should be used only for their intended purposes, and screening instruments are designed solely to identify children who need more extensive evaluation. However, early childhood programs sometimes use screening tests for other purposes because they are quickly and easily administered. Perhaps a program chooses to conduct screenings once at the beginning of the year and then again at the end of the year to compare scores and make statements about children's learning—and the success of the program. Misusing screening tools in this way risks drawing faulty conclusions about children's learning. You will read more about the misuse of assessment tools in chapter 12.

> **Screening tests** are most frequently used with preschool and kindergarten children, although infant screening instruments do exist. Frequently used screening instruments include
> - *Ages and Stages Questionnaires (ASQ)*, Brookes Publishing Company
> - *Denver II Developmental Screening Test*, Denver Developmental Materials, Inc.
> - *Early Screening Inventory— Revised (ESI-R)*, Pearson Education
> - *Developmental Indicators for the Assessment of Learning (DIAL-3)*, AGS Publishing

- **Does your program use a screening instrument? If so, which one?**

- **Is it being used to identify children who may need further evaluation?**

- **Who is responsible for follow-up?**

Reflect on Your Practice

Well-known **readiness tests** include

- *Cognitive Skills Assessment Battery (CSAB)*, Teachers College Press
- *Boehm Test of Basic Concepts*, 3rd ed. (*Boehm-3*), Psychological Corporation
- *Metropolitan Readiness Tests*, 6th ed. (*MRT 6*), Psychological Corporation

Readiness

Readiness assessment tools show whether or not children are prepared for particular experiences or programs. For example, a readiness test might assess whether a child is ready to learn to read or is prepared to start kindergarten. Most often, readiness assessments are standardized tests designed to predict whether a child will succeed in a particular area, often reading or math.

Two issues of concern are related to readiness tests (NAEYC, 1995):

The quality and trustworthiness of results is often in question. A child's score on a reading-readiness test should only relate to how well he or she can read at a future time. Unfortunately, some commercially available readiness tests have unacceptable technical properties (reliability and validity; see chapter 12), and the tests results do not actually predict the child's ability to read (Puckett & Black, 2008).

The validity of some tests is in doubt. Some programs and districts develop their own readiness assessment instruments for children who are about to enter kindergarten. These assessment tools generally have not been validated. Despite this lack of validity, their results are sometimes used to delay a child's entrance into kindergarten. Extensive research shows the negative effects of delaying children's entrance to kindergarten (Graue & DiPerna, 2000; Marshall, 2003). Readiness tests should only be used for their intended purposes and only if they have proven reliability and validity.

Diagnostic Evaluation

Diagnostic evaluation uses multiple methods and tools to determine whether a child has a delay or disability and may be eligible for special education services. These assessment tests are administered by special education and medical personnel, including school psychologists, social workers, speech and language pathologists, pediatricians, occupational therapists, physical therapists, and/or mental health specialists.

Evaluation results, along with input from the family and classroom teacher, are used to create Individualized Family Service Plans (IFSP) for infants and toddlers or Individualized Education Programs (IEP) for children ages 3 years and older. These plans document the child's needs and the services to be provided on the basis of those needs.

- **Have you ever been involved in the diagnostic evaluation of a child?**
- **Who was involved?**
- **What was the outcome?**
- **How did you contribute information to the team?**
- **How was the child's family involved?**
- **How did the evaluation information assist you in teaching this child?**

Reflect on Your Practice

Program Quality

When the purpose of the assessment is to measure program quality, the assessment instrument may focus on the learning environment rather than the child. Some instruments rate dimensions of the classroom environment, for example,

- physical space
- interactions between teachers and children
- program structure
- availability and use of different types of materials

The particular items on each instrument differ according to the authors' definition of best practices in early childhood programs.

- **What experiences, if any, have you had with assessments of program quality?**
- **What aspects of the program were assessed?**
- **What instruments were used?**

Reflect on Your Practice

Teachers and administrators can use many instruments to assess **program quality**. Some program-quality assessment tools are specialized. The *Early Language and Literacy Classroom Observation Toolkit (ELLCO)*, Brookes Publishing, focuses on how a classroom supports literacy learning (e.g., oral language use and availability of reading materials).

Other, more general program-assessment tools include
- *Assessment of Practices in Early Elementary Classrooms (APEEC)*, Teachers College Press
- *Classroom Assessment Scoring System™ (CLASS™)*, Brookes
- *HighScope Program Quality Assessment (PQA)*, HighScope Press
- *Early Childhood Environmental Rating Scale-Revised (ECERS-R)*, Teachers College Press
- *Infant-Toddler Environmental Rating Scale (ITERS-R)*, Teachers College Press

Using a Variety of Assessment Tools

You typically use several types of assessment to support children's learning, and the results from one assessment tool often inform choices about using another. The following vignettes illustrate how assessment sometimes unfolds in the classroom.

In a program for children ranging in age from 4 months to 5 years, teachers use a developmental **screening** tool with infants, toddlers, and preschoolers at the beginning of the program. Most children "pass" the screening and therefore do not require any further diagnostic assessment. Several children need to be screened again, because the screeners did not think the results were accurate. Two children require **diagnostic assessment**. Their teachers coordinate the follow-up to be sure that more extensive evaluation happens in a timely manner. Teachers at all levels assess as children are learning, using an observational assessment tool **(formative assessment)**, and they prepare for progress reports three times during the year **(summative assessment)**.

In February, David, a preschool teacher, prepares narrative reports for families. He gathers his observation notes about each child, literacy and math checklists, and the children's portfolios. Over the next 2 weeks, David prepares progress reports on each child, documenting how much children have learned since the last report **(assessing progress)** and informing families about whether their children are meeting expectations for 4-year-olds **(assessing performance)**.

Lisa, a kindergarten teacher, administers a reading **readiness** test to determine appropriate literacy activities. To identify children's current skills, she also uses various methods of **formative assessment**, including observations and a literacy checklist. Using information from this ongoing assessment, Lisa plans activities for some children to enhance their comprehension of books and strengthen their knowledge of the alphabet. For others, she prepares to begin using the district's kindergarten literacy program.

In which vignettes are teachers using more than one type of assessment tool? Do teachers use information from one type of assessment to inform their choice of another type? How does this happen?

- Do you have experience with various types of assessment? Which ones?

- Did you use the tools for their intended purposes?

- How did you explain the purposes of your assessment instruments to families?

Reflect on Your Practice

Key Ideas to Remember

- Assessment is a cyclical and systematic process that helps you get to know children and enhance your teaching.

- Distinguishing the different types of assessment (i.e., learning and development, screening, readiness, diagnostic, and program quality) is important so that you can select and use the right ones for your purpose.

- When an assessment instrument is not used for its intended purpose, the results may not be valid.

- As a teacher, you use assessment formatively, in an ongoing way, to improve children's learning.

- You also use assessment to summarize children's *progress* and *performance* at the end of an instructional unit or reporting period.

References

Early Head Start National Resource Center. (2000). *Technical Assistance Paper No. 4: Developmental screening, assessment, and evaluation: Key elements for individualizing curricula in Early Head Start programs.* Washington, DC: ZERO TO THREE.

Graue, M. E., & DiPerna, J. (2000). Redshirting and early retention: Who gets the "gift of time" and what are its outcomes? *American Educational Research Journal, 37*(2), 509–534.

Marshall, H. H. (2003). Opportunity deferred or opportunity taken? An updated look at delaying kindergarten entry. *Young Children, 58*(5), 84–93.

McAfee, O., & Leong, D. J. (2007). *Assessing and guiding young children's development and learning* (4th ed.). Boston: Allyn and Bacon.

McMillan, J. H. (Ed.). (2007). *Formative classroom assessment: Theory and practice.* New York: Teachers College Press.

Meisels, S. J., & Atkins-Burnett, S. (2005). *Developmental screening in early childhood* (5th ed.). Washington, DC: National Association for the Education of Young Children.

Mindes, G. (2007). *Assessing young children* (3rd ed.). Upper Saddle River, NJ: Pearson Education.

National Association for the Education of Young Children, & National Association of Early Childhood Specialists in State Departments of Education. (2003). *Early childhood curriculum, assessment, and program evaluation: Building an effective, accountable system in programs for children birth through age 8.* Washington, DC: Authors.

National Association for the Education of Young Children. (1995). *School readiness: A position statement of the National Association for the Education of Young Children*. Washington, DC: Author.

Neisworth, J. T., & Bagnato, S. J. (2004). The mismeasure of young children: The authentic assessment alternative. *Infants and Young Children*, *17*(3), 198–212.

Popham, W. J. (2008). *Transformative assessment*. Alexandria, VA: ASCD.

Puckett, M. B., & Black, J. K. (2008). *Meaningful assessments of the young child* (3rd ed.). Upper Saddle River, NJ: Pearson Education.

Shephard, L. A., Kagan, S. L., & Wurtz, E. (1998). Goal 1 Early Childhood Assessments Resource Group recommendations. *Young Children*, *53*(3), 52–54.

Snow, C. E., & Van Hemel, S. B. (Eds.). (2008). *Early childhood assessment: Why, what, and how*. Washington, DC: The National Academies Press.

CHAPTER 3

Classroom-Based Assessment: The Cycle in Use

Now that you have the big picture of assessment, let's open the classroom door to see the assessment cycle in use. Let's look at how teachers use assessment in their classrooms to enhance both teaching and learning; build relationships with children; strengthen communication with families; and become better, more effective professionals.

Ask Questions
- What do you want to learn?
- What decision do you have to make?

1

Assessment Cycle

Collect Data
2
- What information should you collect?
- How will you obtain it?
- How much do you need?

Take Action
4
- Given what you now understand, how will you use what you learned?
- How will your plans change?
- What strategies will you use?
- What are your next steps with this child or group of children?

Interpret Data
3
- What does the data, or information, mean?
- What do you learn about each child from the data?

Watch how Belinda, an infant–toddler teacher, uses the cycle as she interacts with children.

> Belinda is sitting on the floor among several children who are busy playing with various toys. As she cuts a picture from a magazine, Zach and Sarah crawl over and take some paper. They begin to tear, crumple, and toss it. Once or twice, Belinda tries to take the paper away, but she then asks herself why the children are so interested in the paper. Is this a behavior she wants to stop or one she should encourage? Taking some newsprint from a shelf, she sits back down and hands them the paper to tear and crumple. Zach and Sarah are completely occupied, manipulating the paper, watching it fall, tearing and crumpling. It occurs to Belinda that she is observing the babies exploring, using their senses, and developing eye–hand coordination and fine-motor control. What's more, these are items on the checklist she uses. She decides to put some other types of paper out when the children get tired of the newsprint, and she wonders what similar items she can provide for the babies to explore safely.

Toni and her director, Monique, have had a series of conversations about 4-year-old Thomas, who Toni thinks is having difficulty engaging in choice-time activities. Over time, she uses the assessment cycle to review what she knows, collect new information, interpret his behavior, and, after talking with Monique, put a new plan into action.

Let's eavesdrop on their most recent conversation.

> *Toni:* I have some new insights from my observation notes about Thomas. I think it's interesting that, when he arrives at 7:30, he begins playing with puzzles, building with Duplos®, and looking at books. He focuses on each activity for about 10 to 15 minutes, and then he moves on. At around 8:15, when all the other children have arrived and are getting involved in choice-time activities, Thomas begins running around, knocking things over. He goes from one thing to the next.
>
> *Monique:* Why might this be happening?
>
> *Toni:* Well, after observing, I think there are two possibilities. Perhaps my expectations for his attention span are unrealistic and he needs more structure after 45 minutes of concentrated play. Or maybe he gets distracted as the room becomes crowded and busy.
>
> *Monique:* What kind of structure do you think will help him?

Toni: I think we should add a small-group activity when my assistant arrives. Maybe we'll include movement in the gross-motor room or a snack in the adjoining space. Perhaps an art activity or a small-group reading in a shared space in the building would interest him.

Monique: Those are great strategies! Let me know how they work with Thomas and the other children. Keep me posted.

Larry, a kindergarten teacher, uses the assessment cycle as he plans for and carries out a small-group math lesson.

Larry has organized a small-group experience for five of the children in his kindergarten class. The lesson involves sorting, describing, and naming three-dimensional shapes. He wants to learn what the children already know about these shapes and give them the opportunity to learn new information. His clipboard, sticky notes, and camera are ready so that he can document children's actions and language. Larry puts the materials on the table and encourages the children to explore them for a few minutes. All the children are deeply engaged during the free exploration period. After a few minutes, he begins to focus the lesson, inviting the children to begin sorting the shapes in different ways. Emily continues to build. Boris watches the sorting process for a minute or 2 and then goes back to building. The other three children, Klaudia, Philip, and Ryan, are busily grouping the shapes, asking questions about the shapes' names, and describing how the shapes are similar and different. Louis tries unsuccessfully to get Emily and Boris to join the others.

Now, let's look at how Larry uses each part of the assessment cycle to learn about children and improve his instruction.

What questions does Larry want to answer through this small-group activity? He wants to learn what children already know about three-dimensional shapes.

How does he collect data? He records notes about what individual children do and say, using sticky notes on a clipboard. He takes some photos of the children's sorted objects and captures their dictation. For example, he writes about Boris, "B stacked six cubes to make a tower." For Klaudia, his note says, "K sorted 3-D boxes in two ways: by shape and by size; said, 'This one looks kinda like a triangle.'"

How does he interpret the data? During the lesson, he recognizes that the children are at different levels of knowledge and understanding of three-dimensional shapes. Boris and Emily need more open exploration before they can sort and describe.

How does Larry take action? He adds the collection of three-dimensional shapes to the science area so that the children can explore them independently. He photographs the sorted collections and displays the photos to inspire other children to sort the shapes. He makes a point of connecting with Emily and Boris during choice-time to talk more about three-dimensional shapes. He also invites the children to bring boxes of different sizes and shapes from home.

In these examples, notice that the teacher is curious about each child and actively investigates to answer questions. Now that you have seen how much there is to learn from classroom-based assessment and how it is integrated with curriculum and instruction, let's go into your classroom and focus specifically on how you can use the assessment cycle each day. We'll also consider more stories about other teachers who use the assessment cycle.

Asking Questions

The classroom-based assessment cycle begins with your questions:

- What do you want to know about the children?
- What are you curious about?
- What decisions do you need to make?
- Do classroom dilemmas need to be resolved?
- How can you help individual children build on their strengths?
- Are any children struggling to learn?

Your questions will range in scope, depth, and breadth. They will also depend on the knowledge you want to gain about your classroom and the children in it. You may want to know whether children are accomplishing curricular goals and whether they are meeting program standards. Questions may be narrow: How can I entice Jayne to participate in circle time? Why is Marc having such trouble learning to write his name? How can I make it easier for him to do so? Questions can also be broad: How do children show they are flexible thinkers? Some questions may concern the entire class: Are children making progress in math? Other questions may focus on individuals: What does George understand about geometric shapes?

Why does Carrie sometimes start the day contentedly but other times very upset?

It may be easier to think of assessment questions in terms of the decisions you make each day:

- Should I intervene and help Joni join a group of children, or should I give her more time to find an activity on her own?

- Should I quickly finish the story because children are starting to squirm, or should I just stop and return to it later?

- Which equipment should I change to accommodate toddlers' drive to climb?

- Should we continue our study of water or move on to the children's new interest in trash and garbage?

Think about your own classroom or another classroom in which you observe.

- **List two or three classroom decisions you or the teacher made.**

- **What information did you gather before you made the decisions?**

- **What did you decide?**

Reflect on Your Practice

If you are like many early childhood educators, you might have said that teachers decide what to teach, how to group children, when to introduce a new concept, when to end an activity, and when to let it go a little longer because the children are highly engaged. These decisions and many others that are an integral part of effective teaching can be grounded by assessment information. To make good decisions, you must collect and interpret information. Research suggests that teachers make decisions every 2–3 minutes (Shavelson & Stern, 1981). You are assessing all day long!

Various factors influence the decisions teachers make and, equally important, the questions they ask. For example, at the beginning of the year, teachers ask questions and make decisions that enable them to get to know their students, teach classroom rules and routines, and determine children's initial levels of skills and knowledge. When you begin a new unit of study, you make decisions about what you are teaching, how you are pacing it, and your class's basic knowledge about the topic. At the end of the unit, you ask questions to figure out whether or not the children grasped what you wanted them to learn. Your curriculum and state standards also affect the assessment information you need. Making decisions about what to assess will be addressed more fully in chapter 4.

As you begin asking questions and gathering data, even more questions may arise. After collecting all the information, you interpret it and develop a plan of action based on your interpretations. Sometimes your plan of action is effective, and you can move on to new questions. At other times, your actions may not accomplish your goals. However, this process of asking questions and gathering data *does* provide you with more information that leads to new questions—and the cycle begins anew. Experienced teachers know that assessment results suggest new questions as often as they provide answers and help them make decisions.

Cindy, a preschool teacher, describes her evolving process of questioning children's limited use of the art area in her classroom. Notice how her questions change over time.

> I observed that the children in my classroom were tentative in their explorations of materials in the art area. They didn't choose materials on their own. Instead, they used the art materials only when I put things out on tables. I wondered about their previous experiences with art materials. What background did they have with creative exploration? Did they use art materials at home? Were they allowed to get materials on their own? Did a parent have to set something out? I asked families and found out that some children used materials independently at home but others did not. I studied the art area. I moved furniture around, had the children help me with the setup, and showed them the materials and how they could use them. Children used the area more for a week or 2, but it didn't last long.

I thought about children's creativity and problem solving in other areas of the classroom. This led me to observe more. I noticed that children were thinking imaginatively but not always where and how I expected. They were very inventive in dramatic play; made up stories using small manipulatives; and used paper and other materials to make shoes, hats, and fishing poles to support their play scenarios. They preferred using art materials in other areas of the classroom. I put trays of art materials in other areas so they didn't have to interrupt their play to get things.

Cindy's initial question about the use of the art area turned into a broader question about children's inventiveness and creativity. She found answers to her question by talking with children, families, and team members. She observed children in all areas of the classroom. As she acquired new information, she kept asking questions, gradually deepening her understanding of the children's imaginative play and ways to support and enrich that play.

Collecting Data

Teachers collect data in multiple ways to find out what they need to learn and what they need to teach. Data, or evidence, to answer questions is collected through observations, language and work samples, interviews and conversations, photographs and drawings, and other sources. Other adults, including family members, paraprofessionals, and other educators, may also contribute information.

The evidence collected for classroom-based assessment is visible and tangible; you can see and touch it. Moreover, it is available for review at a later time. In the previous example, Cindy, who collected observation notes about children's choices and the use of the art area and other classroom spaces, asked family members to complete questionnaires. She also interviewed her teaching team. Her documentation provided an extensive record of objective data. In chapters 7–9, you will learn more about how teachers gather and document information through observation notes, checklists, rating scales, and portfolios.

Think about your own classroom or another classroom in which you observe.

What assessment data is collected?

Reflect on Your Practice

Assessment is a *cyclical process* that involves more than a single step. Teachers often use several assessment methods, rather than a single tool or method, to find out what they want to know. For example, Karen, a kindergarten teacher, observes children as they write in journals and during choice time. She also collects samples of their written work. By collecting different types of information from a variety of sources, Karen increases the accuracy of the assessment (see chapter 12).

Having a reasonable amount of evidence of children's learning is essential to formative assessment. However, data alone is not enough. After collecting data, teachers must figure out what it means. This part of the assessment cycle requires the teacher to interpret information about what children said and did.

Interpreting Data

Merriam-Webster's dictionary (2008) defines *interpreting* as, "to explain or tell the meaning of." Teachers review the data to make inferences and draw conclusions. What does the evidence tell you? What does the data mean?

You may have several ideas or hypotheses about the meaning of your data. For example, Paul has observed that children seem distracted during circle time. They are moving around, talking, poking each other, and giggling. He has several hypotheses:

1. The children may be hungry because circle time is just before lunch.
2. Circle time may be too long at this point in the year.
3. Perhaps circle time experiences should be more active.

When you are open to multiple interpretations of the evidence, you have many avenues to investigate. Be curious. Remaining open to multiple interpretations of the data increases the likelihood that the conclusions you eventually reach will be useful.

Think about the children in your classroom or other children you observe.

- Observe a child for a few minutes and make a tentative interpretation of your data.

- What are some other ways to interpret the same information?

Reflect on Your Practice

Interpretation generally involves comparison. When you assess children's reading comprehension, you use standards or expectations that are based on their ages and previous experiences. When Rhonda assesses 3-year-old Tameka's gross-motor skills, she compares the child's performance to what is expected of 3-year-olds who are developing typically. Child development research, state standards, and program expectations provide the yardsticks for comparison.

Sometimes you interpret children's behavior while it is underway. Your immediate response is based on what you understand about what you see and hear. For example, Kara, an infant–toddler teacher, notices Bradley (20 months) and Josh (18 months) pushing cars on the carpet. She hears Bradley say, "My car," in a tense voice. Knowing that Josh has a history of biting when frustrated, she immediately moves closer to the two boys, ready to help Josh protect his car in a socially acceptable way.

In other situations you have time to reflect on the data, figure out what it means, and plan what to do next. Here is an example:

> Early in the school year, Dan has collected many observations that show preschool children's understanding of counting and quantity. He has observed children counting napkins and cups for snack and dividing the bear counters so everyone has the same amount. He has also observed children count during story time and as they sing. As he reviews what he observed, he wants to know who can rote count, who uses one-to-one correspondence, and who understands that six is more than four. After he interprets his data, he can plan learning activities to match each child's current understanding of number and quantity.

Taking Action

Once you have ideas about what the evidence means, you can create a plan of action. What will you do as a result of the information? Here are several possibilities:

- change the daily schedule
- add or remove materials or adapt their display
- change the room arrangement
- develop new questions to ask children
- alter your interactions with a child
- adapt the methods you use to teach a particular concept
- plan new learning opportunities

The Cycle in Use

This chart presents examples of the assessment cycle in use. Each column shows one step of the cycle. Once you choose a strategy to try (column 4), you will again collect data and determine its effectiveness—and the cycle goes on. How does this work in your classroom?

Ask Questions	Collect Data	Interpret Data	Take Action
Tameka, age 3, seems reluctant to try gross-motor activities. Is it because of delayed motor skills or lack of experience?	Document what Tameka does in the obstacle course area.	After watching other children for 2 days, Tameka participated in every station of the obstacle course on the third day. She can walk on a low balance beam, crawl through a tunnel, throw a medium ball with two hands, and jump five times in a row. Skills observed seem age appropriate. Tameka watches before she is ready to participate.	Give Tameka time to observe others before expecting her to participate in gross-motor activities. Continue to observe.
Sam, age 4, has difficulty making some speech sounds. He frequently plays alone. Does he play alone because speaking to other children is difficult for him, or are there other reasons?	Observe Sam during choice time and during small-group activities for a week.	This week Sam played alone every day during choice time. Observations during small-group times show that he tries to communicate with other children when a teacher is present.	Support Sam's interactions with others during small-group time more consistently, clarifying his speech for other children. Assign an adult to support his play at choice time and try to help Sam play with at least one other child.
Before we begin a study of our school, what do children already know about it?	Chart children's responses to the question, "What do you know about our school?"	All children said that they come to school to learn, but they had trouble giving examples of what they have learned. No one talked about the building or the people who work in our school.	Plan a unit to include people who work in schools, rooms in the school building, and other things children can learn about our school.

Think about assessment as a cycle that helps you answer questions and make decisions. Complete the chart that follows with examples from your classroom or from a classroom that you know well.

Ask Questions	Collect Data	Interpret Data	Take Action

Key Ideas to Remember

- Assessment in the classroom is a part of—not separate from—your curriculum, interactions with children, and teaching strategies.

- Assessment is an active process that begins with you. What do you want or need to know about the children in your class?

- There are many different ways to gather data about young children. What methods will you use?

- Once you have data on the children, your first task is to determine how to organize it so you can review it regularly. After that, your next task is to figure out what the data mean, perhaps considering several possible interpretations or hypotheses.

- As the classroom decision-maker, how will you use your interpretations to support children's learning?

References

Mish, F. C., et al. (Eds.) (2008). *Merriam-Webster's collegiate dictionary* (11th ed.). Springfield, MA: Merriam-Webster, Inc.

Shavelson, R. J., & Stern, P. (1981). Research on teachers' pedagogical thoughts, judgments, decisions, and behavior. *Review of Educational Research, 51*(4), 455–498.

CHAPTER 4

Ask Questions
Take Action 4   Assessment Cycle   2 Collect Data
Interpret Data

Asking Questions

Now that the assessment cycle is fresh in your mind, let's narrow our focus and think about the first part of the cycle: asking questions. Questions identify assessment content. When teachers have a clear understanding of what they want to assess, the assessment cycle is more likely to produce useful results. Classroom assessment can help you answer important questions such as these:

- What do children know, and what can they do?
- How does each child approach learning tasks?
- How can I address a classroom problem or challenge?

This chapter describes the questions that early childhood teachers ask and the decisions they make as they answer them. Because teachers' questions change as they get to know children in their classrooms, this chapter also addresses how teachers' questions change during the school year. The chapter ends with guidelines for focusing assessment activities.

Assessing What Children Know and Can Do

The assessment process helps you learn about children's knowledge and skills. You can be guided by expectations in these areas:

- child development
- curricular content
- standards

A clear understanding of each area will make you a more knowledgeable and effective assessor. You will know what to look and listen for as you collect data, and you will have a basis for analyzing what children do and say.

Child Development

Many early childhood assessment tools are designed to gather data about developmental accomplishments. Researchers have helped us understand what we should expect children to do at various ages and the order in which certain skills and behaviors emerge. Your success in assessing development depends on your knowledge of how children grow and learn.

Consider this example:

> Regina has observed that Margie (26 months) says, "Me do it," on a regular basis. This morning, Regina hears her say, "I do it" for the first time. Regina recognizes that this change in Margie's language is noteworthy. She shares what she observed with Margie's dad at the end of the day.

For curricular and assessment purposes, development is often divided into areas, or domains. You may be familiar with these areas:

- social–emotional development
- cognitive development
- communication
- motor development

The National Association for the Education of Young Children and the National Association of Early Childhood Specialists in State Departments of Education (NAEYC & NAECS/SDE, 2003) discuss development somewhat differently in their position statement, *Early Childhood Curriculum, Assessment, and Program Evaluation: Building an Effective, Accountable System in Programs for Children Birth through Age 8.*

They identify these areas:

- physical well-being and motor development
- social and emotional development
- approaches to learning
- language development
- cognition and general knowledge

As you can see, educators think about developmental areas, or domains, in many ways. Keep in mind that development is integrated. Although we assess one domain at a time, children use skills and behaviors from many domains simultaneously.

In some assessment tools, domains are subdivided to assist you in understanding and assessing development. For example, motor development may be divided into gross- and fine-motor (or large- and small-muscle) development. Sometimes this domain is referred to as *physical development*. Language development is frequently subdivided into receptive language (i.e., how well children understand language) and expressive language (i.e., how well children express themselves). In other assessment tools, the entire domain is referred to as *communication*.

These smaller parts of developmental domains may be subdivided into more specific skills, or indicators. Indicators provide a focus for assessment. It is impossible to assess a construct as broad as "a child's expressive language" in a useful way. However, teachers can assess, for instance, whether a child speaks in full sentences, asks questions, and uses pronouns.

When teachers assess children's development, they may ask questions such as these:

- Lori, 13½ months, has just started to walk. How can I give her more opportunities to walk in the classroom?

- Kami, 3½, is very quiet. Does he understand what I say to him?

- I wonder why the 5-year-olds in my class do not follow directions. Are the directions I give too complicated for them? Am I not making my expectations clear?

Think about the children in your classroom or caregiving group, or other children you observe.

- What questions do you have about their development?

- How could the answers to these questions influence your instructional practices?

Reflect on Your Practice

Curricular Content

Bowman, Donovan, & Burns (2000) showed that young children can understand and do more in the areas of math, science, and literacy than we previously thought. This has led to a greater focus on content as an appropriate part of curriculum for young children (NAEYC & NAECS/SDE, 2003; Snow & Van Hemel, 2008).

As a result, curricular goals and objectives are frequently used to define expectations for young children's learning. Goals and objectives are usually organized by subject, content, curricular, or developmental areas. Teachers focusing on content, for example, might assess children's learning in literacy, math, social studies, science, the arts, and so on. In contrast, a teacher focusing on development might concentrate on language development, cognition, and general knowledge.

Many teachers focus their assessment questions on curricular content:

- I have observed Jerry, 19 months, fill and dump containers repeatedly, look carefully at the wheels on toy trucks (wondering how they make the truck move), and watch as the lights go on and off. What else does he do to explore and figure things out? What other opportunities could I offer to engage him in this way?

- How are my preschoolers demonstrating scientific knowledge and skills at the discovery table?

- I have just introduced standard units of measurement to my kindergartners. Who is using the rulers and measuring tapes to solve problems? Who needs more support to use them effectively?

Think about the children in your classroom or caregiving group, or other children you observe.

- What do you know about their learning in various subject, or content, areas?

- What more do you need to know?

Reflect
on Your
Practice

Standards

Standards are also used to describe expectations for children's learning at different ages or grade levels. They have been developed and adopted by states, school districts, and educational programs. Until 2010, the term *standards* most often referred to state standards. Fifty states and the District of Columbia have adopted early learning standards for preschool children, and 25 states have standards for infants and toddlers (U.S. Department of Health and Human Services, 2010a). The National Governors Association Center for Best Practices and the Council of State School Officers (2010a, b) have introduced voluntary national standards for K–grade 12 in the areas of literacy and mathematics. As of this writing, 46 states and the District of Columbia have adopted them.

States refer to early childhood standards by many different names, (NAEYC & NAECS/SDE, 2002) including *early childhood development education standards, early childhood education framework, standards or indicators of quality, curricular goals and benchmarks, early learning foundations, early learning developmental standards,* and *foundation blocks for early learning curriculum guidelines.*

Another set of standards, the *Head Start Child Development and Early Learning Framework* (U.S. Department of Health and Human Services, 2010a), describes what children should know and be able to do by the end of their time in the Head Start program. The Head Start framework is divided into 10 domains that apply to all children: Physical Development and Health, Social and Emotional Development, Approaches to Learning, Logic and Reasoning, Language Development, Literacy Knowledge and Skills, Mathematics Knowledge and Skills, Science Knowledge and Skills, Creative Arts Expression, and Social Studies Knowledge and Skills. Another domain, English Language Development, applies only to children who are dual-language learners.

Whatever the title, early learning standards and K–12 standards help define what children should know and be able to do by certain ages or grade levels. Most of these standards focus on children's learning rather than on what adults do to foster learning. Some do both. Once a program is established and children are participating, what are the desired outcomes for children? What should children know and be able to do as a result of the program? The use of the word *outcome* focuses our attention on the end product: what we expect to *result* from a program or an instructional unit.

Three types of standards are common:

- *Content standards* define what students should know or be able to do. These are often broad statements of learning that cover several ages or grade levels. Because they are very broad, they are not usually directly measurable. You could not create an assessment tool or plan curriculum based on content standards.

- *Benchmarks* define expectations for a particular age, grade, or developmental level. They identify the steps necessary to meet the higher-level standards and may be written in measurable terms.

- *Performance standards* tell in measurable terms how children can demonstrate their knowledge and skills. They focus on how well children know or are able to perform the tasks identified by the standard. A performance standard defines the degree to which content standards and benchmarks have been achieved. Some states have developed performance standards for young children.

Teachers focusing on early learning standards ask critical questions such as these:

- My state standards tell me that babies require time for exploration. Are all my infants actively exploring their environment?

- One of the Head Start early learning framework indicators states, "Observes and discusses common properties, differences, and comparisons among objects." Although I have observed children exploring and using different scientific tools, can they describe the similarities and differences of various objects?

- Rhyming is one of the benchmarks in my state standards for kindergarten literacy. How well do my children understand rhyming? Can they tell whether or not two words rhyme? If I give them a word, are they able to produce another that rhymes with mine?

> - Does your state have standards for preschool children? For infants and toddlers?
> - How do standards influence what you assess and what you teach?
>
>
> **Reflect** on Your Practice

In summary, you may focus on development, curricular content, or standards when assessing what children know and can do. Be aware that these overlap and that the terms are occasionally used interchangeably.

Assessing Children as Learners

When assessing development, attainment of curricular goals, or achievement of standards, teachers gather similar information about all of the children in the class or caregiving group. That type of assessment focuses on *what* each child knows or can do. Although children may show their knowledge and skills in different ways, the teacher is interested in whether or not each child has acquired the same set of knowledge and skills.

Teachers also focus on *how* children learn by examining each child's approaches to learning, interests, prior knowledge, and attitudes. Teachers need answers to questions such as these:

- Is the child persistent? Does he continue trying something new until he is able to do it?

- Does the child observe the activity before participating?

- Who loves science? Who has a great deal of background knowledge about scientific topics?

- Who works slowly and steadily?

- Who is the first to help another child who does not know what to do?

- Who becomes so engrossed in exploring anything mechanical that it is hard to divert her attention to something else?

- Who takes the initiative and thinks of new ways to use materials?

Teachers use the answers to such questions to decide how to scaffold children's learning.

Information about children's ways of interacting with people and using materials are generally referred to as *approaches to learning*. The National Education Goals Panel identified approaches to learning as a critical domain for school success (Kagan, Moore, & Bredekamp, 1995). As teachers assess approaches to learning, they consider these characteristics:

- flexibility
- persistence
- creativity
- curiosity
- imagination
- initiative

Researchers have conceptualized other learning characteristics in various ways:

Working approach Chen and McNamee (2007) use the term *working approach* to describe how children engage in school activities.

Multiple intelligences Many teachers find Gardner's model of multiple intelligences helpful. Gardner (1999) describes learners as having different levels of eight types of intelligence: bodily–kinesthetic, interpersonal, linguistic, logical–mathematical, naturalistic, intrapersonal, spatial, and musical. These intelligences are useful in describing the ways children interact with and in the world.

Dispositions Some researchers talk about dispositions, or habits of mind, that affect learning (Katz, 1988). Carr (2001) assesses five main dispositions, including taking an interest, being involved, persisting despite difficulty or uncertainty, communicating with others, and taking responsibility.

Whether or not we think consciously about approaches to learning, working approach, personality, or multiple intelligences, information about a child's experience and style as a learner influences the way a teacher interacts with the child. Consider the following examples that show how teachers adjust curriculum and instruction according to their assessment of how children learn.

Becky is considering a study of insects because her 4-year-olds seem fascinated by ants on the playground. She begins by assessing children's attitudes, prior knowledge, and interest in insects. She finds out that several children fear insects and decides not to begin the study with an investigation of an ant farm or a visit to a beekeeper, which were her initial thoughts. Instead, she stays focused on the playground ants and encourages children to join the study at their own paces.

Geraldo, a kindergarten teacher, decides not to start a mini lesson on a new math concept right before the class goes to the large-motor room. He makes this adjustment to the schedule because Janine, who works slowly and methodically, has difficulty transitioning to a new activity until she has finished what she is doing.

From these examples, you can see how understanding children's approaches to learning enables you to individualize your teaching approach and to assist each child most effectively.

Here are examples of teachers' questions about individual children as learners:

Hannah, 4 years old, gets immediately involved with building or creating things during choice time, and she struggles to move to the next activity at the end of the time. What strategies can I use to help her transition more smoothly from one activity to the next?

Terry, a child new to my kindergarten, arrives each morning and briefly visits each area to watch for a moment. After observing, he moves on, eventually joining a group or beginning an activity. Is this his way of adjusting to the classroom? What is his style of working? Does he need to see everything available to him before selecting an activity, or does he need some support in order to make a choice?

Think about a child in your classroom or caregiving group, or another child you observe.

- How would you describe his or her approach to learning?

- How might a teacher use knowledge of this child's approach to learning to give greater support to the child?

Reflect on Your Practice

Assessing to Solve Problems

Even the most seasoned early childhood teachers have instances when the events in the classroom feel challenging—even overwhelming. Perhaps one child has suddenly become silent, sending up a red flag. Maybe you notice that children are having an argument about who gets to build with the arch-shaped blocks. Maybe children are having a hard time choosing with whom to play. Whatever the problem, it is important to identify the issue and then collect the information that will help you understand *what* is happening and *why*.

When the challenge involves only one child, the teacher can review the assessment information collected about the child to see whether or not it sheds light on the problematic behavior. By gathering data about the child's behavior (at different times of the day, in different areas of the classroom, in large- and small-group activities, and when playing alone or with others), you will gain insights about the behavior. Talking with the child's family may provide critical background information about the child's behavior at home.

Kelly, a Head Start teacher of 4-year-olds, was puzzled by Jason, who enrolled in her program just 3 weeks earlier. In Kelly's class, children sign in every day by writing their names on a clipboard right inside the classroom door. Kelly writes,

> At the end of every day, I take the children's sign-in sheet and record attendance in my book. By Thursday of the week before last, I noticed that Jason was present every day but had not signed in once. I decided to remind him last week. It's not that I care so much about taking attendance that way, but it usually encourages children to practice writing their names.
>
> On Monday, I noticed that he walked right by the sign-in sheet. I said to him, "Jason, remember to sign in, please," and I continued to interact with children as they entered the classroom. At the end of the day, I found that my reminder hadn't helped; he still hadn't signed in. On Tuesday, I told Jason that I noticed he hadn't been using the sign-in sheet and I wondered why. He said he forgot. I decided to observe him to find out what was preventing him from signing in, and I thought I would look at other samples of his writing.

On Wednesday, he came in, glanced at me, and went right to the truck and big-block area. Later in the day, when I was sitting with a group of children putting puzzles together, I asked Jason whether he would like to join us. Instead, he went to the book corner. While observing him for 2 more days, I noticed that he avoided fine-motor activities if he could. When he had to use small manipulatives, he had a lot of trouble. He never chose drawing or other writing or art activities, so I didn't have any samples of writing or drawing. Since it was early in the year, I didn't want to press him further to find out more about his writing skills.

I decided that I would help Jason sign in and explain to him that I didn't expect him to write his whole name right now, that everyone was just learning how to write his or her name. I did that on Monday, and I showed him how to make a *J*. He made an approximation of the letter and went on to other activities. Tuesday, I reminded him to sign the first letter of his name, which he did readily. On Wednesday, he signed in without my prompting and called me over to look at "my *J*" when he was done.

I'm going to continue to get Jason involved in more fine-motor activities, especially simple ones where he can be successful. A month or 2 from now, we'll focus more intently on name writing. Right now it's more important that he develop some fine-motor control and feel successful.

Teachers use assessment information to solve problems in the classroom with individuals and groups of children. Kelly reviewed information she already had about Jason and decided she needed more. After several days of observation, she had an idea about what might be affecting Jason's behavior and acted on it. Her tentative hypothesis—that Jason's fine-motor control was not well-developed—may be correct. She will continue to assess Jason's fine-motor skills and make more detailed plans to help him develop greater control and coordination.

When classroom problems arise, teachers ask questions such as these:

- Why is this happening? Every morning, as families arrive, there is always a time when several babies cry at once. What is going on?

- Usually the block area is abuzz with actively engaged children. Yesterday, I had to intervene three times to help different children solve conflicts. Was this a single-day problem, or is there a larger issue with either the block area or the children?

- At the end of the day, cleanup time in our kindergarten room is always hectic. What are the causes? What can I do to make this routine run smoothly?

Think about a recent challenge in your classroom or another classroom you observe.

- **What questions do you have?**

- **What data could you collect to help you understand the problem?**

Reflect on Your Practice

How Teachers' Questions Change Over Time

Teachers ask three basic types of questions as they assess young children. They seek information about children's knowledge and skills and children's approaches to learning. Sometimes they need particular information in order to resolve classroom challenges. During the school year, particular types of questions sometimes become more significant than others.

Before the school year begins or before meeting a child, you will usually have very basic questions. At this point, a review of the available information about each child will give you a clearer picture. Focus on information pertaining to each child's family structure, health concerns, allergies, primary language(s), and who picks up the child after school.

During the first few weeks of school, as you are teaching children about classroom rules and routines, your questions center on getting to know the children as individuals and learning how to make them feel secure. Who immediately learns the schedule?

Who needs to be reminded of what happens next? Who transitions easily to a new activity? Who participates easily? Who watches first and needs a little extra help to begin participating in the daily life of the classroom? Who has previous experience with particular materials? Who approaches new activities enthusiastically? Finding answers to these questions—and more—about children's individuality and distinctive approaches to learning is the starting point for nurturing relationships with children.

Throughout the year, you will continually ask, "How can I promote each child's learning and development?" Much of your assessment will focus on developmental areas, curricular content, or your program's standards. You will continue to assess children's approaches to learning and use assessment to solve classroom challenges.

As the year progresses and you introduce new topics or concepts, you will devote some of your assessment efforts to **pre-** and **post assessment of units, studies,** or **projects.** Pre-assessment enables teachers to answer questions about children's attitudes, prior knowledge, interests, and understanding of topics. For example, when kindergartners are learning about community helpers in social studies, it is important to find out what they already know about community helpers. There's no sense teaching things children already know! It may be as simple as completing a KWL chart with your group. At the end of a project, teachers want to know whether children have met the learning objectives.

Before progress reports are due, your questions center on how much children have learned, whether they are making progress, and whether they are meeting—or exceeding—expectations for their age or grade. You will review and reflect upon the information you have gathered about each child, make ratings, write narratives for progress reports, and plan for the future. You will think about how to communicate your knowledge of the child's learning to his or her family, the questions you want to ask the family, and the issues you wish to discuss. This is part of summative assessment (discussed in chapter 2).

At the end of the year, teachers again reflect on the child's learning, complete reports, and prepare for conferences, much as they did for mid-year progress reports. The end of the year also offers the opportunity to take a longer view and reflect on the child's progress. Many teachers view the year's-end assessment report as a chance to celebrate the child's learning!

Teachers cycle back and forth between formative assessment, which occurs during the time children are learning, and summative assessment, which pulls together assessment information at the end of a period of time. Your assessment questions and activities change throughout the year.

Guidelines for Deciding What to Assess

Having more information about a child can be very useful. However, assessing everything is not practical in the busy world of teaching. Given the purpose of classroom assessment—to get to know children and foster their learning—you strategically select what to assess, how much evidence to gather, and how timing affects assessment information. Here are some guidelines:

Only assess learning that is important enough to teach. Aligning assessment with curriculum enhances teaching and learning. The information gained from the assessment process often translates into modification of the curriculum and changes in teaching strategies. If you are not planning to teach a particular skill, do not assess it.

Focus on your fundamental questions, not specific activities. Whether or not children can string beads, stack small cubes, or use lacing cards is not the actual focus of assessment. Such activities help children develop eye–hand coordination and fine-motor strength and control. These underlying areas are what you are trying to assess. Stringing, stacking, and lacing are specific activities that require children to use fine-motor skills. It is good practice for teachers to regularly ask themselves why they are planning particular activities, being sure their curriculum fosters what they want children to learn. Assessment should focus on the children's learning, not on the specific tasks.

Think about how much information is enough. When your question is about children's eye–hand coordination, you need several examples of eye–hand coordination in order to formulate an answer. However, you do not need a record of every fine-motor skill the child has demonstrated since the beginning of the year! Similarly, when you know a child can speak in full sentences or count by rote to 20, it is unnecessary to continue to document these accomplishments.

Be realistic about how many different items you can assess. Time limitations restrict how much information you can collect. For example, children who begin a program 3 weeks before family–teacher conferences will not have as complete a progress report as children you have known for months.

Consider how timing affects what you assess. Just as your teaching changes throughout the school year, so does your assessment. Before school opens, when your children are simply names on a page, your approach to assessment is very different from your approach after completing a study of the neighborhood and assess to find out what children have learned. Even though the assessment process is ongoing, your questions change from the beginning of the year to the end.

Assess learning and development that is important to a child's life. If something is simple to assess, it is generally insignificant. Think about the emphasis that many preschool teachers place on naming colors. It's very easy to gather information about which colors each child can name, but color names are not very important to most adults. In assessing the aspects of children's development that matter most to their continued learning, it would be more useful to collect information about children's classification skills than about their knowledge of color names.

Generally, things that are harder to assess tend to be more important, such as critical thinking, initiative, problem solving, intellectual curiosity, drive, and persistence. These qualities matter throughout one's life and must therefore occupy a central place in high-quality assessment. When you are determining what to assess, ask yourself, "Will this matter when the child is 25?" If the answer is no, it probably should not be at the top of your list of assessment questions.

Be sure the information is useful. Because the ultimate purpose of assessment is to promote children's learning, we want the information we have collected to be useful. *Functional assessment* is based on data gathered during everyday routines in the child's natural environment, whether at home or in the classroom (Bagnato, Neisworth, & Munson, 1997; Dichtelmiller & Ensler, 2004; Greenspan, 1996; Meisels, 2001). Assessment information describes how the child functions in his or her environment. The focus is not exclusively on whether or not a child has a particular skill, but rather on how he or she uses the skill in daily life. Maintaining a focus on the functionality of the skills and knowledge targeted by assessment goes a long way to making sure that assessment is meaningful and developmentally appropriate.

Key Ideas to Remember

- Information gained from the assessment process can answer many different types of questions. You may have questions about children's skills and knowledge, the manner in which children learn, and the challenges you face in the classroom.

- You will notice that your questions change as the year progresses.

- Stay focused on asking significant questions—ones that matter to a child and his or her family—rather than questions that are easy to answer.

- Effective teachers are very clear about what they are teaching and why. Effective teachers are equally clear about what they are assessing and why.

References

Bagnato, S. J., Neisworth, J. T., & Munson, S. M. (1997). *Linking assessment and early intervention: An authentic curriculum-based approach.* Baltimore: Paul H. Brookes.

Bowman, B. T., Donovan, M. S., & Burns, M. S. (Eds.) (2000). *Eager to learn: Educating our preschoolers.* Washington, DC: National Academy Press.

Carr, M. (2001). *Assessment in early childhood settings: Learning stories.* Los Angeles: Sage Publications.

Chen, J. Q., & McNamee, G. D. (2007). *Bridging: Assessment for teaching and learning in early childhood classrooms, PreK–3.* Thousand Oaks, CA: Corwin Press.

Dichtelmiller, M. L., & Ensler, L. (2004). Infant/toddler assessment: One program's experience. *Beyond the Journal.* Retrieved June 16, 2007, from http://journal.naeyc.org/btj/200401/dichtel.pdf

Gardner, H. (1999). *Intelligence reframed: Multiple intelligences for the 21st century.* New York: Basic Books.

Greenspan, S. I. (1996). Assessing the emotional and social functioning of infants and young children. In S. J. Meisels, & E. Fenichel (Eds.), *New visions for the developmental assessment of infants and young children* (pp. 231–266). Washington, DC: ZERO TO THREE: National Center for Infants, Toddlers, and Families.

Kagan, S. L., Moore, E., & Bredekamp, S. (1995). *Reconsidering children's early development and learning: Toward common views and vocabulary* (Goal 1 Tech. Planning Group Rep. No. 95-03). Washington, DC: National Education Goals Panel.

Katz, L. G. (1988). What should young children be doing? *American Educator, 12*(2) 28–33, 44–45.

References, *continued*

Meisels, S. J. (2001). Fusing assessment and intervention: Changing parents' and providers' views of young children. *Zero to Three*, *21*(4), 4–10.

Mish, F. C., et al. (Eds.) (2008). *Merriam-Webster's collegiate dictionary* (11th ed.). Springfield, MA: Merriam-Webster, Inc.

National Association for the Education of Young Children, & National Association of Early Childhood Specialists in State Departments of Education. (2002). *Early learning standards: Creating the conditions for success.* Washington, DC: NAEYC.

National Association for the Education of Young Children, & National Association of Early Childhood Specialists in State Departments of Education. (2003). *Early childhood curriculum, assessment, and program evaluation: Building an effective, accountable system in programs for children birth through age 8.* Washington, DC: Authors.

National Governors Association Center for Best Practices, & Council of Chief State School Officers. (2010a). *Common core state standards for English language arts & literacy in history/social studies, science, and technical subjects.* Washington, DC: Author. Retrieved June 24, 2010, from http://www.corestandards.org/assets/CCSSI_ELA%20standards.pdf

National Governors Association Center for Best Practices, & Council of Chief State School Officers. (2010b). *Common core state standards for mathematics*. Washington, DC: Author. Retrieved June 24, 2010, from http://www.corestandards.org/assets/ CCSSI_ELA%20standards.pdf

Snow, C. E., & Van Hemel, S. B. (Eds.). (2008). *Early childhood assessment: Why, what, and how*. Washington, DC: The National Academies Press.

U.S. Department of Health and Human Services. (2010a). *The Head Start child development and early learning framework: Promoting positive outcomes in early childhood programs serving children 3–5 years old*. Washington, DC: Author. Retrieved December 20, 2010, from http://eclkc.ohs.acf.hhs.gov/hslc/ tta-system/teaching/eecd/Assessment/Child%20Outcomes/ HS_Revised_Child_Outcomes_Framework.pdf

U.S. Department of Health and Human Services. (2010b). *State early learning guidelines*. Retrieved February 4, 2010, from http://nccic.acf.hhs.gov/resource/state-early-learning-guidelines

Collecting Data: Observing Young Children

After identifying the questions they have about children's learning, teachers move into the second phase of the assessment cycle: collecting data. Observation is the most powerful and frequently used method of data collection, especially for early childhood educators.

Observation means intentionally watching and listening to learn about children. I find it interesting when defining the term for practicing teachers that some react by saying, "But, Margo, I observe children all the time. I'm never *not* observing them!" In response, I share this with them: When I'm working every day, I *see* the view through my office window, but I am not *observing* the details. I cannot give a detailed description of the view or how it changes over time.

Although the act of observation might seem simple, the "ordinariness of observing is both its power and the reason [why] it is problematic" (Green & Dixon, 1999; p. ix). Teachers are quite familiar with watching and listening to children. They do it daily. However, observation to assess development and learning requires teachers to watch and listen with particular attention. Observing for assessment purposes means not only becoming aware of what children are doing, but also carefully watching and actively seeking information with the *intention* of answering questions about children's learning.

Observation is a powerful tool that provides you with information you need to be an effective teacher. In *The Power of Observation* (Jablon, Dombro, & Dichtelmiller, 2007), the focus is on using observation to build relationships with children. In this chapter, you learn how to use observation to gather data for the purpose of assessing children's development and learning.

The Power of Observation (Jablon et al., 2007) describes an observation cycle in four steps: asking questions; watching, listening, and taking notes; reflecting; and responding. The assessment cycle in *The Power of Assessment* is similar, but it is designed to be used with various methods of assessment.

Observation Cycle	Assessment Cycle
Ask questions	Ask questions
Watch, listen, and take notes	Collect data
Reflect	Interpret data
Respond	Take action

Observation as a method of data collection is a powerful assessment tool. Here's why:

- Observation enables you to relate to each child as an individual with a unique set of needs and strengths.

- Observation provides specific examples to help you understand what children know and can do.

- The information you collect during observation enables you to adapt instruction to better meet children's needs and strengths.

- It helps you see progress as children gain new knowledge and skills over time.

This chapter explores the following subjects:

- guidelines for observing
- recording observations
- managing your observation data
- planning for observation and documentation
- talking with children about observation

Guidelines for Observing

It takes time and experience to become an effective observer. The following guidelines highlight strategies for observing children for assessment purposes:

Be objective. Watching children objectively—without preconceptions—enhances the accuracy and validity of your observations.

Strive to be as objective as possible as you observe children. Record only what you see; not what you expect or hope to see. Try to resist forming immediate impressions that can lead to labeling children or their behaviors. Instead, each time you observe, watch children with an open mind. *The Power of Observation* describes observation as an "attitude of openness." This mind-set will help you view children without prejudice.

Focus on facts—things anyone observing the same situation would agree upon—to achieve objectivity. If it can be debated, it is not a fact. Picture Jon, 20 months, sitting at the snack table. He just spilled his juice on the floor. Everyone would agree that he has spilled his juice; this is a fact. The debatable point is *why* this happened: Was it an accident? Was it on purpose? Was it an experiment to see what happens? Record *who, what, when, where,* and *how,* but wait to consider *why* until you have more information.

Read the following observation note:

6/25/10

Adam can throw and catch very well with a partner and up in the air.

Now compare it with a factual note about the same event.

6/25/10

Adam tossed a beanbag with a partner by throwing underhand and catching the beanbag with both hands. Tosses landed within a foot of his partner. Later tossed beanbag in air and caught it. Continued tossing in air; followed it with his eyes but didn't always catch it (caught it about 60% of the time). Adam walked over to the mats.

A potential limitation of observational assessment is lack of objectivity. Although we try not to let our ideas, feelings, beliefs, and previous experiences influence our observations, this can be challenging. In some cases, what teachers bring to observation—their cultural identity, knowledge of child development, experience with young children, emotions, and inclination to interpret what they see and hear—makes them more sensitive observers (Bulterman-Bos, Terwel, Verloop, Wardekker, 2002). However, watching children objectively and without preconceptions enhances the accuracy or validity of the observations and is an essential skill.

The first observation note summarizes what happens and evaluates it. The second describes factually what happened and provides much more detailed information.

Listen. As teachers, we often forget that listening is another crucial component of observation. As Gronlund and James (2005) point out, even a teacher getting materials out of a cabinet with her back to the room can still keep tabs on classroom action by listening. We learn much about how children think by talking with them and listening to their conversations with others.

Observe at different times and in different situations. When teachers vary the times and places in which they observe, it is likely that their observation records will more accurately describe children's typical behavior.

Just as some of us are morning people but others of us come to life after midnight, children are also affected by the time of day. For example, over time you learn that Tarique's quiet behavior only lasts from when he arrives until about 8:00 A.M., when he is fully awake. If you only observe Kim right before lunch, you may come to think she is overly reactive to the comments of other children and that she is quick to respond physically. Perhaps this is a response to hunger and not her typical way of interacting with her peers. Observing her at other times of the day will give you more information about her peer interactions. Take note of when you tend to observe children and spread your observations over the course of the program day.

Our environment also affects the way we behave. For instance, Jake, a typically rambunctious and outgoing child, appears quiet and withdrawn during the circus assembly. You wonder why and then notice he avoids looking at the clown. His fear of the clown's unpredictable actions has changed his typical behavior. In the same way, the behaviors we are likely to see during circle time are different from the behaviors we may see on the playground or during free play.

In addition to time and place, other factors affect children's behaviors. A classic example is the difference between the duration of children's attention for child-selected and teacher-directed activities. A child who may have difficulty sitting quietly for a story at circle time may look at the same book on her own for 15 minutes. A 3-year-old who cannot sit with a small group of children for a story can "read" a story with his caregiver, one-to-one, with rapt attention for a long time.

An activity's difficulty also affects behavior. We tend to work differently on something that is easy or just the right level of difficulty for us, compared to how we approach a complex activity. For these reasons, in order to get an accurate understanding of a child, we need to observe in different areas of the program at diverse times of the day and in a variety of situations.

Observe over time. In addition to observing in different contexts, it is vital to observe over time. This approach provides more data. As discussed, the more data you gather, the more likely it is that your observation notes describe how the child typically behaves rather than behavior during a one-time event. Remember Jake and the clown? If a teacher only observed Jake's behavior during the circus assembly, most likely the observation notes would not be a good basis for generalizations about his temperament and social–emotional skills. We need to observe *over time* to make sure that we collect enough information about the child. A one-time observation is usually inadequate because the circumstances are temporary.

Teachers also need to observe over time in order to detect progress. Young children learn and grow rapidly. What they cannot do now, they may accomplish next week. If we want to capture a child's progress, we need to observe for the same skills during different time periods. Observation over time is especially important when our purpose is to monitor development or to track the acquisition of particular skills and knowledge.

Record what you observe. Recording your observations increases the accuracy of your data. The most obvious reason to record observations is so we do not forget what we have seen and heard! Even teachers with good memories are hard-pressed to remember specific, detailed information about 15, 20, or 25 children. Beyond the sheer quantity of information, classrooms are busy, complex, multidimensional environments. Hundreds of potentially memorable events occur between your morning observation of Yumi's sounding out a word beginning with *m* and the next time you have a moment to think about Yumi's emerging literacy skills. Having many ways to record your observations is necessary to becoming an effective observer.

Another important reason to document your observations is to have tangible records of what you have seen. When it is time to review your observations in order to interpret them and decide how you will support children's learning, you need concrete evidence to study.

Date observation notes, photos, and video clips. As you are gathering materials and preparing to observe, remember that all observation records must be dated. There is nothing more frustrating than finding a mislaid observation note and not remembering whether it was from 3 weeks or 3 months ago. In order to show children's progress, teachers must know when skills and behaviors were observed. Then they can compare later observations to earlier ones.

Maintain confidentiality. Teachers sometimes worry about leaving notes about children in plain view. It is helpful to get into the habit of using children's initials as a way of protecting their privacy. When discussing observations with families, be careful to omit the names of other children involved. However, if your observation notes are factual, confidentiality is not usually a problem.

Create realistic goals for observing. When it comes to assessment, the more data or observations you have, the better. However, teachers cannot observe and record each instance of a child's use of a particular skill. The process is to look at *samples* of children's behavior, take notes, and then interpret that evidence. From the data, teachers make general inferences and statements about the child's skills and knowledge. For example, on two or three occasions, you observe a child count 10 objects. You assume that these observations of counting accurately represent the child's ability to count.

Moreover, not every skill requires multiple observations. For example, once a child demonstrates that he can skip, you do not have to continue to observe and record evidence of this skill. In order to increase the chances that you have enough data and that they give a comprehensive picture of the child, be objective. Observe at different times and in different situations, and observe over time.

Remember that observing takes time. It is realistic to focus on 3 or 4 children a day, not 15. Perhaps you might plan to watch for three or four different skills, observing all your children during a week. However, it is unrealistic to expect teachers to observe and record each minute of every teaching day. Regardless of how prepared you are, it is impractical to observe everything going on in a busy classroom. Rather than set unrealistic expectations when it comes to observation, set feasible goals, put them in your lesson plans, and concentrate on them.

Review the guidelines for observing.
- **Which do you follow regularly?**
- **Is there one that you need to focus on this month?**

Reflect on Your Practice

Recording Observations

How do you feel about observing and recording children's learning? What works for you? What are your challenges? Many teachers find that seeing what children do is easy, but they struggle with record keeping.

Record keeping is necessary because it preserves the evidence of what children know and can do. Think about your health care providers. How would you feel if your doctor did not make any notes after examining you? What would she review if you came for a return visit? How would anyone know how she determined her treatment decisions? Documented evidence inspires confidence in the accuracy of the decisions you base on that data.

Let's look at when to record, methods to use, and tools that can help make the process work for you.

When to Record

There are three approaches to recording observations in the classroom (Dichtelmiller et al., 2001; Jablon et al., 2007):

In the action Most early childhood teachers are exceptional at multitasking, and this skill is useful for observing. As you interact with children throughout the day, you can record observations by using brief notes, tallies, or matrices that are described in the following section. Because you are also leading activities, talking with children, supervising the room, and helping children find materials (among other things), you only have time to record very brief notes.

Out of the action From time to time, teachers need to step out of the ongoing action of the classroom in order to observe and record. Maybe a quiet toddler rarely asks for your attention, but you want to be sure that you take time to follow his actions. You let your assistant take responsibility for overall supervision of the room and take no more than 5 minutes to observe and record notes during this time when you do not have other responsibilities. With older children, you can signal that you are unavailable for a few minutes and use the uninterrupted time to observe (more about this follows). Be realistic. Observing out of the action for a few minutes—once in the morning and once in the afternoon—is a realistic goal. Being out of the action for 20 minutes is not.

After the fact A few teachers can observe throughout the day and record accurate notes during a break, at lunch, or at the end of the workday. If you can recall people's exact words in a conversation, what they were wearing the last time you saw them, and what they ordered for lunch, you may be able to record accurately after the fact. One teacher told us that he sets a timer for 10 minutes at the end of the day, reviews a class list, and writes whatever he remembers about each child's day. Keep in mind that, as more time elapses between an event and the time you document it, it is less likely that the record will be accurate.

> **Think about your classroom or a classroom that you observe regularly.**
>
> When does the teacher do most of his or her recording? In the action, out of the action, or after the fact?
>
>
> **Reflect** on Your Practice

However you find time to document your observations, you must record them in order to ensure the accuracy of your recall. If you document an observation inaccurately, the decisions you base on those records will be poorly informed. You will base your actions on erroneous information, making them far less likely to support children's learning.

How To Record

There are many possible ways to record observations. I have observed that teachers primarily record observations in six ways. Typically, a teacher will regularly use two or three of the following techniques:

Brief notes When teachers observe in the action, they often record a few short notes, just words and phrases about what they have seen and heard. Later—at the end of the day, during a break, or when filing their notes—they add enough information to these brief notes so that they will be easily understood during review. Taking brief notes is like taking notes during a lecture—you can't possibly write everything, so you note the most important information and fill in additional information later.

Anecdotal notes These are detailed narratives describing an incident or event. Suppose that you notice Carly playing with another child in the dramatic play area. Carly usually plays alone, so you take a few minutes to watch what's happening. When you do not have time to write the entire anecdote while it is happening, record some brief notes at that moment and add more details later.

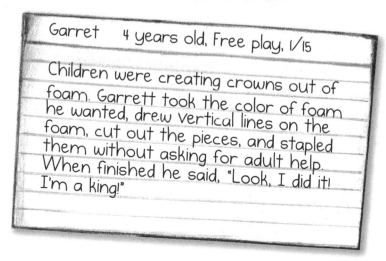

> Garret   4 years old, Free play, 1/15
>
> Children were creating crowns out of foam. Garrett took the color of foam he wanted, drew vertical lines on the foam, cut out the pieces, and stapled them without asking for adult help. When finished he said, "Look, I did it! I'm a king!"

Running records Running records are detailed narrative accounts of behavior or speech recorded sequentially during a given time period. Unlike anecdotal notes that describe a particular event or incident, running records describe all aspects of a child's behavior or speech for a particular period of time. For example, you might use a running record to note what David does in the block area. Running records are most easily kept when teachers have a few minutes out of the action.

Diagrams, sketches, and photographs Sometimes it takes less time to draw a picture of something or to take a photo than it would to describe it in words. Diagrams, sketches, and photographs are particularly helpful when teachers are observing children who are creating things. Sketching the zoo that Shayna built in the block area—complete with animals, food, and zookeepers—may be more efficient and accurate than relying on words alone.

A quick photo using the classroom camera can save time. You can add a brief description later. Digital cameras capture images and are especially useful for image storage. Photos are easily uploaded to a local hard drive. Storing photos on a computer or Web-based system saves physical shelf space in already crowded classrooms.

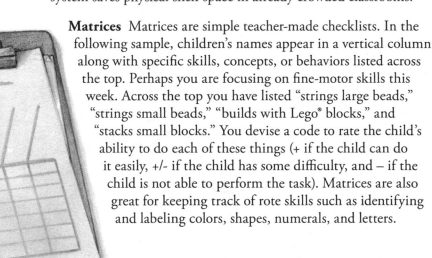

Matrices Matrices are simple teacher-made checklists. In the following sample, children's names appear in a vertical column along with specific skills, concepts, or behaviors listed across the top. Perhaps you are focusing on fine-motor skills this week. Across the top you have listed "strings large beads," "strings small beads," "builds with Lego® blocks," and "stacks small blocks." You devise a code to rate the child's ability to do each of these things (+ if the child can do it easily, +/- if the child has some difficulty, and – if the child is not able to perform the task). Matrices are also great for keeping track of rote skills such as identifying and labeling colors, shapes, numerals, and letters.

Tallies Sometimes you want to know how often a child behaves in a particular way. For example, suppose you perceive that Anna is always hitting or touching someone. You want to see whether or not the facts match your perception, so you decide to count every time she touches another child. You might decide to count touches during a 30-minute period, during a particular activity in the daily schedule, or throughout the entire day. It's simple just to make a tally mark on the daily schedule or a note pad each time the behavior occurs. One teacher put a counter in her pocket and pressed the button each time she or her assistant observed the target behavior. You can analyze the data after finding out how frequently the behavior occurs. Maybe Anna has more difficulty during particular times of the day and needs more support at those times.

Other technology Take advantage of whatever technology is available to you. As technology continues to advance, there are many options for recording children's activities. Digital voice recorders are great for capturing samples of children's language. Digital video can document in real time children's interactions and play scenarios. However, to be efficient, the technology should not require you to transcribe or convert the data into another form. If you must listen again to a recording and transcribe it, you have not saved much time.

Also, personal digital assistants can be useful because the information entered can be downloaded to another computer or uploaded to an online assessment system. However, be conscious of the impact of all technology on your interactions with children.

A streamlined recording process. Regardless of the methods you use, develop a personal shorthand. Use abbreviations and symbols to speed up note taking. Use initials for children's and teachers' names. With matrices, devise codes to rate how well a child is using skills. Do whatever you can to speed up the recording process to capture as many details as possible.

Which of the methods described above have you used?

- Select one that you have not used or do not frequently use. Try it over the next few days.

- How did it work?

- What type of information is it designed to capture?

Reflect on Your Practice

Recording Tools

After teachers determine the observation method(s) to use, they decide what tools to use to record observations. At the most basic level, observers need something to write *on* and *with*. Planning ahead is important because not having the appropriate tools can delay or prevent teachers from capturing important information.

Some of the most commonly used recording tools are described next.

Legal pads Many teachers use 8½-by-11-inch pads or the smaller 5-by-7-inch pads to record observation notes. Some teachers designate a page for each child by creating tabs along the left margin, one for each child. This enables the teacher to quickly find each child's page.

Labels Labels come in all different shapes and sizes. Depending on the size of your handwriting, you might want to use file folder labels or larger mailing labels. One of the nice features of labels is that you can preprint children's names, dates, and even your observational focus on them. This can help you identify when you've missed a particular child or a particular skill.

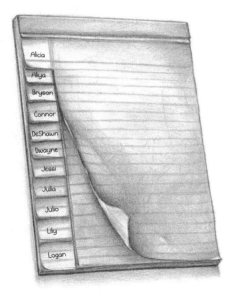

Index cards Index cards also come in different colors and sizes, lined and unlined. Some teachers file them in small file boxes; others punch a hole in the corner of each card and attach them with metal rings. Depending on your style, you might want to color code by domain or subject area. For example, you may find it convenient to record motor skills on blue cards and cognitive skills on white ones. Some teachers tape overlapping index cards (one per child) inside a file folder. They keep all children's observation notes together and easily replace a child's card when it is full. It is also easy to notice when there are few notes on a child's card.

Sticky notes Like index cards and labels, sticky notes also come in a huge variety of colors, sizes, and shapes as well as lined and unlined versions.

Teacher-made observation forms The possibilities are endless. You can design forms to go with activities, centers, routines, specific curriculum objectives, developmental indicators, or early learning standards. If you design your own forms, be sure to include a place for the date.

Pen or pencil If you attach a pen or pencil to a clipboard on which you have secured forms, cards, or paper, you'll always be prepared to write observation notes.

Some teachers wear aprons or smocks with large pockets. This is great for observing because pens or pencils can be tucked in pockets along with sticky notes or index cards.

- How do you record observations? What materials do you use?

- Do your tools change depending on what and where you are observing?

- Try at least one new tool this week.

Reflect on Your Practice

Having matrices prepared in advance or the right index cards where you can find them can make the difference between actually observing and only thinking about observing.

Managing Observation Data

The purpose of documenting your observations is to be able to use the information at a later date. Many teachers collect lots of data, but much of it is disorganized and hard to use. Here are some strategies to manage data collected by observing:

Designate a place to put your documentation at the end of each day. This may be a basket or an envelope that contains all of the notes you have not yet filed. If you have taken photos or made video clips, upload them to a file you have created for each child.

Allocate a few minutes at the end of each day to make sure your observation records are in that designated place. Leaving work with notes still in your pocket increases the likelihood of losing them and decreases the probability of getting them into children's files.

Sort your observation records by child every 2 or 3 days. If you do this regularly, your pile of observation records will still be manageable. You will have all the information you need about each child in one place, ready to review.

Organize your observation records to learn about individual children and the group. You might make a file for each child, including notes from home, notes from other teachers or consultants, observation notes, scores or reports from evaluators, and any other information about the child. Many teachers subdivide the file by developmental domains or subject areas.

You also want to look at observational data across children to see, for example, how the class is progressing with reading comprehension skills. This is why it is critical to organize your observation records for each child by developmental domain or subject area. If you want to find out how well your children understand stories, you have to be able to access every child's record related to story comprehension. By scanning your records on each child in a specific area, you can pinpoint where the class is as a whole and plan appropriate activities.

As mentioned earlier, most teachers have several types of observational data, including matrices with data for an entire group of children. Where do you file them? Rather than copy the matrix for each child's file or transfer each child's information into an individual file, teachers often use a separate folder for group observations. When you review your observation records by child, remember to check the group file for additional information.

- How satisfied are you with the organization of your observation records? Can you find information you need quickly?

- Is there a new strategy you want to try for managing your notes?

Reflect on Your Practice

Planning for Observation and Documentation

To observe regularly, you must plan it. Sometimes you want to observe children in an open-ended manner. At the beginning of the school year or when a new child enters your program, you might observe to learn what you can about how this child experiences his or her environment. This is called *open observation*. Open observation is valuable, so many teachers put a reminder to do it in their written plans.

At other times, you observe with a specific focus in mind. One benefit of focusing is that you do not have to observe everything at once. Adding a section to your lesson plan form, noting who and/or what you plan to observe that week, helps you integrate observation into your practice.

When teachers observe and record with a specific assessment focus in mind, they look for

- evidence of children's accomplishments related to developmental domains, curricular areas, or early learning standards
- information about each child's approach to learning
- data that will help solve specific classroom dilemmas

Observing Development, Curricular Objectives, and Standards

When content is the focus and you need information about all children in your classroom, plan in two ways for observation:

Focus on curricular goals as you plan learning activities. Often, you begin by planning a particular learning experience. As you develop a lesson plan, refine learning goals for the children, and identify your instructional strategies, think about what you want to learn about children as they participate in the experience. To plan for assessment, you have to choose the methods and tools you will use to document your observations. Whenever possible, it helps to specify whom you will focus on so that you can be sure that you eventually observe all children. Consider this example:

Learning Experience   Week of April 10

Walking in the neighborhood during outside time to observe and talk about the springtime environment

<u>Learning Goals</u> - Children will...

1. Observe and describe living things. (e.g., plants, flowers, trees, insects, birds, etc.)

2. Listen for sounds of living things in the environment.

3. Use their senses to examine the environment. (e.g., sight, hearing, smell, touch)

4. Talk about their observations.

5. Use new vocabulary related to living things.

6. Ask questions and gather more information to answer them.

<u>Instructional Strategies</u> - Pam and Laura will...

1. Read a story about going on a neighborhood walk (<u>Mouse's First Spring</u>, <u>It's Spring</u>, or <u>The Boy Who Didn't Believe in Spring</u>).

2. Talk with children before we go and have them predict what they might see and chart their ideas. (Review the chart before each walk.)

3. Encourage children to look closely, touch objects with varied textures, smell a variety of objects.

4. Ask questions: What do you notice on the ground/in the sky/up in the tree? What do you hear? How does that feel? What does that remind you of?

5. Tell children the names of particular flowers, trees, birds, insects, etc.

6. Encourage them to ask questions.

Observation Plan: Use matrix. On each walk, Pam will observe three children, and Laura will observe two.

Pam has identified scientific thinking and language development as a curricular focus for the following week. She wants to engage her group of fifteen 3-year-olds in noticing springtime changes in the neighborhood. To do this, she plans to take the group on a series of short neighborhood walks next week.

She begins by identifying specific goals for children's learning on her lesson plan. These include using language and expanding their vocabularies, asking questions, and using their senses to observe the neighborhood and examine living things. Next, she considers the instructional strategies she and her assistant, Laura, will use to help children reach these goals, including specific questions to ask the children.

Pam designs a matrix that reflects the learning goals for the children. She and Laura will take the children on three walks and focus on five children during each walk. Pam will observe three children, and Laura will observe two children. In addition, Pam will take an audio recorder to capture children's exact words whenever possible.

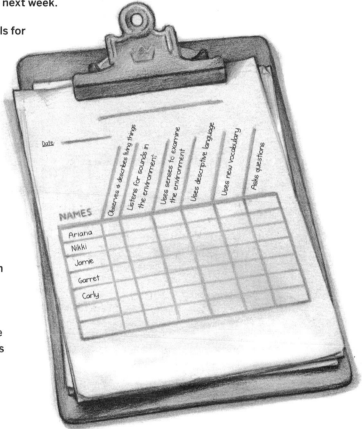

Focus on assessment goals as you plan instructional activities.
In some situations, your plans for observing and recording are
guided by your need to assess how children are performing in
relation to specific standards or curricular objectives. You have
to make sure the learning experiences you plan will provide
opportunities for children to practice these skills and for you to
observe them. Let's look at Tanya, who teaches a mixed group of
3- and 4-year-olds. Carl is her assistant.

Week of October 23   Standards/Learning Goals:

1. Demonstrates balance, control, agility, and coordination

2. Demonstrates ball-handling skills: rolling, throwing, catching, and kicking

<u>Learning Experiences</u>

Monday: Trikes, climber, balance beam, and balls on playground

Tuesday and Wednesday: obstacle course in large-motor room: walk across balance beam,
run on Zig-Zag line, jump over 2 ropes that represent a river, climb stairs and jump down,
crawl through tunnel, run around a circle, hop on 1 foot

Thursday and Friday: ball games on the playground (e.g., rolling balls through children's spread-
out legs, throwing balls so they land inside a hula hoop, tossing and catching a ball around a
circle of children, kicking balls against a wall)

<u>Instructional Strategies</u> - Tanya and Carl will:

1. Observe children.
2. Use mirror talk to validate what children do.
3. Record notes on matrices.

<u>Observation Plan</u>:
Monday: open observation using sticky notes and clipboard

Tuesday and Wednesday: focused observation with Obstacle Course Matrix

Thursday and Friday: focused observation with ball play matrix

---

Next week, Tanya plans to observe children's large-motor skills. Specifically, she wants to learn about children's balance, agility, throwing, and catching. She decides that, on Monday, she will take children outside with gross-motor equipment (e.g., trikes, balance beam, climber, and an assortment of balls).

She will observe openly to get a broad sense of what the children can do. To keep track of what she learns, she will use sticky notes and a clipboard. Next, she plans two additional learning experiences for later in the week so that she can focus more specifically on individual children's skills. She will

– create an obstacle course in the large-motor room

– bring balls of different sizes out to the playground

She makes two different matrices. One lists obstacle course tasks, and the other describes various ball-throwing, -catching, and -kicking tasks. She will also have sticky notes and a pen each time they go outside in case she wants to note additional information.

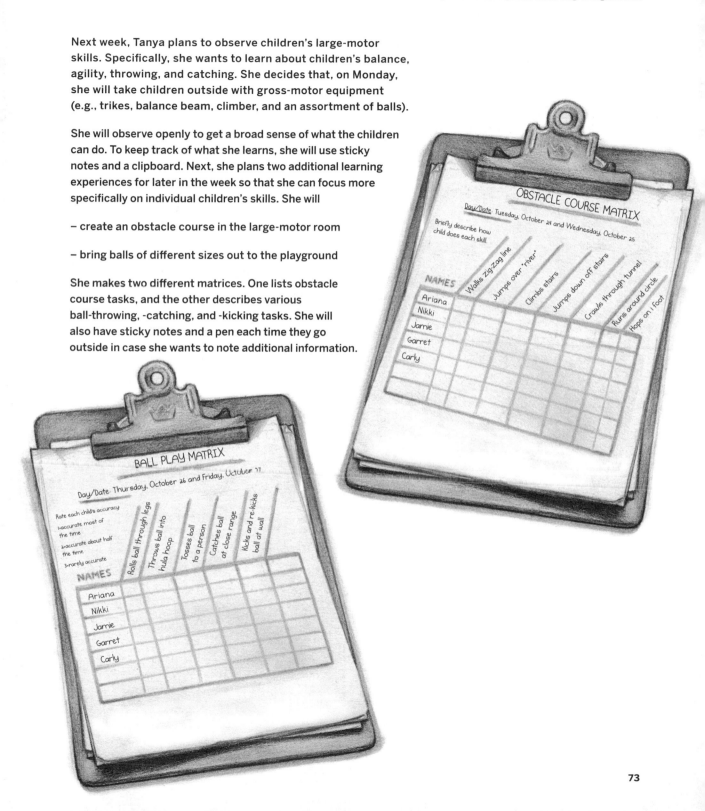

OBSTACLE COURSE MATRIX

Day/Date: Tuesday, October 24 and Wednesday, October 25

Briefly describe how child does each skill.

NAMES	Walks Zig-Zag line	Jumps over "river"	Climbs stairs	Jumps down off stairs	Crawls through tunnel	Runs around circle	Hops on 1 foot
Ariana							
Nikki							
Jamie							
Garret							
Carly							

BALL PLAY MATRIX

Day/Date: Thursday, October 26 and Friday, October 27

Rate each child's accuracy
1-accurate most of the time
2-accurate about half the time
3-rarely accurate

NAMES	Rolls ball through legs	Throws ball into hula hoop	Tosses ball to a person	Catches ball at close range	Kicks and re-kicks ball at wall
Ariana					
Nikki					
Jamie					
Garret					
Carly					

Both planning strategies work. Whether you plan curriculum first and then decide what to observe or vice versa, planning is essential.

When you are planning your activity, take into consideration that some skills and behaviors are easier to observe than others. Taking care of materials, transitions from one activity to the next, pretend play, and small- and large-group participation are behaviors you might see on a daily basis, and you can record a few notes that will jog your memory later.

Other skills and behaviors are more difficult to observe every day, such as describing the properties of objects, classifying items, understanding basic needs of living things, or identifying similarities and differences among families. Teachers sometimes feel that they are "cheating" if they set up activities in order to observe particular skills rather than passively waiting to observe evidence of those skills. Remember that observation is an active process and that observational assessment means intentionally "going after" information. When you plan activities that enable you to observe specific skills, behaviors, and evidence of knowledge, you are maximizing the chance of finding out what you need to know (McAfee & Leong, 2007). As long as the activities are worthy of the children's effort, there is no reason not to set up activities that serve both curricular and assessment purposes.

Objective	Activity	Materials	Observation Plan
Science Center Objective: Distinguish between living and nonliving things	Display a variety of living and nonliving things. Ask, "How can you classify these items into two groups?"	plants caterpillar photos of people class gerbil apple penny cup pencil	Note how each child demonstrates understandings about living and nonliving things and explains his or her groups. Record children's comments and questions. Use sticky notes.

Observing Individuals

When you focus on children's approaches to learning, preparation can be as simple as writing a note to remind yourself of your questions. This note may also indicate where or when to observe so that you maximize your chances of gathering data that will help answer your questions.

Observing to Solve Problems

Like all professionals, teachers have good days and bad days. Typically, a succession of bad days means that something is interrupting the flow of classroom life. Once teachers recognize that they are feeling challenged and a problem exists, observation can help provide information about how to solve the problem. Think about Kat's classroom.

> Every morning as families arrived, there seemed to be a time when several babies cried at once. I noticed it for about 2 weeks before I realized that I really had to figure out what was going on. Mornings were getting off to a difficult start for the children and adults. To find out what was upsetting the children, I decided to observe carefully during arrival.
>
> I observed for several days. Arrival was smooth for several days. No one cried. On Wednesday, it happened again. What was different? At the end of the day, I realized that 9-month-old Ariana was home sick on Monday and Tuesday but back on Wednesday. I decided to focus on her the next day.
>
> I watched Ariana and her mom. As soon as mom moved in to give her a final kiss, Ariana started to cry. I noticed that Jamie and Nikki looked at Ariana and immediately started crying. Then everyone's attention was on the crying babies near the door.
>
> On Friday, I met Ariana and her mom at the door and explained what I thought was happening. I asked Ariana's mom to bring Ariana into the classroom, but explained that she should kiss her good-bye out in the hall. I'd go along, comfort Ariana until she was calm and then bring her into the classroom. That worked perfectly. In fact, I think Ariana calmed down more quickly without the other babies' crying. Problem solved!

In this case, recognizing that there was a problem and making the time to observe were almost all it took to solve the problem.

Talking With Children About Observation

If you are new to observing, you might wonder whether or not to talk with your children about your observation activities. Some teachers feel uncomfortable about letting children know that they are writing notes about them. They try to keep their recording a secret. In fact, there are good reasons to talk about what you are doing:

Talk about learning. If your children are at least preschool aged, talk about teaching and learning regularly. Even young children can understand that you are watching them to find out what they know and can do and that what you learn about them tells you what to do next. Talk regularly about learning and how children are growing and developing (e.g., "Remember when you could only write the *T* in your name? Now you can write the whole thing!"). This helps children develop metacognitive skills—the ability to think about their own learning. (See chapter 8 for more about involving children in assessment.)

Talk about your writing. Explain that you are writing to help you remember what you saw and heard. Young children emulate adults. Early childhood educators know this from seeing their words and behaviors reenacted in the dramatic play area! Soon you might have some children gathering their own observation tools and making notes!

Communicate caring and respect. Taking the time to focus closely on what children are doing communicates that you care. Children learn that what they are doing is important enough for someone to document.

Balance observation and interaction. One issue for teachers new to observation is the difficulty of finding time to write notes or step out of the action to take photos or videos. McAfee and Leong (2007, p. 157) highlight the necessity of "maintaining dual focus," or scanning the classroom overall while also observing and recording. Teachers have accomplished this necessary multitasking in creative ways. First, talk to children about what you are doing so that they understand its importance. Second, teach children to be as independent as possible so they can manage tasks they might otherwise ask an adult to do.

Some teachers encourage children to get help from another child when the teacher is busy. This also builds community in the classroom. Other teachers develop signals that let children know they are busy observing: One wears her observation hat; another writes with a large, brightly colored pen. In various ways and by involving children, teachers have made it easier to get the time they need to record what they see and hear.

As teachers learn to be confident observers, they strive to observe as objectively as possible, recognizing the particular lenses they bring to observation. At the same time, they develop the observation, documentation, and planning strategies that work for them. Once teachers have been observing regularly and have collected observation notes in many areas, it is time for them to reflect on what they know.

Key Ideas to Remember

- Observing for assessment is targeted and purposeful. You identify questions and plan to use various observation strategies to find answers.

- Your observations provide evidence on which to base your assessment decisions. The more information you have, the easier it is to make decisions.

- Becoming an objective and efficient observer takes time.

- Observing only helps improve teaching and learning if you can easily access your observation notes and review them regularly.

- Be open with children about observation. Convey that what they are learning is so important that you are documenting it.

References

Bulterman-Bos, J., Terwel, J., Verloop, N., & Wardekker, W. (2002). Observation in teaching: Toward a practice of objectivity. *Teachers College Record, 104*(6), 1069–1100.

Dichtelmiller, M. L., Jablon, J. R., Dorfman, A. B., Marsden, D. B., & Meisels, S. J. (2001). *Work sampling in the classroom: A teacher's manual* (4th ed.). NY: Pearson.

Green, J. L., & Dixon, C. N. (1999). Foreword. In C. Frank, *Ethnographic eyes: A teacher's guide to classroom observation* (pp. ix–xii). Portsmouth, NH: Heinemann.

Gronlund, G., & James, M. (2005). *Focused observations: How to observe children for assessment and curriculum planning.* St. Paul, MN: Redleaf Press.

Jablon, J. R., Dombro, A. L., & Dichtelmiller, M. L. (2007). *The power of observation* (2nd ed.). Washington, DC: Teaching Strategies, Inc.

McAfee, O., & Leong, D. J. (2007). *Assessing and guiding young children's development and learning* (3rd ed.). Boston, MA: Allyn & Bacon.

CHAPTER 6

Collecting Data: Using Checklists and Rating Scales

Checklists and rating scales offer efficient ways to collect and summarize information about children's accomplishments and behavior. They also help teachers focus and organize the information they collect. Checklists and rating scales can

- help you keep track of what children know and can do

- remind you of what you need to observe

- help you identify the need for more information about a particular developmental area, subject area, or child

- summarize a large amount of information because you translate your documentation about a child's performance into a checkmark, numeral, or point on a scale

- allow you more easily to combine information about children to see your entire class's performance at a glance

Perhaps the greatest benefit of checklists and rating scales is that they enable teachers to recognize the educational significance of the seemingly ordinary things young children do. The 8-month-old child in a high chair who repeatedly drops pieces of her cracker, watching as the crumbs land on the floor, and then looks up to gauge her caregiver's reaction, is learning about the relationship between cause and effect as she interacts with adults. According to the HighScope *Child Observation Record,* that child is "performing an action on an object," "tracking an object," and "repeating an action to make something happen again," all of which are aspects of early logic (HighScope, 2002).

A 3-year-old child filling and dumping containers at the water table is not only enjoying the experience but also learning about weight, capacity, volume, and the properties of materials. According to the *Teaching Strategies GOLD®* assessment system, he is working in the area of mathematics, "comparing and measuring" weight and volume. At the water table, children also "demonstrate knowledge of the physical properties of objects and materials" (Heroman, Burts, Berke, & Bickart, 2010).

Imagine virtually any scene in an early childhood classroom. When children are actively engaged by a rich, developmentally appropriate curriculum, their ongoing behaviors tell the story of their learning. Checklists and rating scales help teachers document that story.

Teachers who use checklists face two tasks: using the lists effectively and efficiently and finding a valid checklist that will help them collect the information they need. This chapter explores

- features of checklists and rating scales
- the effective use of checklists
- accurate ratings
- criteria for high-quality checklists
- the limitations of checklists

Features of Checklists and Rating Scales

A *checklist* is a list of skills, developmental milestones, or specific knowledge. Each skill is referred to as an *item* or *indicator*. Space is provided to note whether or not a child has accomplished each item. Checklists give you *yes* or *no* information, for example, yes, the child can identify shapes, or no, the child cannot name numerals past *10*. You note the presence or absence of a skill, as illustrated in the following "Sample Gross-Motor Checklist."

Sample Gross-Motor Checklist

Indicator	Yes	No
1. Runs with control	√	
2. Gallops	√	
3. Skips		√
4. Walks up stairs with alternating feet		√
5. Climbs on play equipment	√	
6. Walks across low balance beam	√	
7. Jumps 10 times	√	
8. Hops on each foot 10 times		√
9. Throws ball with accuracy	√	
10. Catches large ball	√	

A *rating scale* is a checklist that enables you to describe the extent to which a child demonstrates each skill. You can note the frequency or quality of a behavior, not just its presence or absence, as indicated by the following example. In some cases, rating scales show a developmental progression.

Sample Gross-Motor Rating Scale

Indicator	Always	Sometimes	Never
1. Runs with control	√		
2. Gallops	√		
3. Skips			√
4. Walks up stairs with alternating feet		√	
5. Climbs on play equipment		√	
6. Walks across low balance beam	√		
7. Jumps 10 times	√		
8. Hops on each foot 10 times		√	
9. Throws ball with accuracy	√		
10. Catches large ball	√		

It should be noted that we use the term *checklist* to include both checklists and rating scales.

Checklists may vary in at least three ways:

Breadth Some checklists focus on one developmental domain or subject area; others include all domains.

Content The items, or indicators, on a checklist may focus on developmental milestones, curricular objectives, or early learning standards.

Rating scale The number of points on a rating scale typically range from 3 to no more than 7. Some scales rate how consistently a child performs a skill:

> **3-point scale**—rarely, sometimes, often

> **4-point scale**—seldom, occasionally, frequently, always

Other checklists describe to what extent the child has mastered a skill with ratings scales such as these:

> **3-point scale**—not yet, in process, proficient; or beginning, partially complete, complete

> **4-point scale**—not yet, emerging, developing, mastered

Using Checklists Effectively

A good checklist offers a lens through which you can view children's learning. Your first step is getting to know the checklist with which you will be working. You should become familiar with its items and think about how and where you can gather information about each item. Once you are familiar with the items and their meanings, you are ready to begin using the checklist. Think about how you will find the information you need to make checklist ratings: How will you learn about children's ability to communicate? How will you uncover their understanding of patterns, classification, or size? How will you determine whether a child shows persistence or solves problems? The way gather evidence of learning depends on the type of information you seek. Here are some strategies for using checklists effectively to gather evidence of learning:

Record what you observed. For example, consider the checklist item, "Child takes care of materials." You know that Deanna does this because you recall making notes. You have seen her matching blocks to pictures on the block shelves during cleanup and hanging her coat up when it fell off the hook. Just yesterday she brought you a book because a page was torn. Simply record this evidence and put the notes you have to support your rating in her file.

Review existing documentation. From time to time, you need to examine your notes carefully or watch a video clip to recall information about checklist items. For instance, as you reflect on your records, you realize that Plenette demonstrated understanding of one-to-one correspondence as she set the snack table for eight children and when she counted the blocks in her structure. Your focus while observing may or may not have been on one-to-one correspondence, but you can use what you learned incidentally to make an accurate rating.

Observe intentionally. If your existing observation records do not provide the information you need, observe intentionally to learn more. For example, a checklist asks whether a child uses ordinal numbers, but perhaps you never focused on this skill before. Plan to watch for this behavior. A clear focus for observation often enables you to hone in on what may have always been present but not necessary recognized.

For example, *The Work Sampling System*® checklist (Dichtelmiller, Jablon, Marsden, & Meisels, 2004) for 4-year-olds has a social studies item, "Shows awareness of what it means to be a leader." Maybe you never really noticed children's understanding of leadership. You decide to pay attention when children are chosen to be the line leader and to ask them what they think it means to be the "leader." You start to notice which children take on leadership roles in dramatic play and who always wants to be the "boss." At times, all you need to do is refocus your attention in order to see evidence of particular skills in children's actions and conversations.

Study children's work. Gather evidence for checklist ratings by looking at a child's portfolio. When you want to know about a child's writing skills, look for evidence in journal pages or drawings. Similarly, collages made with various materials in the art center, sketches of children's block designs, and children's paintings can provide information about children's creative representation, an important experience in the HighScope *Child Observation Record* (HighScope, 2003).

Plan activities to gather evidence. You may find it tricky to collect data for particular checklist items. After reviewing the data you already have, plan the following week's experiences so that you have specific opportunities to see particular behaviors and skills. *Teaching Strategies GOLD®* has *Assessment Opportunity Cards™* (Teaching Strategies, Inc., 2010) that present activities during which teachers focus their observations on literacy and numeracy skills. Teachers use the activities to collect specific information about particular objectives.

Plan for assessing with checklists. Think about the information needed to complete your checklist as you plan curriculum for the following week. If you review your checklists regularly, you can see where you need more information. What do you need to focus on next week?

If you decide to observe for evidence related to four or five checklist items, gather it for all of your children during the week. Some teachers focus on one developmental or content area at a time. Others determine the specific checklist items on which to focus by looking ahead and finding out what they are likely to see given their curricular plans for the week.

Sometimes you will realize that you do not have data for any of your children for a specific checklist item. This means that you will need to plan opportunities for children to demonstrate that particular learning. For example, *The Work Sampling System®* checklist for 4-year-olds (Dichtelmiller, Jablon, Marsden, & Meisels, 2004) has this item in the Scientific Thinking section: "Asks questions and uses senses to observe and explore materials and natural phenomena." There can be any number of reasons why you do not have information about this indicator. Perhaps you are not someone who loves science. Maybe you know that Anna constantly asks questions, but it never occurred to you to focus on this with the other children. For whatever reason, you need a bit more structure to get information about children's methods of exploration.

To obtain information, you decide to offer new experiences next week that will encourage children to use their senses and ask questions. You might borrow the class gerbil from next door for a week, make paint with soap flakes, and display a bird's nest that fell into your yard during last week's windstorm. Observe intentionally, focusing on each child's exploration of the new materials. Now you just have to record what you see and hear.

Avoid testing situations. When gathering evidence for checklists, you do not want to set up an early childhood test. "A test!" you exclaim, "I don't test my children!" But how often do we see preschool and kindergarten teachers assessing one child in a corner of the room or even outside in the hall? This might seem like a quick, easy way to get information on rote skills, but it is *on-demand assessment* that offers children only one chance to show what they know. Although some children enjoy the one-to-one attention, others get nervous about why they are being asked to leave the ongoing activities of the classroom. When we collect data only once—at a time that may or may not be good for particular children—our results are often unreliable (see chapter 12).

Gather data for checklists in naturalistic situations. It is best to gather assessment data from situations in which children are participating comfortably. Doing so enables you to sample children's behavior more reliably. When assessment is woven into the regular activities of the classroom, it is known as *curriculum-embedded assessment*. Whether children are involved in free play, participating in large- or small-group activities, or outside on the playground, you can gather evidence of their learning in order to make checklist ratings.

Complete checklists over time. Checklists can be completed gradually over the course of several weeks. Sometimes teachers want to have the most current information, so they wait to make checklist ratings until several days before they are meeting with families or preparing progress reports. This puts undue stress on the teacher and rarely produces added benefits. When you report to families, you can describe how the child performed during the reporting period and include dates to show when you made particular ratings.

When you complete checklists over time, the information you gain can be used to influence your curricular plans and interactions with children. If you wait to complete checklists for several weeks or months, you lose the opportunity to use that information to adjust your planning.

If you are currently using checklists to assess children's learning or if checklists are used in a classroom you know well, think about the following questions:

Reflect on Your Practice

- Did the teacher collect evidence to support those ratings?

- Did the teacher plan how, when, and where to observe particular indicators?

- Did the teacher make ratings based on children's behavior during ongoing classroom activities?

- Were the checklists completed over time?

Making Accurate Ratings

Completing checklists or rating scales accurately depends on knowing how much data is sufficient, understanding what ratings mean, and knowing how to choose among them. You also need to know the difference between *not applicable* and *not observed*.

How much data is enough? Unfortunately, there is no easy answer to this question. It does not make sense to require, for example, four observations for each indicator. For behaviors that teachers observe daily, behaviors for which they have some recorded evidence, or behaviors for which they recall unrecorded evidence, four new observations might be a waste of time. Then again, a teacher could have four observations of Miki's attention span but still need more information to figure out what makes Miki attend easily on some days and not at all on others. Arbitrary requirements to record a particular number of observations do not acknowledge teachers' professionalism or the differences among items or indicators.

You certainly need adequate evidence to feel confident about making ratings. When a behavior or a skill is not demonstrated frequently, you need more than one observation to be sure the behavior is really a part of the child's working knowledge or skills. If you credit a child for a skill he can only perform occasionally, the checklist rating is unreliable. When you have doubts or are vacillating between ratings, stop and collect more evidence. Rather than gather a particular number of observations to support each checklist rating, try to stay focused on learning about the child.

Understand the meanings of ratings and how to choose among them. Your use of checklists and rating scales is valid and reliable only if you fully comprehend what the ratings mean and how to choose among them. How often does a child have to do something to move from "sometimes" to "frequently"? What does "seldom" mean? Does the child exhibit the behavior or skill consistently and independently, or does he require cues from you to complete the task? When selecting checklists, look for those that clearly define the rating scale.

It is also important to use the existing ratings and not to create new points on a rating scale by marking between two ratings. This is not the time to hedge your decision by making a checkmark between two points. Evaluate your evidence and choose a rating. If you cannot base a decision on the evidence, gather more information.

Know the difference between *not applicable* and *not observed*. Be careful not to confuse ratings that indicate a child cannot perform a skill with ones that indicate you have not observed the child performing it. There is a distinct difference. Some ratings scales use "not applicable" or "not observed" to mean that the teacher does not have evidence of the child's performance of the item. Sometimes the teacher does not know what a child can do because she or he did not focus observations on the specific item. Sometimes the teacher did not provide opportunities for children to demonstrate the skill. These are entirely different situations from those in which a child had opportunities to demonstrate a skill but the teacher observed that the child did not do so.

Criteria for High-Quality Checklists

Checklists are readily available to early childhood teachers in many forms. They are commercially available and can be found as stand-alone tools or as part of more complete assessment systems. Many teachers and programs create checklists to meet specific needs. As you search for a published checklist or develop your own, you will want to keep the following six criteria in mind:

The content should be purposeful. Every checklist reflects a particular view of what is important to assess. The content of the checklist you use should measure what you want to know about children. In a program for 2-year-olds, you may select a developmental checklist because it aligns well with your play-based program. However, a kindergarten teacher might opt for a developmental checklist that also includes math, science, and social studies items that reflect his or her curriculum. Be certain that the checklist you choose is based on current knowledge about how children learn and develop.

Items should be clearly defined. Items on your checklist should be easy to understand, observable, and specific. Consider this example: A mathematics item on a kindergarten rating scale is, "understands numbers," but no additional explanation is provided. How will a teacher know how to rate this item? Does it mean rote counting? Does it require a child to use one-to-one correspondence while counting objects in a set? Is it about quantity—knowing that a set of 15 objects has more than a set of 4 objects?

There are two problems with this item: First, it is not specific! As you just saw, there are many ways to interpret the wording. Second, "understands" is not directly observable. We can only see behaviors that indicate understanding. This item is neither observable nor specific enough to have the same meaning for everyone using the checklist.

If an item can potentially be interpreted by teachers in different ways, it must be accompanied by an explanation—or a set of criteria—to clarify its meaning. Otherwise, the reliability and validity of the ratings will be questionable.

Consider the following example:

> An item on a motor checklist for toddlers (12–24 months) is "Uses a spoon."
>
> Darren, 14 months, occasionally gets some food onto the spoon and into his mouth. Jessie, one of Darren's caregivers, thinks this means he is using a spoon.
>
> Ralene, another caregiver, does not consider a child able to use a spoon until the child gets most of the food onto the spoon and into his or her mouth.

Unless the checklist specifies *how* to interpret this item, these caregivers cannot be expected to use the checklist reliably.

Items should evaluate meaningful learning. Many checklists include only easy-to-rate items. For example, it is easy to use checklists to keep track of rote skills such as whether or not a child can count to 20 or how many upper- and lowercase letters a child can identify. However, it is much more difficult to find evidence of children's problem-solving abilities, level of initiative, or understanding of leadership.

There should be a reasonable number of items. The overall length of the checklist must be manageable. For each item on the checklist, you need to collect evidence in order to make a rating. When selecting a checklist, consider *how much* data is needed in order to make ratings for 18, 20, or 25 children. Long checklists typically end up unused and at the back of a file drawer. Moreover, when overly lengthy checklists are used, teachers are often tempted to make ratings from memory—without collecting or reviewing evidence to support them.

The points on the scale should be clearly defined. Two issues must be addressed for a rating scale to be used reliably:

- **Accuracy and practicality** A scale of 3–5 points is practical to use. However, it is often difficult to be accurate and to make the intricate discriminations needed when using 6- or 7-point scales.

- **Even or odd number of points on a scale** Scales with an odd number of ratings allow teachers to avoid making a decision by using the middle rating. On a 5-point scale, for example, 3 is the midpoint. In contrast, with a 4-point scale, there is no tempting middle rating; the teacher must decide whether a skill is basically present or absent.

The format should be well-organized. A logically organized checklist makes it easier to use. Many checklists are organized according to developmental areas. Some present items to show the sequential order in which children typically develop skills. Adequate space should be allocated for making ratings and including comments.

Validity and Reliability of Checklists

To be practical and valuable, checklists and rating scales, must measure what *you* need to know. This may be tied to curricular objectives or state benchmarks. If a checklist claims to assess literacy development but is limited to children's interest in books and how they interact with them, it is not a *valid* literacy checklist. It does not measure the entire domain of literacy skills.

Checklists also need to be *reliable*, which means the results should be consistent regardless of who is completing the checklist. Checklist items should be clear and defined well by explanations and criteria so that they are understood and interpreted in the same way by all teachers.

Using checklists reliably requires that ratings be supported by evidence. Furthermore, checklists are deceptively simple because it is possible for a teacher to complete them from memory. When ratings lack documented evidence, there is no way to determine whether all teachers used the checklist the same way (see chapter 12).

Five factors related to human tendencies can affect checklist reliability:

- *Generosity error* occurs when teachers give higher ratings than children actually deserve because they feel uncomfortable giving lower ratings or worry about families' reactions.

- *Severity error* happens when a teacher errs on the low side, giving lower ratings than the evidence supports.

- *Central tendency error* operates when a teacher overuses the middle, or central, rating on a scale.

- *Halo effect,* or overall impressions of a child, can affect how teachers rate that child's skills. For example, 5-year-old Jennifer actively participates in classroom activities. She is verbal, has many friends, and seems to be accomplishing all the goals of kindergarten. When her teacher begins to focus on math, he is surprised to learn that Jennifer shows limited skills related to quantity and measurement. He just assumed that Jennifer's math skills were at the same level as her other skills. This is known as a *halo effect* because the teacher does not allow anything to interfere with his overall positive impression of Jennifer.

- *Fatigue* affects the accuracy of ratings. We all tire, so it is always a good idea to work on only a few children's checklists in one sitting. Take your time. Use it to reflect on the ratings and to create new plans for each child. It is unrealistic to think you can work with many files thoughtfully in one sitting.

Take some time to examine a checklist you use or are considering using. Ask yourself these questions:

Reflect on Your Practice

- Is the content meaningful for your class? Does it address what you want it to assess?

- Does the checklist include more than easy-to-assess items (e.g., more than rote counting, naming colors, and identifying shapes)?

- Are the items so clearly defined that everyone using the checklist will interpret them the same way?

- Is the format clear and easy to use?

- Are the points on the rating scale clearly defined?

- Is the length reasonable, given the number of children in your class?

Limitations of Checklists

Checklists provide information about whether or not children have acquired particular skills or behave in specified ways. However, checklists cannot portray *how* children perform those skills. While checklists provide useful information, they do not provide a picture of the child's actual performance. If two children receive the same rating, you might assume that they perform tasks in the same way. This might not be true. For example, Diontaye and Lynn receive credit on their teacher's checklist for writing their names. However, Diontaye writes all seven letters quickly and uses an uppercase *D* while Lynn writes slowly, pauses periodically, and painstakingly draws each letter. The qualitative differences that distinguish how they write their names will be sacrificed if teachers rely solely on checklists and rating scales. Portfolios, described in chapter 7, are useful if you want to know *how* children perform tasks and create products.

Key Ideas to Remember

- Using a checklist is an efficient way to keep track of children's knowledge and skills because it focuses and organizes your observations.

- A checklist will be useful to you if it assesses what you want to measure with clearly defined, meaningful items. Carefully review any checklist to be sure it matches your early learning standards and curriculum.

- High-quality checklists provide clear directions about how to make ratings.

- Checklist ratings are only valid and reliable if they are based on evidence (observations, work samples, etc.).

- With young children, it is especially important to gather evidence for checklist ratings when children are participating comfortably in typical classroom activities.

References

Dichtelmiller, M. L., Jablon, J. R., Marsden, D. B., & Meisels, S. J. (2004). *The Work Sampling System: Preschool–4 developmental guidelines*. Parsippany, NJ: Pearson.

Heroman, C., Burts, D. C., Berke, K., & Bickart, T. S. (2010). *Teaching Strategies GOLD® objectives for development & learning: Birth through Kindergarten*. Washington, DC: Teaching Strategies, Inc.

HighScope Educational Research Foundation. (2003). *Preschool child observation record* (2nd ed.). Ypsilanti, MI: HighScope Press.

HighScope Educational Research Foundation. (2002). *Infant-toddler child observation record*. Ypsilanti, MI: HighScope Press.

Teaching Strategies, Inc. (2010). *Teaching Strategies Assessment Opportunity Cards™*. Washington, DC: Author.

Ask Questions

Take Action

Assessment Cycle

Collect Data

Interpret Data

CHAPTER 7

Collecting Data: Creating Portfolios

A *portfolio* is a purposeful, well-organized collection of a child's work. It assembles concrete evidence that answers questions about the child's learning. Portfolio collection is an example of curriculum-embedded assessment, because the materials in portfolios come from everyday activities (see chapter 6). As children participate in the classroom, documentation of their activities and the products they create become items in their portfolios. As you review portfolios, you acquire new insights about the children in your classroom and fresh ideas about how to approach teaching. Portfolios are a bridge between teaching and assessment.

Portfolios are an example of authentic assessment, which is a type of performance assessment that engages children in using thinking and problem-solving skills similar to those of successful adults. Authentic activities are meaningful to children's lives in- and outside of the classroom. They require children to use prior knowledge, investigate actively, and make decisions. Children perceive authentic activities to be worthwhile, so such activities tend to engage children at higher levels (Jablon & Wilkerson, 2006).

Authentic assessment focuses on the application of skills in real-world contexts. For example, writing an article for a class newspaper is an authentic performance task because class news is meaningful to children's lives. Memorizing addition and multiplication facts is not an authentic task, but using those facts to figure out how many pencils are needed when three children are each to get two pencils is authentic. Adding time limits sometimes increases the authenticity of tasks for older children, for example, when they are researching and writing newsletter articles as though they were reporters working under a deadline. However, children should still be given time to plan and complete their work, be able to use appropriate tools and resources, and have opportunities to revise their work. When that is so, work samples from authentic tasks make exceptional portfolio items.

Although there are many different types of portfolios, this chapter focuses on portfolios designed for formative assessment. Referred to as *process* (Puckett & Black, 2008), *working* (Wortham, Barbour, & Desjean-Perrotta, 1998), *learning* (Shores & Grace, 1998), or *current-year* (Gullo, 2005) *portfolios*, these collections of work focus on the child's emerging processes and development of knowledge and skill over time. Learning portfolios offer a unique opportunity for children to be involved in the assessment process as they select portfolio pieces and reflect on their personal growth.

Portfolios support your assessment activities by
- providing meaningful information about what children know, the skills they have acquired, how they approach tasks, and their unique personalities
- organizing evidence of children's learning
- supporting evaluative ratings
- illustrating children's accomplishments for families and others beyond the classroom
- presenting a context for regular teacher reflection on children's learning in order to differentiate instruction
- offering opportunities to talk with children about what and how they are learning

This chapter explores several aspects of portfolio creation:
- purposes of portfolios
- what goes into portfolios
- collecting items
- selecting items
- thinking about the work in portfolios
- involving children and families in collecting items

> Generally, early childhood portfolios are not used as a summative assessment method. This contrasts with the portfolios of older elementary- and secondary-age students. Their portfolios, or the items in them, are often graded or evaluated with rubrics. Most early childhood teachers do not score, or rate, individual portfolio pieces or assign grades to entire portfolios. Given our focus on using assessment to improve teaching and learning, it does not make sense to reduce a rich collection of a young child's work to a grade or summative evaluation.

Purposes of Portfolios

Portfolios are defined in a variety of ways (Gullo, 2005; Kingore, 2008; McAfee & Leong, 2007; Puckett & Black, 2008), and each definition invites us to think about the purposes for keeping them. Take a moment to think about professional portfolios.

Think about your own professional portfolio or one belonging to an artist, photographer, or interior designer whom you know.

Reflect on Your Practice

- **What is the purpose of the portfolio?**
- **How do the included items serve that particular purpose?**

Much like professional portfolios, early childhood portfolios are used for many different reasons, including documenting achievement of objectives or standards, a child's progress, best work, representative work, or the uniqueness of the child. Portfolios do not contain all of the work that children do. They only include items related to the purposes that you identify.

Here are some of the many purposes of early childhood portfolios:

Show a child's achievement of objectives or standards. Programs often use portfolios to document children's accomplishment of objectives. Some portfolios cover a single subject or developmental area. For example, a class may have writing portfolios tied to curricular objectives. Other portfolios are intended to show what children know across the curriculum and may contain work from several different areas. Portfolios are also used to demonstrate mastery of early learning standards and benchmarks, with work showing the child's performance as it relates to each standard or benchmark.

Show a child's progress. Progress portfolios document a child's development and learning over time. They contain similar types of work from several times during the school year. This allows comparison of earlier work to later effort and tracks a child's growth. Many progress portfolios show work that is representative of the child's performance at the beginning, middle, and end of the year.

Present a child's best or representative work. Portfolios may be made up entirely of a child's best work, rather than the range of work characteristic of the child at a given time. These portfolios, sometimes known as *showcase portfolios*, include final products that may have been revised over time.

"Shouldn't all portfolios show the child's best work?" you might ask. Essentially, teachers have a choice between selecting "best work" or work that represents how the child typically performs. The decision depends on your purpose for collecting the work. If your goal is to collect pieces that inform teaching in an ongoing way, your portfolios will be comprised of work selected over time that is representative of children's everyday performance. If your focus is on documenting the child's highest level of accomplishment, perhaps to pass on to his or her next teacher, then you will want to create showcase portfolios of best work.

Demonstrate a child's individuality. Portfolios designed to include examples of the child's skills and accomplishments, approaches to learning, particular interests, struggles, and strengths create a detailed sketch of the child as a learner. Such portfolios may include evidence of a child's best efforts, emerging skills, and first demonstrations of particular skills. Some suggest that portfolios are a child's self-portrait, telling the story of his or her learning (Wortham, Barbour, & Desjean-Perrotta, 1998).

If you are currently using portfolios in your classroom or if portfolios are used in a classroom you know well, think about the following questions:

Reflect
on Your
Practice

- Why are portfolios used in this classroom? What is their primary purpose?

- What types of items are included in the portfolio? Do the items reflect the purpose for portfolio collection in that classroom?

What Goes Into Portfolios

The following list includes examples of the concrete items that are often included in portfolios as samples of work.

Early Childhood Portfolio Items		
• drawings	• participation charts describing what a child did on a particular day	• teacher's or child's sketches of the child's creation
• journal pages and other writing samples	• child-made books	• descriptive observation notes about children's activities or creations
• observation notes that capture children's spoken language	• child-created game with dictated rules	
• children's dictation (stories, lists, questions, etc.)	• child-made maps	• paintings, collages, and other artwork
• initial, revised, and final versions of projects	• printouts of computer activities	• transcriptions of interviews
• photos of children engaged in an activity	• solutions to math problems	• charts and graphs
• photos of block structures or other three-dimensional creations	• woodworking projects or photos of woodworking projects	• digital voice recordings (of conversation, songs, fingerplays, dramatic play, etc.)
• child-made signs or labels used in play	• reading logs (lists of books read to the child by the teacher)	• video clips

Let's look at some guidelines to help you identify portfolio items that will provide meaningful assessment data.

Items must match your purpose. The purpose of the portfolio has the greatest influence over which items to include. If, for example, the purpose is to show children's literacy development, the portfolio should contain items that show appreciation for books, knowledge of print, word-recognition skills, emerging writing skills, and so on. A standards-based portfolio would include items related to each standard. For a portfolio to be a useful representation of a child's work, the items must reflect the purpose of the portfolio.

Progress portfolios contain work showing the child's development of particular skills, behavior, or knowledge over time. Items show what a child did or said during what Kingore (2008) refers to as "repeated tasks," defined as "learning experiences that children complete at one point in time and then later complete again to note gains in skills or achievements" (p. 61). For instance, if you want to determine whether or not a kindergarten child is making progress in emergent writing, you may want to collect journal pages from October, February, and May. You might see many drawings with teacher dictation in the October pages, drawings and some letters in February, and drawings with written captions in May.

For "best work" portfolios, you would collect multiple samples of similar work—several writing samples, for instance—and then meet with the child to select the best sample.

Alternatively, if your purpose is to show the individuality of each child, focus on including samples that represent a child's interests, strengths, significant accomplishments, struggles, and approaches to learning. I once had a child in my class who hated to touch any messy, wet, squishy substances. The first time he hesitantly put one finger into finger paint and then made a line on a piece of paper, I saved a copy of that painting to document his risk-taking and initiative.

Consider ownership and use of portfolios. When children are very young, teachers take greater control over creating items and organizing portfolios. A number of teachers include checklists, progress reports, test scores, evaluations, and other school-related—and sometimes confidential—information about the child in the portfolio. However, if your intent is to use portfolios to talk with children about their learning, use another file for items that are not samples of the child's work. Lists and reports have little meaning for the child. What's more, children feel greater ownership of their portfolios if they contain only their work.

Portfolios should not look alike. In developmentally appropriate classrooms where teachers value individuality, each child's portfolio will be different and reflect his or her uniqueness. This does not mean that each child's portfolio will be entirely different from every other child's. There are at least three ways to think about the degree of similarity among children's portfolios:

- **Same learning, same tasks** With this approach, all children perform the same task. For example, you might have children draw a family portrait three times during the school or program year. Each time children draw the portrait, they also dictate or write information about the drawing. By the end of the year, each child's portfolio will include three family portraits.

- **Same learning, different tasks** All children's portfolios include evidence of the same learning, objective, or standard, but children demonstrate their learning differently. For example, a teacher, might want evidence of counting and of understanding quantity in each child's portfolio. Here are some sample items that might be included to show learning:

  - a photo of a child distributing crackers at snack time, with notes about what the child said as she counted crackers

  - a language sample from two children spontaneously talking about how to make sure they each got the same number of red blocks

  - a photo, with notes, of a child counting while bouncing a large ball and trying to bounce more times on each try

  Each child's portfolio will include evidence of counting skills, but, as shown on the next two pages, the particular items will vary.

Brisilda (4 years)
April 3

On a spring nature walk, the children were fascinated by butterflies. I created a worksheet showing six different kinds. Some children colored the butterflies. Brisilda counted them aloud, pointing at them one by one. Then she wrote a numeral by each butterfly. She asked, "How do you write a *2*?" I modeled it on a separate piece of paper, and she wrote it twice. Then she continued, writing the numerals *3* through *6* next to the other butterflies. I asked, "How many butterflies would there be if there were one more?" She answered, "Eight."

Alexander (4 years)
April 12

I asked A. to take some cubes out of the basket and count them. He reached in with both hands, took out 10, and then lined up 9 of them. Starting on his right, he pointed to each one and counted aloud, 1 through 9. The tenth cube (the white one) was not counted.

Zach (4 years)
April 12

Zach watched Bryce line up and count the colored cubes. Then Zach went to the math shelf and brought the basket of counting bears to the table.
He lined up seven bears, starting on the left. He pointed and counted,
"1-2-3-5-8-6-10."

- **Different learning, different tasks** An item is included in only one child's portfolio because it represents something that only engaged—and was only significant to—that particular child. For example, I taught a 4-year-old who was very interested in dinosaurs for several months. Her portfolio included several drawings and photos of small block and tile representations of dinosaurs, demonstrating her intense interest in them. Representations of dinosaurs were not in other children's portfolios.

Portfolios will not be carbon copies of one another in early childhood classrooms. Although they may show similar types of learning, the ways children express their learning vary, depending on their skills, interests, and approaches to learning. Portfolios "assist teachers in their quest to honor the diversity of students and discover the strengths of each learner" (Kingore, 2008, p. 13).

If you are currently using portfolios in your classroom or if portfolios are used in a classroom you know well, think about the following questions:

Reflect on Your Practice

- What types of children's work are currently saved?
- How did the teacher decide what to save?

Items should be informative. In some ways, portfolio collection might seem rather straightforward: Teachers have questions about children's learning, so they collect children's work to help answer them. Then they review the work to see what it tells them, and they use this information to adjust their planning. The assessment cycle works exceptionally well when portfolio items provide rich, comprehensive information about learning.

However, collecting portfolio items that offer insights about teaching and learning can be challenging. Teachers must find concrete ways to show children's ongoing learning and accomplishments. Portfolios use tangible items (e.g., a journal page, a photo of a block structure, a drawing) to represent internal, invisible processes of thinking and learning.

Teachers study expressions of children's thinking and learning in order to know whether they are developing and learning as expected. Children express their learning in diverse ways, including writing, speaking, drawing, and dramatizing, just to name a few. Examining children's creations and how they express themselves offers a window into their thinking. Using a video camera is a dynamic way to document how a child engaged in a task.

Portfolio items vary widely in their effectiveness. Some portfolios are highly informative, telling us a great deal about a child's learning. Others make us wonder why someone bothered to assemble and save certain items. Consider these points when making children's portfolios as meaningful as possible.

Items should tell a story. Comments, also referred to as *annotations* or *captions*, aid us in understanding a portfolio item by providing background information about the piece. Below, note how much more we learn when a teacher annotates a painting.

With its emphasis on children's work or products, portfolio collection exemplifies **performance assessment** (see chapter 6). In performance assessment, the focus is on the integration and application of skills in real-world contexts. Consider two approaches to assessing children's knowledge of language conventions. Teachers using a traditional approach might ask children to state the rules of grammar or identify complete sentences. In contrast, using a performance-based approach, teachers would ask children to apply what they know about grammar and complete sentences in their written accounts of a recent class trip. This task enables the teacher to continue to teach writing, while observing the child's application of language skills. The writing samples can be included in the portfolio.

Amaya Creager   4/26/10

"This is the baby's cow tail. Mouth nose, cheeks and the eyes. It's name Amaya. Amaya lives on a farm."

"That's my name."

Edward Peguero   4/26

"Duck, pig, cow hen, sheep. I asked which was his favorite animal. He said, 'All of them.'"

(Edward was looking at a picture of farm animals as he painted his version.)

Current Study: Farm Animals

As Amaya & Edward were painting, 4/26/10

Amaya asked Edward, "What are you painting?"

Edward explained, "This is the ear. This one is upside down. His face is sideways."

Current Study: Farm Animals

We have to know something about the items in order to understand them. All items should include the child's name and the date of the learning experience. A few quick notes from the teacher explaining how the piece came into being, or describing the child's process, are incredibly useful. You might add comments that answer the following questions:

- Did the child do the work spontaneously, or was everyone doing it?
- Did the child work alone or with others?
- Was it done all at once?
- What was important about how the child worked (e.g., drew very quickly, moved the paper 45 degrees to the right, used left hand, switched hands)?
- Did the child comment about his or her work?
- To what curricular objective(s) or benchmark(s) does the piece relate?
- Why was the piece selected for the portfolio?

Kingore (2008) advises teachers (and older children) to write captions on work to increase its assessment value. Captions succinctly describe the activity and list the objectives or standards related to the work. Teachers can photocopy the captions and attach them to work included in all children's portfolios. When teachers upload an item to a child's online portfolio in *Teaching Strategies GOLD®*, they can connect the item to an objective in the system. *The Work Sampling System*™ portfolios include specialized sticky notes to help teachers quickly annotate items.

Although the relevance of portfolio pieces might be apparent to teachers when the item is created, over time teachers may forget the circumstances surrounding the item (Hanson & Gilkerson, 1999). Annotating items may feel like a chore, but it emphasizes to the child that the work is significant and models another use of writing. For parents, comments or captions on the work enhance its meaning.

Include items that represent all types of learning. It is tempting to gather only those items that are easy to collect. For example, finding work that shows a child's emergent writing skills is rather straightforward: You just gather writing samples and put them into the portfolio. All too often, though, verbal skills are over-represented in portfolios because they are easy to document. It can be challenging to show a child's understanding of number and quantity or their level of gross-motor development. Nevertheless, try to have all types of learning represented if the purpose of the portfolio is to focus on all domains of learning.

Use child-generated work whenever possible. Some items provide more information than others because the child—and his or her personality—is better represented by items created during meaningful activities. Consider the worksheet below. Think about a child's experience while completing this worksheet. Who has done most of the work: the worksheet publisher or the child? When children's responses are limited to circling pictures or drawing lines to correct answers, the worksheet does not show much about the child's thinking and learning.

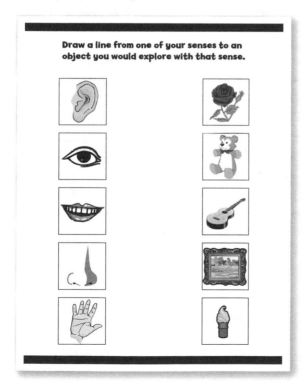

In contrast, photographing a child and taking notes about how he or she solved a math problem with manipulatives affords a much more comprehensive portrait of the child as a problem-solver. However, there is an exception to the general rule: Teacher-created worksheets can be very appropriate to include in a portfolio, but only if they were designed to align closely with the curriculum and encourage active engagement on the part of the child.

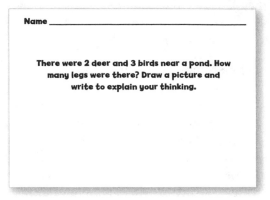

Name _____

There were 2 deer and 3 birds near a pond. How many legs were there? Draw a picture and write to explain your thinking.

Look for items that show multiple skills. Work demonstrating how children integrate multiple skills gives teachers more information than work illustrating a narrowly defined skill. Journal entries, for example, offer information about children's interests, show us how children express ideas, reveal vocabulary levels, show stages of writing development, and display how children use the conventions of print. In contrast, documenting an experience in which a child identifies capital letters by circling them on a page provides information about only a single, narrow skill. Truly informative portfolio items provide evidence of multiple skills and various content areas.

Show the evolution of work. A teacher recently showed me a 4-year-old's drawing with swirling, circular lines in many different colors. Fortunately, the teacher had taken a photograph of the child as he was working and made some notes about the moment. Interestingly, before obscuring the drawing with other strokes, the child had sketched a circle and a square and attempted a triangle. Including the final drawing without comments would not have accurately represented this child's drawing ability or knowledge of shapes. With older children who are learning to revise their work, including first attempts, revisions, and final products imparts more information about the child's process of learning.

Collecting Portfolio Items

Teachers are ready to begin collecting portfolio items when they have clearly identified a purpose for collection and have ideas about the types of items that will serve that purpose. To manage the portfolio process, you need to plan for work storage and determine how to collect the items. Finally, it is helpful to be clear about how much work to collect.

Special Considerations for Infant, Toddler, and Preschool Portfolios

In some ways, portfolio collection for very young children does not make sense. At this age, it is more important for teachers to focus on process, not product. Our job is to provide a rich environment and challenging activities that wholly engage children's attention. We focus on experiences, not work products. When children are making collages at the art table, we are interested in how they explore the materials and go about assembling their collages, not the quality of the collages when they are "finished" or when the child is ready for a new activity.

Having purposeful collections of young children's work may not initially seem sensible. However, if we slightly shift our thinking about portfolios, they can assist our assessment of younger children. Instead of focusing on "work" and "products," we focus on play and process. We capture children's learning by documenting their play activities. Since younger children do not create many things that can be put into a portfolio, photographs and video become important ways to illustrate what babies, toddlers, and preschoolers are learning.

Additionally, teachers sometimes create "word pictures," (Dichtelmiller, Jablon, Dorfman, Marsden, & Meisels, 2001, p. 83). These anecdotes describe how a child engaged in an activity. Note what Joshua's teacher wrote about him in the word picture shown below.

These portfolios are still purposeful and organized, but they are more *about* the child than *by* the child.

Infant portfolios, in particular, may contain language samples, anecdotal observation notes, photographs, video clips, and daily schedules with the infant's activities described. The adult does the work to capture the child's development and learning in a tangible format.

> Joshua, 1 years old, 10/9
>
> Joshua returned to the classroom after doing his special exercises with the physical therapist, Mariata. I was sitting on the floor with a group of children, doing a floor puzzle. After saying good-bye to Mariata at the door, Joshua quickly walked up to the group and, with a big smile on his face, announced, "Here I am." After we greeted him, he sat down and joined us in finishing the puzzle.

Word picture about Joshua

Where Will You Put Children's Work?

Successful portfolio collection requires the teacher to manage the flow of work in the classroom.

Portfolio containers We have discussed what goes into portfolios, but where are the items stored? Early childhood teachers have used the following to contain children's work:

- accordion or expandable files
- hanging files with file folders inside
- file folders
- three-ring binders with dividers
- pizza boxes
- poster board, folded and stapled to create oversized envelopes
- pocket folders

When deciding what to use, think first about accessibility. If you store portfolios in a metal file cabinet, they are not easily accessible to young children. Instead, use plastic crates or file boxes. Next, judge how much space you have to store portfolios. If you have many oversized items, a three-ring binder will not work for you. If you have little storage space, finding room for 10–18 pizza boxes might be impossible. Some teachers have a regular-sized portfolio for each child in an expandable file that is outfitted with file folders. They also use large poster board envelopes to store the class's oversized pieces (illustrated below). Photographs of work samples are easy to store in an online system.

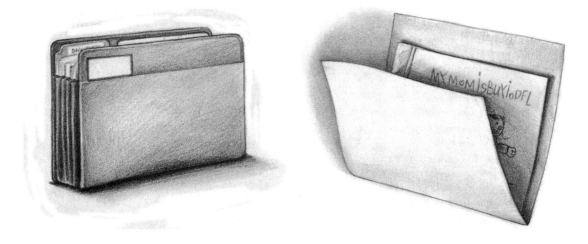

At this stage, decide how you will organize the items in each child's portfolio. Will you group items by date, subject area, domain, or standard? Depending on how many different types of learning the portfolio documents, you may want to show how the items are organized by including a table of contents for each child's portfolio. While this approach will require a little more time at the outset, it will save you from later having to search through 10, 12, or 15 items to find the one you want. Another tip is to lightly number the items in pencil so it will be easy to put them back in order after working with them.

Digital storage of portfolio items can be effective as well. For young children whose writing is just emerging and who create three-dimensional pieces, you will also want to maintain portfolios they can handle and look at on their own. Older children will enjoy looking at their portfolios online as well as in a format they can hold.

Work folders or baskets You need a work folder or a collection basket for every child to temporarily store work (i.e., potential portfolio items) until it goes into a portfolio or is sent home. Some teachers put all items in one place and then sort them, sending some home and keeping others in a work folder. You can ask older children to put specified pieces into their work folders and then make portfolio selections at a later date. The point is to make sure the work you think might eventually become part of the portfolio is in a safe place.

Include the child's name and the date of the experience it documents on anything put in a work folder. Some teachers make date stamps available for children to use when they put work into folders. The date on the stamp gets changed each day when the class talks about the calendar. Updating the stamp is usually a popular job.

Ways to Collect Items

There are two basic ways to collect children's work:

Planned collection When you have determined the type of learning that you want to represent in your portfolios, you can plan activities that engage children in that learning. As part of those activities, you can provide children with opportunities to demonstrate their skills and knowledge. If you want to know about children's understanding of stories, for example, plan to read several stories aloud to them and have children read books on their own. After reading stories, provide children with opportunities to show their understanding of them. You might make available flannel board pieces for retelling the stories, provide props to dramatize them, encourage children to illustrate or write the stories in the art area, or ask children to record their telling of the stories. Then, you will have tangible portfolio items that show children's understanding of stories. Look at the following chart to see what you might put in a portfolio.

Learning Activity	Portfolio Item
Flannel board retelling	Photo with notes about what a child said or did; video recording
Dramatic retelling	Photo with notes or video recording
Drawing/writing	Drawing with dictation or child's writing; photo of work
Verbal retelling	Written transcript of the recorded retelling

I am not suggesting that every child in your class must retell the same story, retell a story in the same way, or retell one on the same day. (That would be more like an on-demand test than authentic performance assessment!) If you are interested in story comprehension, then you might encourage children to respond to different stories over the course of several weeks. Children with strong expressive language skills might retell a story verbally, while children like Jamie, who loves to draw, might use mostly pictures. Children like Zachary, who never ventures into the dramatic play area, might use the flannel board to retell the story. *How* a child shows us what he or she understands is not important as long as we are getting information about story comprehension. Portfolio assessment honors the fact that children not only learn in different ways, but they also most comfortably express their knowledge in different ways.

You might ask at this point, "But aren't we going to encourage Jamie to use language and Zachary to express himself through drama and movement?" Of course we are! But right now story comprehension is our focus. How children show their understanding of the story is not our major concern. When we notice that Zachary never ventures near the dramatic play area, we might set a goal for him to participate in a structured role play with teacher support and incorporate that goal into future curriculum plans.

Spontaneous collection Suppose that, during a week when one of your assessment goals is story comprehension, you notice that Liam and Desmond—two 3-year-olds who usually play near one another but not together—have started talking to each other and occasionally trading pieces as they build with blocks. You realize that this is a new accomplishment for both of them and decide to document it. You might take a photograph, make a video recording, or write a word picture that vividly describes their interaction. This illustrates their development of new peer-interaction skills. Perhaps you see Jamie drawing a detailed picture of a train and telling Sasha about *The Polar Express* movie he saw over the weekend. You collect this drawing because it shows Jamie's strength in drawing.

Selecting Portfolio Items

Once you have collected some work, photos, or drawings, it is time to make decisions about which go into the portfolio. There are four selection issues to think about: *when* to select portfolio items, *who* selects the items, *how* to select, and *how many* pieces to select. Remember, you are looking for pieces that represent children's learning, standards, or individuality, depending upon the purpose of the portfolio.

When? According to the child's age and how much work is produced, you might review the pieces in the work folder every 2–4 weeks. Regardless of whether or not your selection process involves children, do not wait too long. You do not want to face such an enormous pile of work that the task becomes overwhelming. Moreover, you do not want the pieces to be very old because young children might not remember them.

Who? As often as possible (depending on the ages of the children), teachers and children should select some portfolio items together. Being involved in selecting items strengthens the child's sense of ownership of the portfolio. Even more significantly, when portfolios are part of formative assessment, the goal is to use assessment information to improve teaching and learning. Giving children the opportunity to reflect on their work affects their learning because they begin to think about themselves as skillful, competent learners.

How? Teachers use various approaches as they begin selecting pieces for specific portfolios. Periodic review of what has been collected about infants and toddlers helps you decide what to keep in each child's portfolio. For preschool portfolios, teachers help individuals or small groups of children select the work to be included. In groups of three or four children, kindergartners can review the work for their folders. For example, with some practice and clear direction, children can find the pieces about stories in their folders and pick the one that best shows their knowledge of a story. Children might review several paintings and select the one they like best for the portfolio, verbally explaining the reason for their preference to an adult. Teachers often use parent helpers or other volunteers to assist with portfolio selection. Sometimes teachers devote one of their centers to portfolios.

How much is enough? Structured portfolios are the most effective. When a portfolio has structure, its purpose is clear and the items are well organized. Structure enables us to understand the meaning of the collected work. Resist the urge to save everything. I once knew a teacher who started collecting work and ended up with portfolios so vast she said she needed a moving van to take them home! When that happens, teachers become overwhelmed, often giving up portfolios altogether. Keep in mind your purpose for portfolio collection and limit the number of items you collect. If you select carefully, fewer items can tell more. Twenty carefully chosen items can give more information than 50 random items hastily inserted into a file folder.

If a portfolio is a collection of typical work, rather than best work, it needs to include a large enough sample to give you confidence that the chosen pieces actually represent the child's typical performance. Otherwise, the portfolio may not be a reliable indicator of the child's performance.

If you are currently using portfolios in your classroom or if portfolios are used in a classroom you know well, think about the following questions:

Reflect on Your Practice

- What type of container is used for children's individual portfolios? How is oversized work handled?

- What is the system for collecting work for portfolios? Are work folders or baskets used for storing work temporarily?

- How often are items selected for portfolios?

- What is the child's role in selecting work for his or her portfolio?

Thinking About the Work in Portfolios

Portfolios give you opportunities to review and reflect on children's work at least three times. At each point, you gain new ideas about specific objectives for individual children, curriculum modifications, instructional methods, and strategies to motivate children.

Think about children's work when it is created. As children work, you interact with them, look at their work, and observe what they do and say. You might comment on what they are doing, as well as teach them new skills related to their activities. Over the course of your interactions, you challenge them to try something new.

> Min-Jee, a child with limited English skills, is at the fish tank. You wonder what she is doing, so you take a quick photo. Then you watch her move to the art table, find paper and colored pencils, return to the fish tank, and start drawing blue fish.

At the time, you make a mental note to add her drawing and the photo to her portfolio. You are amazed by the length of time she is spending on one activity and remind yourself to talk with her about the fish during the next quiet moment in the classroom. As the teacher in this example, you are documenting something about Min-Jee's approach to learning and her interest in fish, which you plan to use to engage her in conversation to promote her English-language skills.

Think about children's work during the collection and selection of portfolio items. Take a few minutes to study each piece as you organize each portfolio. This can be done either on your own or with children. During this process, you will undoubtedly see something new that gives you an insight about a child or a great idea for an activity. For example, Jared's last two journal pages included letters from his name as well as drawings. You wonder what he is learning about letters and plan to talk with him tomorrow during journal writing to find out what he knows about the letters in his first name. You might also introduce some new letters.

Review completed portfolios. Take the time to review each child's entire portfolio every 4–6 weeks. Portfolios can only help you learn about children when you take the time to review each piece and think about what the collection of work tells you about each child. Teachers often do this in preparation for family–teacher conferences. However, if you plan a regular time to sit with children's portfolios—maybe once a month—you will have the opportunity to review all the evidence about a child and ponder its meaning.

"Once a month? 20 portfolios? Is that realistic?" you might asking. Yes, it is realistic. It is a big task, but the payoff is well worth the work. You may want to review five portfolios a week after the first month of school. Reviewing the portfolios before planning your lessons each week will give you useful information. Have a note pad to record the ideas that emerge as you look at the children's portfolios. It is wise to allow yourself time to think about the children and your teaching when you can concentrate—not on the way to the grocery store or walking to the office to drop off permission forms. Quiet reflection will pay off in more targeted planning for the entire class.

If you are currently using portfolios in your classroom or if portfolios are used in a classroom you know well, think about the following questions:

Reflect on Your Practice

- How and when do you reflect on children's portfolios?
- Do you think you are taking full advantage of the benefits of portfolios for learning about children's thinking and accomplishments?

Involving Children and Families in Portfolio Collection

Portfolios are perfectly suited to involving children and families in assessment. Having something concrete to look at together is a superb learning tool for young children, who primarily interact with the world in tangible ways, and for their families, who enjoy and appreciate learning what their child does at school.

Portfolios are powerful communication tools that help family members appreciate and celebrate their child's development. It is easier for many parents to understand the development of children's writing skills by looking at a sequence of their child's writing samples than by reading words on a checklist. Portfolio items are tangible, so parents and teachers have access to the same information about children's learning, and the items help focus discussions on the child's development and learning. Moreover, portfolios are positive; they display what children can do. Although they sometimes provide evidence that a child's skills do not meet age-level expectations, the portfolio displays a set of acquired skills that can be celebrated. Families love to talk with people who know their child in a way different from the way they do and who can contribute a different perspective. For instance, by studying journal pages, drawings, and photographs together, you have a good chance of building positive relationships with families.

Let's look at how you can support children's ownership of portfolios and use portfolios to partner with families.

Supporting Children's Ownership of Their Portfolios

One of the benefits of portfolio collection is that it focuses children's attention on learning, especially for children in kindergarten and the early primary grades. You will want to talk with children about their work and explain what they are learning and why. If you are clear about the learning in any activity and communicate your expectations for the activity to children, they will begin to internalize your expectations and gradually develop their own criteria for defining acceptable work.

When you include them in each step of portfolio development, children are more likely to feel a sense of owning the portfolios. Here are some ways to cultivate children's sense of ownership:

Teach children about portfolios. A sense of ownership is less important for infants because the teacher manages the portfolio. However, toddlers, who love things that are "mine," can understand that they have a special book for particular things. From 3 years on, if the portfolio is set up collaboratively, children will recognize their own portfolios, know they contain their work, and take pride in them. Children can create cover pages for their portfolios, and older children can write their names on their binders, folders, or boxes to enhance feelings of ownership.

Include children in filing work. After you introduce portfolios to children and create the containers, have children immediately file some work. Depending on the collection procedures in your classroom, children can learn where to put work to save it. Four- and 5-year-olds can be taught to put the newest pieces in the back of their folders so the items are always in chronological order. If you place a date stamp next to the work folders, children will eagerly date their work before they file it. The more organizational tasks the children do, the fewer you have to do. Along the way, children's connection to their work deepens.

Invite children to help select items. When it is time to select pieces for the portfolio, you will choose some and children can help select others. It is critical not to present a young child with a huge pile of work. Even when you use portfolios, some work can be sent home immediately. The idea is to give a child 2–4 pieces and ask him or her to identify particular kinds of work: What is his or her favorite piece? What was most difficult to create? This will help you to discover something new about each child.

Consider including children in family–teacher conferences.
Children may join a traditional conference, or you may teach
them how to share their portfolios with their families. Some
programs conduct "portfolio nights" in addition to family–teacher
conferences. On these occasions, several children at a time share
their work with their families as the teacher moves around the
room, joining each family for a few minutes. At the end of this
event, some teachers ask the family to write their child a letter. This
letter is meant to communicate the parents' reactions to the child's
presentation of his or her work. Parents' letters are often heartfelt
and speak directly to the child about how much the parents value
school and what the child is learning there.

Because a portfolio contains a child's work, the child owns it. He or
she takes it home at the end of the year or when moving to a different
classroom. Some programs keep the portfolio for the child's next
teacher, who reviews it with the child and then sends it home. As
children get older, they can take more control of their portfolios.
As they do so, they develop a stronger sense of owning the
portfolio. Personal investment in the portfolio enhances children's
sense of themselves as competent learners. Collecting and saving
work, photographs, and other items communicates to even a very
young child that the child and his or her activities are valued.

Using Portfolios to Involve Families

Portfolios benefit families by providing new avenues of communication
between parents and children—as well as between parents and
teachers. You can show what children are learning by displaying
portfolio items on bulletin boards and publishing portfolio work in
a class newsletter. Ask families to do activities with their children
and then put evidence of those child–family activities in the children's
portfolios. Moreover, if you suggest a few questions for families to
answer at the end of the family activity, the documentation
becomes an even more meaningful addition to the child's portfolio.
Ask, "What did your child learn from this activity? Was this
activity interesting?"

Looking at a child's creations, seeing photographs of a child, reading a detailed anecdote about something a child has done—these are very positive experiences, especially for parents. Portfolios provide a firm basis for strengthening the parent–teacher relationship because they focus on the child in a very positive way.

Here are more considerations for involving families:

Communicate the purpose and power of portfolios. When you inform parents that you use portfolios, explain what portfolios are and why they are an important. Do this during a "curriculum night" or in a featured newsletter article.

Share portfolios with families at conferences. Conferences are usually short (in some cases 10–15 minutes). Given time constraints, it is important that you have already selected the samples you are going to share with parents. These pieces should be flagged with sticky notes so they can be located quickly. You should double check that your comments on the work are legible and communicate precisely what you mean. Some teachers encourage family members to look through the entire portfolio after their conference or while they are waiting to begin the conference. It frustrates parents when they are not seeing everything there is to see! Except perhaps for the initial one, conferences can focus on progress the child has made. By selecting items that demonstrate the same type of learning, you can compare the child's first work to similar work completed several months later. What better way is there to show the child's growth? A year-end conference can address progress the child has made over a longer period of time and should celebrate the child's accomplishments.

Three Approaches to Early Childhood Portfolios

There are several ways to approach portfolios for young children.

Focused Portfolios™

Focused Portfolios™ (Gronlund & Engel, 2001) is an approach to portfolio collection for children from birth through age 5. This approach is structured, giving direction about what to collect, how frequently to collect items, and forms that facilitate collection. Teachers assemble 10 pieces per child, two or three times a year. The pieces may be photographs accompanied by anecdotal notes, work samples with anecdotal notes, or observation notes. *Focused Portfolios*™ include items representing favorites, friends, families, and developmental milestones. They are individualized portfolios that focus on developmental or curricular goals.

The individualized part of this approach focuses on favorites, friends, and family. Teachers learn about children's "interests, talents, and passions" (Gronlund & Engel, 2001, p. 10) by documenting their favorite activities. Collecting information about children's friends provides information about developing social skills. The family section recognizes the family's contribution to the child's learning and invites families to add to the portfolio. Gronlund and Engel provide many different examples of ways to elicit family contributions (e.g., each family takes home a disposable camera and takes a limited number of photos of everyday family times, or a family writes a story about the arrival of a new pet). For those families who cannot directly contribute to the portfolio, teachers should take a more active role by photographing drop-off or pick-up routines, or by taking dictation from the child about a relative's visit.

The remaining items in *Focused Portfolios*™ center on the child's reaching developmental milestones. Gronlund and Engel provide a list of widely accepted milestones, which are divided into age groups: birth to 8 months, 8 to 18 months, 18 to 24 months, 24 months to 3 years, 3 years, 4 years, and 5 years. Infants' and toddlers' portfolios track their abilities to show interest in others, demonstrate self-awareness, perform gross- and fine-motor tasks, communicate, act with purpose, use tools, and express feelings. Preschoolers' portfolios focus on thinking, reasoning, and problem solving; emotional and social competency; language and communication; gross- and fine-motor development; reading and writing development; and creativity.

Developmental Milestones Collection Form
Version #1 Infant/Toddler

Child's Name _____ Age _____

Observer _____ Date _____

Check off the *areas of development* that apply:

This photo, work sample and/or anecdote illustrates the following *developmental milestone(s)*:

❑ Shows interest in others
❑ Demonstrates self-awareness
❑ Accomplishes gross-motor milestones
❑ Accomplishes fine-motor milestones
❑ Communicates
❑ Acts with purpose and uses tools
❑ Expresses feelings

_____

_____

_____

_____

Check off whatever applies to the context of this observation:

❑ Child-initiated activity
❑ Teacher-initiated activity
❑ New task for this child
❑ Familiar task for this child
❑ Done independently

❑ Done with adult guidance
❑ Done with peer(s)
❑ Time spent (1–5 mins.)
❑ Time spent (5–15 mins.)
❑ Time spent (15+ mins.)

Anecdotal Note: Describe what you saw the child do and/or heard the child say.

From *Focused Portfolios: A Complete Assessment for the Young Child*, by G. Gronlund and B. Engel. Copyright 2001 by Gaye Gronlund and Bev Engel. Reprinted with permission of Redleaf Press, St. Paul, MN.

The Work Sampling System®

The Work Sampling System® (Dichtelmiller et al., 2001; Meisels, Jablon, Dichtelmiller, Marsden, & Dorfman, 2001) includes a structured method of portfolio collection for children from age 3 through sixth grade. The system focuses on showing the quality and progress of children's work and thinking across the curriculum. Work is collected throughout the year and is summarized three times during that period.

The Work Sampling System® Portfolio contains two types of items, each with a distinct purpose. *Core items* reflect learning in Language and Literacy, Mathematical Thinking, Scientific Thinking, Social Studies, and the Arts. In each of these domains, teachers identify particular skills or concepts to guide the collection of work. Three samples of each skill or concept are collected throughout the year in order to document the child's progress. *Individualized items* are selected to show the child's unique approach to learning, interests, and significant accomplishments or talents.

Child _____		
Teacher _____ Age/Grade _____		**Core Item Collection Plan**
School _____		

Directions: List the areas of learning in the spaces below. Make a copy of this form to include in each child's portfolio. As you add each Core Item to the portfolio, check off the appropriate collection period.

Domains		Areas of Learning	Collection Period
II Language & Literacy	1	Understanding and interpreting literature	Fall _____ Winter _____ Spring _____
	2	Using letters and symbols to represent words or ideas	Fall _____ Winter _____ Spring _____
III Mathematical Thinking	1	Applying the concepts of patterns and relationships to problem-solving	Fall _____ Winter _____ Spring _____
	2	Using strategies to solve number problems	Fall _____ Winter _____ Spring _____
IV Scientific Thinking	1	Observing and describing scientific phenomena	Fall _____ Winter _____ Spring _____
	2	Questioning, predicting, and explaining in a scientific investigation	Fall _____ Winter _____ Spring _____
V Social Studies	1	Collecting and understanding information about self and family	Fall _____ Winter _____ Spring _____
	2	Recognizing similarities and differences between self and others	Fall _____ Winter _____ Spring _____
VI The Arts	1	Using an artistic medium to express ideas and emotions	Fall _____ Winter _____ Spring _____
	2	Exploring a variety of artistic media	Fall _____ Winter _____ Spring _____

The Work Sampling System.
© 1994, 2001 NCS Pearson, Inc.

From ***Work Sampling in the Classroom: A Teacher's Manual***, by M. L. Dichtelmiller, J. R. Jablon, A. B. Dorfman, D. B. Marsden, and S. J., Meisels. Copyright 2001 by NCS Pearson. Reprinted with permission of Pearson PsychCorp™, San Antonio, TX.

Teaching Strategies GOLD®

Teaching Strategies GOLD® (Heroman et al., 2010), which is used for children from birth through kindergarten, asks teachers to create a portfolio for each child. They collect evidence, including teachers' observation notes, work samples, audio and video clips, drawing and writing samples, and photographs of children engaged in various activities. These items document children's behaviors and skills related to the objectives in all areas of development and learning. For social–emotional, physical, language, and cognitive development as well as literacy and mathematics, teachers are guided to collect materials related to the developmental progressions provided for these domains. Teachers can document the progress of children with developmental delays or disabilities by using the same tool, because they can see the progressions for each of the objectives. There are also two objectives for English language acquisition that direct teachers to collect portfolio items related to receptive and expressive language skills in English.

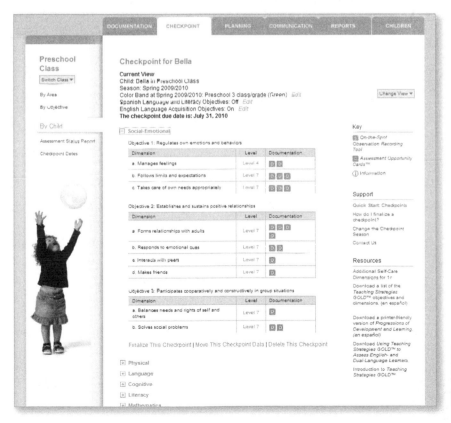

From *Teaching Strategies GOLD®* [Electronic version], by Teaching Strategies, Inc. Copyright 2010 by Teaching Strategies, Inc. Reprinted with permission of Teaching Strategies, Inc., Washington, DC.

Key Ideas to Remember

- Portfolios provide you with a powerful communication tool that focuses attention on children's learning.

- Well-organized, purposeful portfolios convey a picture of a child's skills and knowledge as well as the child's learning processes.

- Always identify your purpose for portfolio collection and then limit the samples you collect to those that serve that purpose. Remember, less is usually more when it comes to portfolio collection.

- By reflecting on children's portfolios, you gain new awareness of their skills, strengths, and challenges. Transform this awareness into more differentiated teaching.

References

Dichtelmiller, M. L., Jablon, J. R., Dorfman, A. B., Marsden, D. B., & Meisels, S. J. (2001). *Work sampling in the classroom: A teacher's manual.* Upper Saddle River, NJ: Pearson Education.

Gronlund, G., & Engel, B. (2001). *Focused portfolios.* St. Paul, MN: Redleaf Press.

Gullo, D. F. (2005). *Understanding assessment and evaluation in early childhood education.* New York: Teachers College Press.

Hanson, M. F., & Gilkerson, D. (1999). Portfolio assessment: More than ABCs and 123s. *Early Childhood Education Journal, 27*(2), 81–86.

Heroman, C., Burts, D. C., Berke, K., & Bickart, T. S. (2010). *Teaching Strategies GOLD® objectives for development & learning: Birth through kindergarten.* Washington, DC: Teaching Strategies, Inc.

Jablon, J. R., & Wilkinson, M. (2006, March). Using engagement strategies to facilitate children's learning and success. *Beyond the Journal*, March 2006. Retrieved May 26, 2006, from http://journal.naeyc.org/btj/200603/JablonBTJ.pdf

Kingore, B. (2008). *Developing portfolios for authentic assessment, PreK-3: Guiding potential in young learners.* Thousand Oaks, CA: Corwin Press.

McAfee, O., & Leong, D. J. (2007). *Assessing and guiding young children's development and learning* (4th ed.). Boston: Allyn & Bacon.

Meisels, S. J., Jablon, J. R., Dichtelmiller, M. L., Marsden, D. B., & Dorfman, A. B. (2001). *The Work Sampling System* (4th ed.). NY: Pearson.

Puckett, M. B., & Black, J. K. (2008). *Meaningful assessments of the young child* (3rd ed.). Upper Saddle River, NJ: Pearson.

Shores, E. F., & Grace, C. (1998). *The portfolio book: A step-by-step guide for teachers.* Upper Saddle River, NJ: Pearson.

Teaching Strategies, Inc. (2010). *Teaching Strategies GOLD®* [Electronic version]. Washington, DC: Author.

Wortham, S. C., Barbour, A., & Desjean-Perrotta, B. (1998). *Portfolio assessment: A handbook for preschool and elementary educators.* Olncy, MD: Association for Childhood Education International.

CHAPTER 8

Helping Children Think About Their Learning

Chapters 5, 6, and 7 focus on how teachers collect evidence of children's learning. As they observe or collect work samples, teachers interact with children. In fact, we interact with children throughout the day, but rarely do we talk with them about the core subject of classroom life: learning. Yet, part of our job as teachers is to make young children aware of their learning so that eventually they will be able to take the initiative and guide their own learning. The assessment process gives you an opportunity to talk about learning. Just as you use assessment tools to study children's learning, you can also use them to help children recognize, appreciate, and assess their own learning.

Teachers who value the emergence of children's critical thinking and problem-solving abilities can use assessment to foster reflective discussions about learning and create a "culture of thinking" (Ritchhart & Perkins, 2008) in their classrooms. Even young children can begin to identify their strengths, interests, and struggles as learners and become critical thinkers and problem solvers.

This chapter addresses ways to involve children in thinking about their own learning. It begins with a brief explanation of metacognition. Then it discusses ways to promote children's metacognitive, critical thinking, and problem-solving skills by creating a "culture of thinking" in your classroom.

This chapter defines *metacognition* and discusses these five useful strategies:

- creating an emotionally supportive classroom climate
- talking about learning and assessment
- giving children high-quality feedback
- teaching children to reflect and make choices
- using portfolios to promote reflection

Metacognition

Flavell (1971) defines *metacognition* as "an awareness of one's own cognitive functions, the ability to reflect on, monitor, and control them." Others define the term as "knowing about knowing" (Brown, 1978) or thinking about one's own thinking.

Having an awareness of one's own thinking is necessary for critical thought and problem solving and is related to higher cognitive functioning (Larkin, 2000). Consider the following example:

> My friend avidly solves crossword puzzles. When I asked her about completing the Sunday puzzle in the *New York Times*—one of the most difficult puzzles of the week—she said she consciously tells herself to look at the clues in multiple ways. She gave the example of the word *still*, which can mean "quiet," "unmoving," "yet," or "something in which you make alcohol." When she gets nowhere with thinking about *still* as meaning "quiet," she tells herself to think about it in another way.

As my friend monitors and guides her own thinking to solve the puzzle, she is using metacognitive skills. Similarly, when children develop an awareness of themselves as strategic thinkers and learners, that awareness advances their ability to solve problems.

Metacognition is necessary to transferring knowledge and skills from one situation to another. Without knowing that you possess a skill, it is sometimes difficult to apply it to a new situation (Burke, 2005). Our goal as educators is to provide children with skills that they can generalize, rather than skills that can only be applied exactly as they were taught. For example, we encourage children to set the table for snack—asking them to count spoons and make sure each person has one—because we want them to be able to apply counting skills and their understanding of one-to-one correspondence in a variety of situations.

Early childhood teachers help children develop metacognitive skills when they guide them to become aware of their own thinking strategies. In a school district with a kindergarten initiative on metacognition, teachers label children's thinking strategies as "comparing," "sequencing," or "searching systematically." A teacher might point out, "Sara, when you said the red apple was larger than the green one, you were comparing them." Through repetition and consistently pointing out examples throughout the day, children become adept at recognizing and labeling their own thinking as well as the thinking of their peers.

When teachers ask children to plan, predict, connect, question, hypothesize, and reflect (Epstein, 2003a, b), they are providing opportunities for children to think critically. Children often use metacognition when they talk about learning, discuss portfolio items, and set goals for future work.

Creating an Emotionally Supportive Classroom Climate

Becoming a critical thinker and problem solver depends not only on children's natural abilities but also on "how the person invests those abilities" (Ritchhart & Perkins, 2008). Children must feel emotionally safe and supported in the classroom for them to be willing to think critically, reveal their thinking, and admit mistakes. Obviously, if a child is laughed at or disparaged when she says, "I thought the caterpillar had to get to a magic place and then he turned into a butterfly," she may not be willing to talk about her thinking in the future.

Puckett and Black (2008) describe "psychologically safe classrooms" as characterized by the following features (p. 149):

- challenging, yet reasonable and enjoyable expectations
- child empowerment
- mutual respect between the teacher and children and among the children
- freedom from embarrassment, guilt, ridicule, and negative or hurtful interactions
- encouragement of risk taking and freedom to make mistakes
- reasonably stress-free

Maria, an experienced kindergarten teacher, describes one way she helps children learn to manage frustration and take risks.

> Over the years, I developed a strategy that helps children feel comfortable about taking risks and making mistakes. I tell stories about myself as a kindergartner. When I sense that some students are struggling, I tell a true story, an embellished version, or a purely fictional account about my having had the same struggle as a child. The children have responded to this so well that it has become a big part of classroom life. They call these "Maria the Kindergartner" stories and beg me to tell them! They nudge one another, saying, "That's just like me!" and their hands shoot up to tell me their stories. I elaborate on what I did, how I felt, how I got the help I needed from a friend, a parent, or a teacher. I talk about how I took a risk and how I got better and better even though I made mistakes.

Think about your classroom or a classroom you know well.

- Do children feel free to make mistakes and take risks?

- How do you empower children to take initiative, follow their interests, and direct their learning?

- How could your classroom be more supportive of children's learning?

Reflect
on Your
Practice

Talking About Learning and Assessment

Each day, teachers talk with children about what they will experience that day. We help 3- and 4-year-olds learn the daily schedule by using pictures and repetition. This is so they can anticipate experiences and feel in control of their lives. We want them to develop the ability to predict what happens next, so we tell them we will visit their home tomorrow, that cleanup starts in 5 minutes, or that on Thursday a dentist will visit. However, we less frequently talk with children in ways that support their ability to direct their own learning. Let's look at how we can also talk with them about learning and assessment.

Talking About Learning

According to McAfee and Leong (2007), children should know what they are learning, why, and what they have yet to achieve. Therefore, talk about learning with children before you introduce new skills and topics. For example, you might show a picture of a baby—perhaps the sibling of a child in the class—and ask whether the baby can walk. You can point out that at some point most people learn to walk. Follow this by saying, "Now that you are in school, you will learn many new things, just as you learned how to walk when you were a baby. Today, we're going to learn…" When you introduce new topics and skills, or when you observe that a child has acquired a new skill, refer back to this conversation. Children who are aware they have learned something in the past will have a more confident approach to learning in the future.

Natasha talks openly to her preschoolers about different rates of learning.

> At the beginning of the year, we read *Leo the Late Bloomer*, by Robert Kraus, and talked about the varying rates of development in our class. We have a tone-setting discussion about both encouraging and accepting our classmates as each begins to bloom throughout the year. The lesson involves children's sharing ways in which they know they have already "bloomed", what they are working on, and what their goals are (academic, self-help, sports, etc.). As the children share, the others use class signals that indicate "same" or "Me, too." Those who are just beginning to bloom see that they are not alone, and the children begin to identify with one another. It is not uncommon to hear a child who, after observing another child, blurts out happily, "Ms. Green, _____ has bloomed in writing *Es*!" Then the class applauds spontaneously.

Talking About Assessment

Although children are at the center of assessment activities, not all teachers share the assessment process with them. Many well-meaning teachers keep assessment activities secret from children. This approach makes assessment seem mysterious and deprives children of opportunities to think about their own learning. For instance, some teachers cover their observation notes so the child cannot see what is written. Others keep children's portfolios in a file drawer, making these collections only accessible to themselves. Some teachers do not explain to children what happens at family–teacher conferences.

Instead of hiding your assessment process from children, let them know that you assess to find out what they know and can do. Tell them that assessment enables you to decide how to help them learn what they do not yet know. When children ask why you are watching or listening to them and then writing notes, explain that you want to remember exactly how they write their names or what they told you about their family reunion. Most young children react positively when they find out their teacher is interested in their accomplishments and that she writes about them! Some time later, you might see yourself reenacted in children's dramatic play. You may see a child reach into his or her pocket for a pad of paper and then quickly scribble some notes.

A student teacher in a preschool classroom reported this incident:

> Manny asked me what I was writing, so I explained that I was writing what he was doing and saying so that I could remember. He said "Okay," and kept working. Later, he came back to me and said, "I'm playing with trucks now. Did you write that down?" and "You should write this down: 'I'm building with blocks.'" He kept following me all day, making sure I knew (and wrote about) what he did.

Consider using some of the following strategies:

Talk with children about how their skills are developing. For example you might explain, "When we first learn to cut, we just snip. Look, you can do that now. Soon you'll be able to cut that picture out by yourself."

Talk about how you find out what children understand and can do. Openly describe the processes of assessment. You might say, "When you made your picture, I saw that you have learned how to hold a pencil with your fingers. Do you remember when you used to hold it in your fist, like this?"

Help children appreciate their unique combinations of strengths and needs. Comment respectfully about who is good at what and where each child struggles. Everyone in the class has strengths and weaknesses. Communicating the idea that it is okay if you are terrific at puzzles but not great at counting is positive for everyone.

It is important to tell 4-, 5-, and 6-year-olds about upcoming family–teacher conferences and to share with them what you will tell their parents. If children do not attend conferences, they may be confused and anxious about why their parents are coming to school when they are not. It is a sign of respect for children—even young ones—to include them in conversations that concern them (Mooney, 2005). As you interact with children, take the time to take the mystery out of assessment by helping them understand how it works and how they can be involved.

Talking With Children Individually

Excellent early childhood teachers talk frequently with children throughout the day. Much of this talk is in groups: Teachers give directions, present new information, and discuss what is going to happen next. Teachers also talk with children individually. In fact, I often challenge teachers to have a 1-minute conversation with each child every day. This does not mean calling children to you for a conversation. You can talk at greater length with several children when you greet them in the morning. Then, later in the day, speak with several others individually when you are outside or during choice time. Maybe you can converse with each of the others when they are getting ready to go home. The point is to make sure you "see," or connect with, each child every day and talk about classroom activities and learning.

Think about the children with whom you work or other children you know well.

- How will you begin to talk with children about their learning?

- Will you speak with groups of children or one-to-one?

Reflect on Your Practice

Giving Children High-Quality Feedback

As they talk with children, teachers regularly provide feedback by commenting on children's behavior, skills, knowledge, and attitudes. However, in many classrooms, feedback is vague. Children are praised in general terms whenever they succeed at something: "Good job," "Good work," and "Nice."

This type of feedback is not very useful for several reasons. When children hear "good job" frequently and tied to many different behaviors, how do they feel when the teacher does not say, "Good job"? I have often seen babies turn to their parents each time they drop a block in a bucket, expecting adults to clap for them. Meaningless reinforcement inspires children to act for external rewards rather than internal satisfaction.

Instead of offering children rote, generic statements of praise, encourage them by giving specific feedback. Here are some ways to offer meaningful feedback:

Focus on a clear message. When feedback is unclear, children do not know what they should continue or stop doing. For instance, imagine that a child runs to the art area to finish a collage, nearly colliding with several children who are working on a floor puzzle. Asking him, "Are you sure you want to do that?" does not give enough information for him to know whether he should reconsider finishing the collage, running through the room, or interrupting other children's activities.

Be specific. Specific feedback communicates exactly what the child did or did not do. For example, Stacey's comment to Kari, "You figured out how to make wheels for your car," is much more informative than saying, "Good job on your car."

Communicate the learning goal. Focused feedback may be a question or a comment. It can direct the child's attention to the parts of learning the teacher thinks are important. For example, Becky is working with 4-year-old Jack, who is determined to zip his own coat. She notices his repeated but unsuccessful efforts; goes to him; and says, "Jack, you are working hard on that zipper. Be sure to hold both parts of the zipper together on this side before you put in the tab on the other side." If children are using manipulatives for counting, your feedback should focus on counting rather than the fact that a child selected all the red pieces to count (Brookhart, 2008).

Focus on attitudes, feelings, and the child's learning process.
When you say, "You're working very hard on that. Is there another way you could do it?" or, "You stacked those blocks four times! You really want to make that structure taller," you draw attention to children's efforts and motivation to learn (Good & Brophy, 2008). Effective feedback addresses children's learning and motivation at the same time (Brookhart, 2008).

When children receive specific feedback, rather than a generic "Good job," they know what they have done well, how they have succeeded, or what to pay attention to in order to improve.

Examples of Feedback
Model your feedback after the following comments heard in various early childhood classrooms:
- "Wow, Aisha, you're walking all by yourself!"
- "You worked a long time on that painting. I notice you used many different colors."
- "I see that your building keeps falling. Why do you think that is happening?"
- "I see you only used red blocks. Why did you do that?"
- "Hmmm, you have an extra box of juice. How do you think that happened?"

Think about the children in your classroom or other children with whom you work.
- List several examples of clear, specific feedback focused on your goals for children's learning.
  - ___
  - ___
  - ___
- List several examples of clear, specific feedback focused on a child's feelings, attitudes, or process of learning.
  - ___
  - ___
  - ___

Reflect on Your Practice

Teaching Children to Reflect and Make Choices

Early childhood teachers are accustomed to asking children to reflect on their feelings and social behaviors (e.g., "How did it make you feel when Rory took your book?"), but they are less familiar with asking young children to reflect on their learning (Mindes, 2003). Epstein (2003b) defines *reflection* as "remembering with analysis." Teachers often ask children to recall activities from earlier in the day or week, a field trip, or the time when Sam's mother came to class with a baby lamb. In these examples, children may be asked to remember something but not to analyze or think critically about what they remember.

For example a teacher might say, "Let's talk about our field trip to the fire station, yesterday. What did you see?" Instead, the teacher could say, "Let's talk about our field trip to the fire station, yesterday. What tools did you see that firefighters use to put out fires?" Both examples ask children to recall the field trip experience, but only the second example asks them to analyze something about the field trip.

Teachers support children's cognitive self-awareness and ability to think about what they've learned by modeling reflection and asking questions.

Modeling Reflective Thinking

Early childhood educators regularly model behaviors, skills, and attitudes that they want children to acquire. For example teachers develop different ways to soothe each infant, and, in time, each infant learns to calm him- or herself. Similarly, in preschool and kindergarten classrooms, teachers develop rules with children but initially take the major responsibility for teaching the rules and making sure they are followed. Over time, the children internalize the teacher's rules and begin to monitor their own and others' behavior. Teachers can also teach children to reflect on their own thinking and learning. Here are some strategies for doing so:

Verbalize your thoughts. Teachers who discuss their own thinking processes, who talk about their mistakes and describe what they do to fix them, and who problem-solve aloud are modeling reflective thinking for young children. When a teacher explains that she is having difficulty choosing among books to read at circle time and tells children that she has decided to read Aaron's book about a castle so that he can take it home that day, she is sharing how she thought about a problem. When you erase several numerals from a note you just wrote to a child's parent and explain that you made a mistake when writing the time for the meeting, you are modeling that it is okay to make mistakes. You are also presenting an important model about how to react emotionally to setbacks.

Model questioning as a problem-solving strategy. Children talk to themselves, using the same types of language they hear teachers use when giving directions or solving problems (Copple, 2003). Eventually, they internalize the language as part of their own problem-solving approach. When you ask, "How can we make sure everyone has time to use the computers?" you model higher-level thinking and give children an example of asking questions when they need to solve problems.

Investigate thinking programs. Some teachers support children's thinking by using various programs, such as the Visible Thinking program (Ritchhart & Perkins, 2008; Salmon, 2007). Developed at Harvard University as part of Project Zero, Visible Thinking includes brief classroom strategies known as "thinking routines," which are used repeatedly to target specific types of thinking. For example, a kindergarten teacher might use the See-Think-Wonder routine to stimulate curiosity about a new topic. The teacher asks three questions: What do you see? What do you think about that? What does it make you wonder?

Using Questions to Foster Reflection

When you ask children open-ended questions, you are rewarded with a glimpse into how a child perceives and thinks about the world. Open-ended questions invite many possible responses. Also known as *divergent questions*, they encourage children to think critically about a topic. They prompt children to reflect on their learning. Consider how children might respond to the following questions:

- What did you notice about the tree near the window?
- Did you notice the leaves on the tree near the window?

The first question, "What did you notice about the tree near the window?" is open-ended. It allows for many different responses that reveal children's observations and interests. The second question, "Did you notice the leaves on the tree near the window?" invites *yes* or *no* responses that end the conversation.

Questioning can provide us with a window into children's thinking, especially when they are genuine inquiries that tell us something we do not already know. Too often, adults confuse children by asking them questions to which answers are already known (e.g., How old are you? What color is your shirt?). This behavior is unique to adult–child interactions.

Consider questions that require higher-level thought rather than rote recall. Here are some examples:

- What will happen next in the story?
- What will happen if we mix the yellow paint with the blue paint?
- What makes you think that?
- What do we need to make the cookies? Why do you think so?
- How did you know that block would stay on top?
- What do you know about butterflies?
- What other book did we read about bears? Which did you like better?
- How can you tell?
- I wonder what would happen if…
- Why do you think that happened?

However, even open-ended questions must be used wisely. Even the most thoughtful child does not want his or her activities to be constantly interrupted. As you know, conversations are not composed of a series of questions, with the adult always asking the questions. Instead, conversations are combinations of questions, responses, comments, and pauses. Commenting on children's actions (e.g., "I notice that your blocks are in two groups.") invites the child to explain his or her actions. Furthermore, pauses can be powerful, particularly with young children who sometimes need more time to process information than we often allow.

Next time you work with young children, be ready to ask several open-ended questions.

Use the space below to write two or three question formats that you plan to use.

- ▪
- ▪
- ▪

Reflect
on Your
Practice

Giving Children Opportunities to Make Choices and Plan

When we give children opportunities to make choices about their learning and plan their activities, we take an important step toward helping them become self-directed, self-monitoring learners. Even toddlers can make choices when given alternatives: "Do you want the drum or the bells?"

Preschoolers can make even more significant choices. For example, a teacher who asks a child how she plans to make the roof of her block house focuses the child's attention on her ability to choose from many options. Children feel empowered when they make choices. They become more able to express their needs and desires and to take charge of their own activities and behaviors.

Children need to practice making meaningful choices, and planning activities *with* them provides children with choice-making experiences. Asking children what the class needs to do to get ready for the veterinarian's visit requires them to recall previous experiences with classroom visitors. They have to apply their knowledge to the current situation. Similarly, brainstorming possible ways to fix the broken tricycle and then selecting the way to try first helps children to see parts of the planning process in action.

Various curricular approaches involve children in planning their own activities. The most well-known example is the HighScope curriculum, which uses a three-step "plan, do, review" process. Children plan their activity, engage in it, and review what they accomplished when they finish (Hohmann, Weikart, & Epstein, 2008). Other curricular approaches, such as the *Tools of the Mind* curriculum (Bodrova & Leong, 2007), *The Creative Curriculum® for Preschool* (Dodge, Colker, Heroman, & Bickart, 2010), and *The Creative Curriculum® for Infants, Toddlers & Twos* (Dodge, Rudick, & Berke, 2011), also emphasize the importance of children's making choices and increasingly complex decisions. When young children regularly make choices, plan activities in a group setting, and prepare their own activities, they are beginning to take responsibility for and direct their own learning.

Using Portfolios to Promote Reflection

In chapter 7, you read about how portfolio collection provides a venue for teachers to reflect on children's work and to make decisions about further teaching. Furthermore, portfolios help facilitate children's reflection on their own work. As children sit together and look at a drawing or select work for their portfolios, discussing their work strengthens relationships among children and with you. Interactive discussions about portfolio pieces facilitate children's abilities to think about their own learning, recognize their strengths, and acknowledge their struggles.

Kay Burke (2005) writes, "Reflection is the heart and soul of the portfolio, but reflection doesn't just happen" (p. 67). Teachers must plan time for reflection, for both children and themselves. If reflection does not occur, then all of the rich evidence collected cannot help children's learning or aid your teaching. Consider how to facilitate children's reflection and then turn to your own.

Encouraging Children to Reflect

Kingore (2008, p. 30) lists the following benefits of actively involving children reflecting on and deciding what goes in their portfolios. Kingore says,

Typically, children

- apply high-level thinking as they analyze alternatives;
- practice decision making;
- begin to develop self-assessment skills;
- assume some responsibility for their learning;
- perceive a more concrete overview of their developing skills and concepts;
- delight in their accomplishments and/or challenge themselves to higher achievements;
- engage in goal setting.

Even very young children can reflect on the items in their portfolios (Smith, 2000). At first, 4-year-olds often respond to questions about why they wanted to put particular pieces in their portfolios with, "I like it." However, after a few months of practicing reflection, they begin to offer more informative responses, such as "It's the best painting I ever did" or "I made it all by myself, even my whole name."

When a teacher sits with a preschooler and reviews several drawings, she is setting the stage for reflection. Asking a preschooler to pick the piece he likes best requires the child to make a decision about his work. Asking why he selected the piece encourages the child to reflect and analyze why he likes his selected piece best.

As they become more mature, children can use the standards they have been taught to reflect on their work. The kindergartner looking at writing samples from the past month starts noticing, with the teacher's guidance, that he has learned to separate words with spaces. As with learning other skills, the teacher first explained what words are and then how they are separated by spaces in a sentence. The child eventually internalizes spacing as one feature of good writing and can identify it in his own work.

Modeling is one strategy used to teach children how to analyze their own work and to be aware of their own thinking and learning processes. For example, you might model "why" questions that encourage children to think about their own decision-making processes. You might ask, "Why did you use a lot of red paint in this picture?" As previously mentioned, modeling facilitates the development of children's metacognitive skills; they begin to think about their own thinking. Metacognition is an integral part of critical thinking and problem solving.

Here are strategies for helping children think about their own work:

Ask questions. When you are selecting portfolio items with a child, or when you are reviewing a child's portfolio with him or her, guide the child's thinking by asking questions about the pieces:

- What do you want to tell me about what you did?
- What is your favorite piece of work? Why?
- How did you make this?
- How did you figure that out?
- What did you most enjoy doing?
- Why did you…?
- What did you like about this writing/painting/block structure?
- Would you like to do this again? How would you do it if you did it again?
- What do you notice about the first page in your journal and this page?
- What did you learn while doing this?

Give directions. Give children specific directions for selecting a piece of work from a small number of items. Use instructions such as these:

- Pick one that was hard to make (or took the most time).
- Pick one that was easy for you to make.
- Find your favorite piece of work that shows your writing.
- Which one shows the best work you can do? What makes it your best piece?
- Select something that shows you can write a letter (or a word).
- Select a piece that helped you learn something new.

Help children set goals for themselves. Five and 6-year-olds, who can regularly talk about their learning and select work for their portfolios, can begin setting goals for themselves. As Puckett & Black (2008, p.163) suggest, teachers support young children's abilities to set goals by using prompts such as these:

- When I finish this activity, I am going to…
- When I come to school tomorrow, I want to…
- I want to learn about…
- Next I want to draw…
- I plan to build…

When setting goals, consider children's interests and strengths as well as skills that are difficult for them. It is natural to want to help Mason set goals to improve his behavior during large-group activities, but it is equally important to encourage him to set goals related to his strengths. If Mason loves writing his first name and writes it frequently, perhaps a new goal is to write his last name or other words that are significant to him.

Asking children to take responsibility for their portfolios sends several important messages. First, it reinforces the ideas that the portfolio belongs to the child and that the child's creations are significant enough to warrant a special way of keeping them. Second, asking children to select work acknowledges their ability to make decisions about their portfolios. Finally, the entire portfolio-creation process, with its focus on reflection, communicates that it is important for children to think about their own learning and set goals for themselves.

Key Ideas to Remember

- The primary reason for involving children in discussions about learning and assessment is to foster children's metacognition, or awareness of their own thinking.

- Metacognition is an integral part of critical thinking, problem solving, and the application of learning to new situations.

- Create a "culture of thinking" in your classroom so that children feel safe to make mistakes and take risks.

- Use language to deepen your relationships with children. Provide specific feedback that contributes to their understanding of themselves as thinkers and learners.

- Support thinking in your classroom by modeling reflection, asking open-ended questions, and encouraging children to make choices and plans.

- Use the full potential of portfolios to enhance children's critical thinking skills. Encourage children to make choices, reflect on work, and set goals.

References

Bodrova, E., & Leong, D. J. (2007). *Tools of the mind: The Vygotskian approach to early childhood education* (2nd ed.). Upper Saddle River, NJ: Prentice-Hall.

Brookhart, S. M. (2008). *How to give effective feedback to your students.* Alexandria, VA: ASCD.

Brown, A. (1978). Knowing when, where and how to remember: A problem of metacognition. In R. Glaser (ed.) *Advances in instructional psychology.* Hillsdale, NJ: Erlbaum.

Burke, K. (2005). *How to assess authentic learning.* Thousand Oaks, CA: Corwin Press.

Copple, C. (2003). Fostering young children's representation, planning, and reflection: A focus in three current early childhood models. *Applied Developmental Psychology, 24*(6), 763–771.

Dodge, D. T., Colker, L. J., Heroman, C., & Bickart, T. S. (2010). *The Creative Curriculum® for preschool* (5th ed.). Washington, DC: Teaching Strategies, Inc.

Dodge, D. T., Rudick, S., & Berke, K. (2011). *The Creative Curriculum® for infants, toddlers & twos* (2nd ed., revised). Washington, DC: Teaching Strategies, Inc.

Epstein, A. S. (2003a). An early start on thinking. *Educational Leadership, 65*(5), 38–42.

Epstein, A. S. (2003b). How planning and reflection develop young children's thinking skills. *Young Children, 58*(5), 28–36.

Flavell, J. H. (1971). First discussant's comments: What is memory development the development of? *Human Development, 14,* 272–278.

Good, T. L., & Brophy, J. E. (2008). *Looking in classrooms* (10th ed.). Boston: Pearson.

Hohmann, M., Weikart, D. P., & Epstein, A. S. (2008). *Educating young children: Active learning practices for preschool and child care programs* (3rd ed.). Ypsilanti, MI: HighScope Press.

Kingore, B. (2008). *Developing portfolios for authentic assessment, Pre-K–3: guiding potential in young learners.* Thousand Oaks, CA: Corwin Press. Material from page 30 is reprinted with the permission of SAGE Publications. Permission conveyed through Copyright Clearance Center, Inc.

Larkin, S. (2000). *How can we discern metacognition in year one children from interactions between students and teacher?* Paper presented at ESRC Teaching and Learning Research Programme Conference, November 9, 2000.

McAfee, O., & Leong, D. J. (2007). *Assessing and guiding young children's development and learning.* Boston: Allyn & Bacon.

Mindes, G. (2003). *Developing decision-makers: Involving kindergartners in their own assessment.* Olney, MD: Association for Childhood Education International.

Mooney, C. G. (2005). *Use your words: How teacher talk helps children learn.* St. Paul, MN: Redleaf Press.

Puckett, M. B., & Black, J. K. (2008). *Meaningful assessments of the young child* (3rd ed.). Upper Saddle River, NJ: Pearson Education. Material from pages 149 and 163 reprinted with permission of Pearson Education, Inc.

Ritchhart, R., & Perkins, D. (2008). Making thinking visible. *Educational Leadership, 65*(5), 57–61.

Salmon, A. (2007). Promoting a culture of thinking in the young child. *Early Childhood Education Journal, 35*(5), 457–461.

Smith, A. F. (2000). Reflective portfolios: Preschool possibilities. *Childhood Education, 76*(4), 204–208.

CHAPTER 9

Partnering With Families

Families play a significant role as contributors and decision makers in the assessment process. Today, early childhood educators usually view families as partners in supporting children's development and learning. This has not always been the case. Families were often viewed as passive participants, that is, as recipients of information and listeners at conferences rather than as engaged contributors to children's learning.

To address ways to partner effectively with children's families in the assessment process, this chapter explores

- establishing collaborative assessment relationships with families
- preparing to share assessment data with families
- conducting family–teacher conferences
- writing narrative reports

Families not only consist of biological or adoptive parents and children, but they also come in many other configurations that include grandparents, aunts, uncles, partners of lesbian moms and gay dads, foster parents, and others who assume parental roles. In *The Power of Assessment*, the word *parent* is used to describe *anyone* who nurtures a child in a familial context and functions as a parent to the child, regardless of his or her legal or biological relationship.

Establishing Collaborative Relationships

Family–teacher relationships are complex, and, in my experience, both new teachers and veterans share apprehensions about working with families. Some teachers bring their notions about how families *should* work to their interactions, just as families may bring their experiences as students to their interactions with educators. Teachers may feel anxious about whether family members think they are competent educators; family members may worry about whether the teacher thinks they are good parents. A number of factors, including your age or personal situation, may affect the relationships between you and children's families. You might be fearful that the family will not take you seriously because you are younger than they or do not have children of your own. What's more, differences in cultural background, socioeconomic status, educational level, or language increase the complexity of family–teacher relationships.

Take a moment to think about how you define *family*.

- **What was important to your family when you were growing up?**

- **What values and beliefs did they hold?**

- **How did they communicate with your teachers?**

- **How do your ideas about families match the families in your program?**

- **What are your concerns about sharing assessment information with families?**

Reflect on Your Practice

So, what can you do to counteract potential tensions inherent in family–teacher relationships? How can you build a trusting relationship in which you will be able to discuss and work together to assess children's learning and development? Here are some important ideas about developing collaborative partnerships with families:

Appreciate the intense feelings parents experience about their child. As Sara Lawrence-Lightfoot (2003) wrote: "To parents, their child is the most important person in their lives, the one who arouses their deepest passions and greatest vulnerabilities, the one who inspires their fiercest advocacy and protection" (p. xxi).

Amy, a graduate student returning to the classroom after the birth of her first child, shared her experience and showed me how powerful these feelings can be.

> After becoming a mother, I looked at my students differently. I realized that each one was someone's child and as important to them as my daughter is to me. Now I am much more sensitive to parents' feelings when they talk with me about their child.

While interacting with parents, keep in mind that praising their child makes them feel good but criticizing their child hurts them. Parents of young children with special needs often wonder whether something they did caused the disability. As educators, we have to honor and appreciate the special relationship between parent and child. We must take into account that the statements we make to parents can take on greater significance than we might intend.

Recognize that each family is unique. There is no "one size fits all" rule for creating collaborative relationships with families. Your way of working with one family may not be helpful with another. By tailoring your interactions to the needs and communication styles of each family, you are more likely to foster partnerships with them.

Get to know each family's style of communication. A family's cultural background contributes to the way family members interact with you. Culture affects the family's view of education and the family–teacher relationship. For example, some parents expect to interact with teachers as partners and will want to collaborate with you immediately. Other parents feel uncomfortable about making suggestions or sharing ideas with the teacher because they consider the teacher to be the expert in school matters.

Two excellent books, *Developing Cross-Cultural Competence: A Guide for Working with Children and Their Families* (Lynch & Hanson, 2004) and *Knowing and Serving Diverse Families* (Hildebrand, Phenice, Gray, & Hines, 2000), draw portraits of various cultural groups. However, keep in mind that descriptions of cultural groups are generalizations about that group. Individuals of the same cultural group can be very different from each other. After gathering background information from various resources such as those, your next step is to talk with family members and learn from—and about—them.

Have realistic expectations for family involvement. We often think of family involvement as attending events at the program or volunteering in the classroom. Although this kind of participation is wonderful and should be encouraged, research indicates that the involvement that most benefits children's achievement is parental support of children's learning at home (Epstein, 2001). Parents encourage learning and achievement when they talk about their child's day, read stories with their child, and have a set place and routine for homework. Like you, parents have numerous demands on their time. Talk with family members about how they can be involved to support their child.

Tell parents how children will be assessed. At the beginning of the school year, early childhood programs usually schedule a session to inform parents and family members about the program's policies and curriculum. That gathering provides an excellent opportunity to present the assessment system that will be used to measure children's development and learning. It is also a good time to give parents a sample progress report so that, at conference time, they will have the background knowledge to understand what you are sharing about their child.

Make regular contact. Positive relationships require communication. Talk with families frequently, not just two or three times a year when you share assessment results formally. Some programs send home information once a week so families learn to expect a packet on a particular day. Other teachers write personal notes once a month to each child's family. Still others call each family every 3 weeks. Whatever your style, be sure to make contact when there is good news, not solely to communicate problems. You will not gain parents' trust if they come to expect bad news each time you are in touch. A spontaneous call, note, or e-mail to communicate an interesting story about a child will brighten every parent's day.

Use a variety of ways to communicate. As you begin to
discover—and get comfortable with—the best ways to
communicate with children's families, you will learn that most
people have a way in which they prefer to keep in contact and
to remain informed. Being flexible with different methods of
communication will demonstrate that you honor families' needs
and diversity.

Some ways of keeping everyone informed include sending home
weekly newsletters with updates about assessment activities in your
classroom, e-mailing parents to tell them about children's activities
and progress, or posting information on your program's Web site.
Over time, you will learn which families prefer a phone call and
which like personal notes. At the beginning of the year, ask parents
how they would like to share information. This might initially seem
to be a lot of work for you, but children benefit when teachers and
families communicate well.

Treat parents of children with special needs gently. Disabilities
are often first identified when a child enters an early childhood
program. During the evaluation process when it is being determined
whether or not a child has a special need, his or her parents
might feel guilt, anger, or that they are at fault in some way. For
this reason, it is especially important to be sensitive to families'
emotions and that you work to develop their trust.

A genuine relationship of trust between a teacher and family
develops when teachers honor the special role of parents and when
parents value the insights and expertise of the teacher. Building
such a relationship takes time, but all of your positive interactions
with family members contribute to a relationship that supports the
child's learning and development. It is much easier to talk with
families about their children's challenges—and successes—when
trust has been established.

Assure families that confidentiality will be respected. Families have rights related to assessment. The Family Education Rights and Privacy Act (FERPA), passed in 1974, assures parents that information about their child is secure and shared only with them. The NAEYC Code of Ethical Conduct (2005) asserts that families have additional rights that include rights to

- understand the assessment system used by their child's program
- regular and respectful communication with their child's teacher about their child's learning and performance in school
- receive information about their child's performance in a language they understand
- have their questions answered and ideas used to improve the child's program

When put into practice, these strategies will help you build enduring relationships with families and children. Furthermore, the following approaches will ensure that conversations about assessment will benefit everyone.

Preparing to Share Assessment Information

As you prepare to share assessment information with families, your first task is to determine what you want to communicate. Consider the following guidelines:

Review the evidence. Give yourself time to review all of the data you collected over time about the child. Although teachers remember a great deal of pertinent information about the children in their classrooms, they sometimes forget the details and specific examples that are meaningful to families. Once you have thoroughly reviewed the evidence about the child's learning, list your interpretations of the information.

Focus on two or three main points. Remember, less is more. Think about your interpretations of the child's behavior and put them in order of importance. Choose no more than *three main points* to share with parents. Because they are highly invested in their children's performance, family members are often unable to process much more than three significant ideas. When teachers are mindful about what they present during family–teacher conferences, they are more likely to leave ample time for parents' questions, concerns, and comments.

Do not diagnose. When you summarize what you know about a child, you make judgments about that child on the basis of evidence collected over a period of time. However, do not make judgments that you do not have the evidence or expertise to support. Classroom teachers are not qualified to diagnose children or to tell parents whether or not a child has attention deficit disorder, is hyperactive, or is learning disabled. If you have concerns, your role is to share specific examples of behavior with the family, ask questions about what the family observes, and make a referral for an evaluation or help the parent get additional information. Remember, your role is to be a resource and to be supportive, compassionate, and respectful.

Be accurate and positive, but never mislead. Focusing on children's growth and progress, early childhood teachers tend to have positive outlooks. Our training reinforces this attitude. We are encouraged to view children's struggles in a positive light, and we often present our concerns about a child to the family with a positive spin. Rather than say, "Melanie gives other children the answers," we would probably reframe that statement and say, "Melanie can't help sharing her answers with others" (Berger, 2004). When we have information to discuss about difficulties a child is experiencing, we are encouraged to "sandwich" it between a strength the child shows and our plans for helping the child resolve a problem. In fact, we are told not to talk about the child's *problems* but to own them as our *concerns*.

Occasionally, we go too far. We present our observations, issues, or concerns so positively that the family does not know there's a problem. When we say, "Jason has his own agenda," rather than say, "Jason does not follow classroom rules," our desire to be kind might mask the fact that Jason's behavior—not following rules—is affecting his learning. Although parents might take our statements very personally, they generally appreciate straight talk about their child's issues. We do both parent and child a disservice by glossing over a child's struggles. Instead, we should help parents put challenges into perspective, appreciate how they may be typical for a particular stage of development, and assist parents in finding additional resources.

When presenting difficult issues to families, the key is to show you appreciate the child and then accurately to present the issue. Focus on being encouraging rather than on being positive. A parent of a kindergartner once told me, "The most important thing is that the teacher conveys that we are in this together." We want parents to have a sense that concrete actions will be taken, that the problem is on the way to being solved.

Identify specific suggestions for each family. Children's learning can be actively promoted at home. You can identify specific activities that families can do in various daily situations with readily available materials. At home, children can count doors, windows, or shoes. As parent and child climb stairs, they can count together. While grocery shopping, a parent can say, "We need three apples," and then ask, "How many apples do I have?" We want children to have a variety of experiences that encourage them to make connections between what they learn in the classroom and what they do at home. Individualize suggestions in ways that acknowledge the individuality of the family and the parents' expertise. For example, if you know a parent loves to bake, you might suggest that the child practice measuring during a baking project.

Encourage families to build on their daily routines. You do not want to make learning, or family participation in that learning, seem like a chore or something they must do *in addition to* what they are already doing. For example, if you know that Terrence and his dad play with their dog, Sparky, every night, suggest that Terrence draw a picture of all three of them and where they play together. This kind of activity will help Terrence practice recall skills and his abilities to express his thoughts. Whenever you ask families to work with their child at home, make sure the activity has the potential to strengthen the deep and special parent–child relationship; family members do not need to duplicate your role as a school teacher.

Some parents feel as though they lack the skills to be their child's teacher at home. These feelings are often compounded when parents have low levels of literacy or when they do not speak the primary language of the classroom. Parents may be unable to participate in certain activities or to provide various resources because they are "families with overwhelming needs" (Klass, 2008). They may not have materials such as paper, pencils, crayons, scissors, cameras, etc. at home. Bear in mind that every family— and every family's situation—is different. Participating in certain activities that support the child's learning at home will be possible for some families but not for all.

Conducting Family–Teacher Conferences

Several times a year, teachers and families meet to share information about children's accomplishments. When conferences take place in the context of supportive, reciprocal relationships, valuable information about children's learning can be exchanged. As you read this story of Tina, a 3-year-old child with special needs, notice how a family–teacher conference had a powerful effect on the child's life.

Background

During Tina's kindergarten screening, the observer noted that Tina exhibited "autistic-like" behaviors. At the time, the staff was unable to test her. On the first day of school, Tina fell apart when her father left her in the classroom. He decided that school would be too traumatic for her, so he did not want her to be in the kindergarten program. During later phone conversations, the option of evaluating and placing Tina in a small, self-contained class was discussed with him and with Tina's mother.

Tina's parents do not live together. Tina lived mostly with her mother, stepfather, and 3-month-old sister. Every day while Mom was at work, Dad took care of Tina and put her on the bus to school. Tina also spent several nights each week with Dad.

Tina was evaluated and identified as being a child with autism spectrum disorder. Her language consisted primarily of echolalia; jargon; scripted speech (e.g., "Help me." "That's Tina's."); and some spontaneous two- to three-word phrases when she wanted something. She did not initiate conversations or answer questions at school.

Family–Teacher Conference

We met with both parents while Tina played with a para educator in the adjoining classroom. During our conversation, Dad described an incident that happened when he and Tina were on a city bus. His retelling of the situation suggested that Tina engaged in conversational speech with him. This piqued my curiosity. He told me that she asked and answered questions and make relevant comments about situations. To me, this seemed out of the ordinary. I told Dad that I had never heard Tina speak that much at school. I gently told him that Tina's primary communication with my team and me was limited to two- to three-word requests and sometimes echoing. Mom indicated that Tina's speech at home with her was similar to what we observed at school. Dad was surprised. He said that he thought maybe she was just shy at school.

While the rest of the team finished sharing information with Tina's mom and dad, I went into the room where Tina was playing and started talking to her. I said, "Tina, Daddy just told me what happened on the bus. He said that you talk all the time at home and that he wants you to talk to me at school. When you come back to school next week, I want you to start talking to me."

"I talk. You listen?" Tina asked in reply. I was stunned by her response.

"Yes," I said, "I'll listen when you talk. Let's shake on it and go tell Daddy." We shook hands, and I took Tina to her Mom and Dad. I told them about the conversation and that she agreed to talk at school.

"Tina, that's great," Dad said. "You're a big girl. You need to talk at school." Tina did not respond. As the meeting was ending, Tina's dad asked her to get her coat.

"Time to go home already?" asked Tina, looking up at Dad.

Tina's story illustrates how important conferences can be to a child's learning. What can *you* do to ensure that family–teacher conferences are meaningful? Thoughtfully prepare for conferences and strategize your actions during each conference session.

Preparing for Conferences

Here are several steps to make sure your conferences are constructive:

Schedule conferences to meet families' needs. Keeping in mind that families have different needs, provide a full range of times and days for them to meet with you. Include some mornings before school, times during the day, and some evenings. Depending on your program, conferences may last from 10–45 minutes per family. You will find it helpful to allocate time between conferences. Even 5 minutes will help you switch mentally from the conference just finished to the one scheduled next.

Think about how to keep track of the length of each conference without making time-keeping too obvious. If a major issue arises that cannot be fully discussed during the regularly scheduled conference, schedule a second meeting. Also be aware that some family members may view time differently from the way you do. They may not think it is as important as you do to begin and end meetings promptly (Gonzalez-Mena, 2007).

Let families know what to expect. For some families, their first conference with you will be their first formal family–teacher conference. To help families feel comfortable, let them know what to expect and how they can prepare. You can explain that at a "Curriculum and Assessment Night" or by sending a note of explanation home for each family.

You will find, too, that it is helpful to send home a copy of the completed progress report before the conference. This is critical, especially if you have concerns about the child's learning. This approach indicates your desire to be open with families and to make it as easy as possible for them to hear difficult information.

Many programs send home a form so parents can gather their thoughts and make notes about what they want to talk about at the conference. Parents are much more likely to share information if we show that we value it and that asking for their input and feedback is not an empty ritual.

Dear Family Member,

Your family–teacher conference for _____

is scheduled on _____

at _____ .

Please use this page to list topics or write notes about what you would like to discuss at your child's conference.

Please bring this form to the conference. I am looking forward to talking with you.

If necessary, arrange for a translator and interpreter. If at all possible when families speak a language different from yours, arrange to have translations of written materials as well as interpreters at conferences. If your program, school, or district does not have translators and interpreters, seek resources in the community or through the child's family. There may be a relative who speaks English fluently and who can translate for the family.

Plan the way you will conduct the conference. Organize your thoughts. Consider the best sequence for presenting the points you want to make.

Here is a sample agenda for a conference:

1. Welcome the family member(s) and share a positive anecdote about the child.
2. Ask parents for input.
3. Share information about some of the child's strengths.
4. Share information about some of the child's needs.
5. Set goals with the family.
6. Plan next steps for meeting those goals.
7. Summarize the conference.

You can plan for most parts of this agenda *before* the conference, but be prepared to change your agenda when a family comes in with a major concern that is not part of what you planned to talk about. Conferences are for communicating and bridging the perspectives of the teacher and the family; flexibility is often essential to a successful conference.

As you prepare, make sure the photos or work samples that you want to show families are tabbed so that you can find them easily. The more specific the information you share with the family, the more readily the parent(s) or other family member(s) will understand what you are communicating about the child.

Finally, try to speak simply, avoiding educational jargon. Terms such as *psychosocial, sensory integration,* or *gross-motor* may be common among teachers, but using them without defining them will not help achieve the goal of clear and supportive communication with families.

Some teachers find it helpful to use a planning form. Here is a sample:

Conference Planning Form

Child's name:

1. Opening
(*It is important to help family members feel comfortable and at ease from the start of the conference.*)

2. Ask parents for input.

3. Key points
(*Describe strengths, concerns, and goals. Limit the number of concerns you present in one conference. Remember the rule about three main points. Be sure to explain what you are doing to address concerns.*)

Strengths:

Concern(s):

Goal(s) for the student:

3. Questions for the family
(*Conferences are conversations. Questions can help engage family members in conversation and enable you to learn from them about their child.*)

4. Closing
(*You want family members to leave the conference feeling positive and knowing that they will be able to talk with you again. How will you close the conference?*)

Know how you will begin. Especially for new teachers, beginning a conference can be the most difficult part. Planning will help. You might start by telling a funny story about the child, sharing a question the child asked, or showing a photograph of the child taken during a favorite activity in the classroom.

Arrange the environment. Think about the messages the conference environment communicates. The teacher who sits behind her desk in a comfortable chair while talking with parents who are sitting on lower folding chairs may be communicating that she is the expert "above" the parents. Although some parents may find sitting in child-sized chairs interesting because they then view the room from the child's eye-level, most appreciate sitting in adult-sized furniture. Whenever possible, sit beside the parents so you can easily look at photographs and examples of student work together.

Decide whether the child will be present at the conference. At the elementary level, child-led conferences are common. Teachers prepare students to meet with their families to discuss their performance and show work samples that illustrate their accomplishments. There are many excellent books and videos about child-led conferences. Although preschoolers and kindergartners can play a role in conferences, I do not recommend child-led conferences at this level. For parents of young children who are just beginning to have regularly scheduled conferences, talking with the teacher, adult-to-adult, is important. These early conferences not only focus on the child's learning but also help the family feel comfortable about participating in the program and in their child's education.

Young children who are involved in conferences are able to share particular samples of work that they have chosen ahead of time with their teacher. When the child has no formal involvement, it is important for the family and teacher to tell the child what happened at the conference. Even young children worry when the adults in their lives talk about them. They find it reassuring when adults talk with them after the conference.

During the Conference

By the time of the conference, you will have determined what you want to convey to families and will have a tentative agenda for doing so. To make conferences as productive as possible, use the following strategies when you meet with families.

Welcome families. Make sure you provide a comfortable place for families who come early. Many families will arrive early because they do not want to keep you waiting. You can show parents that you value their time by providing them with something to do while they wait for their conference appointment. You may have class books available or displays of classroom activities. Some teachers have videos of the classroom running on a loop for families to watch while they wait.

Once you are ready for the conference, introduce yourself professionally and, at least at the first conference, greet the family members formally by their last names: "Hello, Mr. Hudson, Mrs. Hudson." If they indicate that you should use their first names, take their lead and address them more informally. Names are important. If you are unsure of how to pronounce a name, asking for help is better than repeating the name incorrectly throughout the conference. If more people come than you expect, find out how they are related to the child by asking, "How do you know (child's name)?"

Ask questions to learn from parents about their child. Naturally, family members have much to contribute because of their roles as caregivers and the extensive time they spend with their children. Teachers need to know information that will help them provide for the child's safety and well-being while attending the program. However, from an assessment perspective, you also want to learn how the family views the child, their goals for the child, what they know about the child's learning and behavior, and what they would like to know.

Eliciting Information From Family Members

What You Want to Find Out	What You Might Ask
How parents view the child The kind of person the child is	If I had never met your child, how would you describe him to me?
Child's strengths	What is she able to do really well?
Child's needs or parents' concerns	With what does he struggle? Do you have any concerns about him?
Child's interests	What does she like to do at home? Are there certain things she's really interested in?
Parents' goals for the child	What do you want him to learn in the program? What do you think we should work on in school?
Child's behavior at home	How does she deal with transitions at home? What does she do when she has to stop one activity and start another? Are you concerned about any of your child's behaviors?
Presence of special needs	Does your child have any special health problems? How is his vision? Hearing? Have they been checked? Can you understand what your child is saying when he speaks with you?
Communication skills	How does she let you know what she wants?

Share information about the child's strengths. There are many ways to highlight each child's strengths. Here are some questions to ask yourself to identify them:

- What are the child's special skills or strong areas?
- What does she enjoy?
- What are his interests?
- What are her particular ways of learning?
- What makes him unique?
- In what areas is this child meeting expectations for a child of her age?

You might focus on benchmarks and standards and talk about those that the child has met. Parents appreciate how well you know their child, especially when you demonstrate this knowledge by telling a specific story, sharing an observation, and presenting samples of work. Most parents appreciate your showing you know and understand their child. Especially that at the end of the year, conferences should celebrate children's accomplishments.

Share concerns about the child. It is difficult for parents to hear a laundry list of concerns about their child. With this in mind, be judicious and only focus on one or two concerns or areas for growth and improvement, and do so in a constructive way.

To clarify your thinking about a child's struggles, ask yourself the following questions:

- What does this child struggle with?
- In what areas is he not meeting expectations or benchmarks?
- Am I concerned about any of the child's behaviors?
- Has she made progress in this area?
- Are additional resources necessary to help the child succeed?

When presenting information about a child's difficulties to family members, be sure to share your professional knowledge and experience to help families maintain perspective. If Michael does not recognize *all* upper- and lowercase letters but started the year without recognizing any, assure his parents that he is learning and that what you are doing in school is benefiting him. Differentiating between the child's current level of performance and the progress he or she has made is significant for families. Helping families distinguish isolated instances of a behavior from a pattern of behavior is also important. For example, if an 18-month old has had a single incident of biting, the family should not be overly alarmed, given her developmental level and the fact that this is not a pattern of behavior.

For children who are developing typically, *anticipatory guidance* can be useful for families. Anticipatory guidance means talking with families about the behaviors and skills that their children are likely to develop next. This can help focus families' attention on the significant behaviors that will be developing over the next few months.

Answer questions. Answer questions as honestly as you can. When you do not know an answer, tell the family that you will investigate and get back to them. They will respect you for admitting that you do not know everything and trust you to be honest with them in the future.

Set goals with the family. Head Start programs are required to set individual goals for each child in the program, with input from the child's family. However, it is sometimes difficult to elicit information from the family about goals for their child. As teachers, we are familiar with and driven by establishing goals and objectives. However, many families have less experience with focusing on goals and may not have thought about them for their children. Asking family members directly about their goals for their child might not be productive.

Instead, listen for the "deep structure" of your conversations with families (Puckett & Black, 2008). Although families may not be talking about goals, you might interpret what they say in terms of goals. Suppose, for example, that a parent talks about how difficult it is to get his 2-year-old daughter to go to sleep. You might share that she has a hard time falling asleep at school as well and suggest that one goal for Preina is to manage the transition from wakefulness to sleep more smoothly.

By asking targeted questions about specific developmental areas, you can help identify parents' goals for their child in that area. For example, have a conversation with Sam's family about his play skills. Ask with whom Sam plays at home or elsewhere in the community. Find out whether he interacts with other children or plays alongside them. Depending on what you learn, his goal might be to assume a pretend role that complements one other child's role for short periods of time.

When you set goals for children, base them on information obtained during the assessment process. Be sure to establish goals to promote children's strengths and interests, as well as to support development in their weaker areas. A child's goal could be to explore her interest in frogs by reading five books on the topic. A goal for a child who loves to do puzzles might be to continue to develop fine-motor skills by completing more challenging ones.

Plan ways to work together to meet goals. Once you decide with the family on the most important goals for the child, the next step is to talk about how to address those goals. Some are best addressed by the teacher. Eric, 3½, needs help transitioning from one activity to the next. His teacher plans to give him a one-to-one warning a few minutes before it is time to change activities. She will then give him and his friend Allan a specific job to do as they move from one activity to the next. After trying this for a few weeks, the teacher will let Eric's family know how he's doing.

If parents are willing, some goals can be addressed both at home and at school. Another goal for Eric is to begin being interested in books. Once in awhile he will listen to and enjoy a story, but he rarely selects a book to look at on his own. His mother and teacher decide to find more books about different types of trucks and other large vehicles, because Eric loves them. At home, he will read one with a parent as part of his bedtime ritual, and his teacher will try to read a book to him and a few others once a day.

Summarize the conference. At the end of the conference, take few minutes to summarize the main ideas discussed. Some programs have teachers complete a conference summary form to document the highlights of the conference, especially the plans agreed upon to support the child's learning. Here is an example:

Family Conference Summary

Child's name: _____   Date: _____

Family members attending: _____

_____

Family input:

Teacher input:

Goals:

Plans to address goals:

Parent's signature: _____
Teacher's signature: _____

If you have shared items from the child's portfolio during the conference, give family members time to review the entire portfolio after the conference. For many parents, seeing only a few specially selected items will simply whet their appetite for seeing more of their child's work.

Common Conference Challenges

"But he does it at home." Teachers can be frustrated when parents insist that their child performs a skill at home that seems far above the child's present capabilities. When this situation occurs, it is best to listen and resist being defensive. As teachers, we sometimes interpret this comment as, "If you were a better teacher, the child would perform the skill for you, too." We tend to take this kind of comment personally.

Instead, recognize that most family members are not saying anything about the teacher or the program when they make this statement. Remember what we know about young children's behavior: Children behave differently in various situations and environments. Sometimes as new skills are developing, children first try them where they feel most comfortable. This might be at home. It is logical to expect children to behave and perform differently at home from the way they do at school.

Be certain that you and the family are talking about the same behavior. Furthermore, make sure that you are using the same language to define developmental stages and behaviors. For example, when a toddler is just learning to walk, the family may consider their child to be walking when he cruises around holding onto furniture. You may define *walking* as taking 20 or more steps without holding onto anything or anyone.

View discussions with families as opportunities to talk about children's learning. We want children to apply what they learn at school to other environments, so it is very important to involve families in assessment. By talking with family members, we can learn whether children are transferring knowledge and skills from school to home and vice versa.

**"What does this mean? Is she the best in her class?" "Is he an A
student?"** Near the end of a conference, family members might
inquire about how their child's skills compare with other children's.
In response to questions like these, McAfee and Leong (2007)
recommend comparing the child's performance to a hypothetical
child of the same age and experience. For example, talk about what
we expect a typical 4-year-old to do. Remember that most parents
are unfamiliar with classroom-based assessment methods. They
want a measure of how their child is doing comparatively.

**Think about how you facilitate conferences
with families.**

- **How effective is your planning for family–teacher
  conferences?**

- **What new strategy would you like to implement?**

- **How comfortable are you with conducting
  conferences? If you do not feel comfortable, what
  strategy might enhance your confidence?**

Reflect
on Your
Practice

Writing Narrative Progress Reports

When you share information face-to-face, you are able to gauge
parents' reactions from their body language, facial expressions, and
comments. When you are writing reports, you do not know how the
parent will respond. It is therefore critical to craft your comments
carefully. Moreover, progress reports from kindergarten onward will
become part of the child's permanent record, so you want to be sure
that they communicate your message clearly.

Teachers vary in their skill and comfort level when it comes to writing
comments or narratives for reports. Just as some teachers can chat
easily with families, others can fluently describe a child's learning,
writing amusing anecdotes and communicating their own appreciation
for the child. If writing does not come naturally to you, use the tips on
the next pages when you write reports about young children.

Appearance When a parent receives a report about his or her child, the appearance of the report creates a first impression about the teacher and the educational program. Therefore, reports must look professional. They should be either word processed or legibly handwritten, using correct grammar and spelling. Always have someone proofread your reports, because it is hard to catch your own mistakes. Find another teacher and proofread one another's reports. Your proofreader will not only catch spelling and grammatical errors and typos but also might help you clarify ideas. He or she might find sentences that appeared clear to you but that are not easily understood by someone who does not share your knowledge of the child.

Length You do not have to say it all. Before writing a child's report, think about the two or three things that are essential for the family to know about their child. Even when information is in writing, there is a limit to the amount families can assimilate. Focus your writing on these main areas. If the family has other concerns, you can address them during the conference.

Tone Your purpose for writing a progress report is to communicate clearly and simply how the child is doing. Use a conversational tone, avoiding educational jargon and generic statements that could be true of any child. Personalize your comments with specific examples. Families should be able to see *their* child in your report.

Maintain an encouraging tone. When the child is struggling in an area, communicate the problems accurately and assure the family that you will work with them to resolve the difficulties the child is facing. After reading a report or ending a conference, you want the family to feel assured that the issues are being addressed.

Beware of using words and phrases that communicate a negative tone. For example, avoid using extremes, such as *never* and *always*. It is highly unlikely that a child *never* manages transitions successfully or *always* has conflicts with peers. If you are not sure how a parent might react to your report, ask a colleague to read it, taking care to maintain the confidentiality of the information.

Audience The primary audience for progress reports is the child's family, so keep this in mind as you write. For example, if you know that a family with two young children just had a set of twins, you might omit complicated activities to do at home for the next several months. You know that just settling two new babies into life at home will be challenging enough.

When answering questions and talking about children's learning and behavior at school, be sensitive to the effect your words will have on the family. Even though your primary focus is on the child, family systems theory tells us that anything that happens to one member of a family affects the entire unit (Christian, 2006; Minuchin, 1974). You do not want the result of your conference or progress report to be that children are pressured or expected to perform at a level far above their capabilities. If you know that a family tends to be critical of a child, emphasize that child's strengths. In that case, it would be helpful to explain that making mistakes is part of the learning process and that the process is not always smooth.

Format Successful reports follow a three-part format. For each of your main points, begin with an overall statement that describes how the child is doing or outlines the progress the child has made since the last progress report. Then provide evidence or examples that support the broad statement. Finally, end each section— whether it is about an area of strength or weakness—with goals and plans for addressing the area. Plans can encompass the teacher's strategies as well as actions the family can take to support the child.

This three-part format—overall statement, evidence, and plans— provides a structure for a narrative or progress report. Within that framework, personalize each report. Use specific examples that include the child's own words and show his or her interests. Select observation notes from the child's file that best illustrate your main points. The following examples illustrate how teachers have used this basic format.

In November, after using an observational assessment tool for 2½ months, Charmaine, Lila's primary caregiver, wrote this about Lila's social and emotional development:

Lila, 17 months, is developing a strong sense of self and sees herself as part of our group. She cheerfully tells us that many of the objects in the classroom are "mine" and yells, "Mine!" when another child tries to take her toy. She shows pleasure when she has completed a task. She is beginning to do some self-help tasks independently. Recently, Lila went into the bathroom, pushed the soap dispenser, and turned on the faucet to wash her hands. We will continue to support her as she discovers more interests and preferences.

As Lila has adjusted to being in our program, she has started to interact with children and adults. She loves to watch other children as she plays and often brings her toy to where other children are playing. Recently, when Lori started crying, Lila found her purple blanket and handed it to her. Lila has also formed relationships with the adults in the room. She gives me hugs and interacts with the other familiar caregivers in the room. Our goals for Lila are for her to continue developing trust in the adults in the program and continue interacting with the children.

Barb, a preschool teacher, described Julian's physical development this way:

Julian's motor skills are developing as expected for a 4-year-old. He asks to use the gym and to go outside, where he shows balance, agility, and control while moving. He can jump, hop, and gallop as well as demonstrate other basic gross-motor skills. In the area of fine-motor skills, Julian uses eye–hand coordination when he manipulates small objects and builds with small toys, blocks, and construction materials. Building is his favorite activity. We are encouraging Julian to practice with writing tools and scissors, although he is not very interested in them right now.

In this excerpt from the final progress report of the year, note how Sally, a kindergarten teacher, communicates clearly about Marc's behavior and learning. She offers a significant amount of information about Marc's skills and accomplishments. Equally important, she communicates her appreciation of Marc as a learner.

Hillside School Final Kindergarten Progress Report

Child. Marc Katz
Teacher: Sally Menke
Date: June 11, 2008

SOCIAL–EMOTIONAL DEVELOPMENT

Marc demonstrates his creative thinking and passionate interests by initiating and following through on independent projects. He continues to investigate sea creatures, and his comments and questions reveal how much he has learned ("Did you know that…?"). He is motivated to create props for his own play and to initiate art projects. He often tells a story or illustrates a point by drawing or creating simple human figures, animals, and symbols.

It is much harder for Marc to pay attention and exercise self-control during work that involves specific directions. When directions are given to the class, or when he is expected to complete an assignment, Marc sometimes gazes around the room or doodles instead. When I give him directions personally and help him focus on his work, he is very capable of producing high-quality work.

Marc is easily distracted during transitional times and needs many reminders to accomplish classroom expectations such as cleaning up or getting unpacked in the morning. He continues to get upset when things don't go his way. Frequent reminders and positive feedback have supported Marc's progress this year, and he can now follow some classroom routines independently. When we know that our routine will change, we give him ample warning. In fact, we often give him the revised schedule in writing so that he can refer to it. He has formed a strong friendship with a student in the class and seems to enjoy this relationship.

LANGUAGE AND LITERACY

Marc's language and literacy skills are strong. He has a large vocabulary, appropriate grammar, and clear articulation. Marc tells well-organized stories. He is beginning to develop his ideas by providing some supporting details. Marc's listening skills vary, depending on the situation. When he is attentive, he can follow two- and three-part directions. He also has strong phonemic awareness skills, which means listening to individual sounds in words. He can break consonant-vowel-consonant words (such as "bag") into their component sounds and can correctly identify the sounds in blends such as /fl/ or /nd/. These are important skills for learning to read.

Marc's reading and writing skills are on target for the end of kindergarten. He recently identified all of the 14 most-studied sight words and knows others as well. He has become adept at decoding many words composed of consonant-vowel-consonant combinations. He can read easy texts successfully! Marc independently uses his knowledge of phonics, his repertoire of memorized words, and his understanding of the convention of putting spaces between words to produce very legible sentences. You can help Marc continue to grow in this area over the summer by visiting the local library, reading with him each night, and encouraging him to use writing as he plays.

MATH

Marc's understanding of math is also very strong. He is able to represent his thinking with diagrams and graphs; make a key or use labels to identify different parts of a problem; use mathematical language; and present the solutions to math problems through words, drawing, and writing. Marc is able to solve challenging math problems. His understanding of addition and subtraction and his knowledge of number facts exceed kindergarten expectations.

Key Ideas to Remember

- Establish relationships with families before you share assessment information.

- Be sensitive to each family's style of communication. Remember that the parent–child relationship is emotionally intense. Your words may have more power than you intend.

- Present information positively but honestly.

- Think of family–teacher conferences as conversations in which family members have a valuable perspective to share.

- Less is always more. Decide on three main points you want to communicate so that you do not overwhelm families with information.

- When writing progress reports, remember that many family members do not have the background in child development and education that you have. Avoid educational jargon and communicate clearly.

- The format, length, tone, and appearance of a narrative report will influence how well parents understand what you are trying to communicate.

References

Berger, E. H. (2007). *Parents as partners in education: Families and schools working together* (7th ed.). Upper Saddle River, NJ: Prentice Hall.

Christian, L. G. (2006). Understanding families: Applying family systems theory to early childhood practice. *Young Children, 6*(1), 12–19.

Epstein, J. (2001). *School, family, and community partnerships.* Boulder, CO: Westview Press.

Gonzalez-Mena, J. (2007). *Diversity in early care and education* (5th ed.). Washington, DC: National Association for the Education of Young Children.

Hildebrand, V., Phenice, L. A., Gray, M. M., Hines R. P. (2007). *Knowing and serving diverse families* (3rd ed.). Upper Saddle River, NJ: Prentice-Hall.

Klass, C. S. (2008). *The home visitor's guidebook: Promoting optimal parent and child development.* Baltimore, MD: Brookes.

Lawrence-Lightfoot, S. (2003). *The essential conversation: What parents and teachers can learn from each other.* New York: Random House.

Lynch, E. W., & Hanson, M. J. (2004). *Developing cross-cultural competence: A guide for working with children and their families* (3rd ed.). Baltimore, MD: Paul H. Brookes.

McAfee, O., & Leong, D. J. (2007). *Assessing and guiding young children's development and learning* (4th ed.). Boston: Allyn & Bacon.

Minuchin, S. (1974). *Families and family therapy.* Cambridge, MA: Harvard University Press.

National Association for the Education of Young Children. (2005). *NAEYC code of ethical conduct and statement of commitment.* Washington, DC: Author.

Puckett, M. B., & Black, J. K. (2008). *Meaningful assessments of the young child* (3rd ed.). Upper Saddle River, NJ: Pearson Education.

CHAPTER 10

Interpreting Assessment Data

From the previous chapters, you learned how to identify what you want to know about the children in your classroom. You also discovered the best ways to collect factual data to help answer your questions and found ways to include children and families in the assessment process. Now it is time to interpret the information you collected.

Interpretation means figuring out what the evidence tells you so that you can decide how best to take action. When teachers interpret data, they review what they know in order to hypothesize or draw conclusions about children's learning and behavior. They sometimes interpret data immediately. They also review data over time and in a systematic way by examining photographs, video and audio clips, observation notes, transcriptions of conversations or interviews, checklists, or organized collections of work.

This chapter discusses three basic types of interpretation. Each is useful at a different time, and each serves a different purpose:

Responsive interpretation Teachers often interpret their observations immediately so they can respond quickly to classroom situations.

Interpretation for planning Teachers interpret data daily or weekly, in order to plan differentiated instruction and resolve classroom challenges.

Evaluative interpretation Teachers interpret data after several weeks or months in order to evaluate each child's performance and progress. This is done most often in preparation for writing progress reports and conducting conferences with families.

The chapter ends with a section about interpreting data accurately.

Responsive Interpretation

Each day, you make quick, nearly instantaneous interpretations based on what you see children do and what you want them to learn. This immediate, informal interpretation enables you to respond quickly but thoughtfully to classroom situations and events. In many situations you do not need to formally review and interpret data in order to respond. Instead, your interpretations are based on your prior knowledge of children (partially based on your familiarity with previously collected data about your children's learning), your expertise, and curricular goals. Consider this example:

> Joseph and Ricky, both 4 years old, are engaged in an animated discussion about whose bead necklace is longer. Knowing that size concepts and gaining experience with measurement are part of the preschool math curriculum, David, their teacher, intervenes. He asks the boys to figure out how to measure the necklaces. With his help, Joseph and Ricky straighten their necklaces, place them side-by-side, and compare them visually.

David's in-the-moment interpretation of the boys' conversation gave him an opportunity to extend Joseph's and Ricky's understanding of length and measurement.

David's interpretation was immediate. From previous experience, he knew that Joseph, especially, was very interested in relative size. (Which tree near the classroom window is the tallest? Who had the larger piece of cheese at snack?). David made sense of what he saw the boys doing, using his previous knowledge about them and the curriculum. He used that information to decide whether and how to intervene. He decided that this was a "teachable moment," that intervening would enhance, not disrupt, the boys' ongoing activity.

Interpretation for Planning

Although finding time in your busy schedule to systematically review and interpret data may seem daunting, there are many benefits to this kind of interpretation. You may identify new questions about children or find gaps in your data. You may notice that you do not know a particular child very well or do not have enough information about children's problem-solving skills. Putting the immediate demands of the classroom aside in order to think about your children at a more leisurely pace allows you to put information together in a new way. For instance, suppose your data shows that Inez frequently runs around the classroom. At first you think she is ignoring the rules. Upon further reflection, after taking the time to study your documentation, it becomes clear that Inez does not understand your directions to stop running.

Interpreting data to plan learning activities or review how smoothly your classroom is functioning is a very different process from responding in the moment. For this type of interpretation, you must think about when and where you will review the data, look for patterns in the data, and focus on particular information related to curricular goals and objectives.

Think ahead. Find a time and a place where you will not be disturbed. Next, select individual children's files and gather information about specific objectives or domains. When you have what you need, you are ready to think about the information you have collected.

Reflect without a specific focus. Unhurried thinking enables you to see things you may have overlooked during busy days in the classroom. Take an unstructured approach, giving yourself time to think about what the data is telling you about children's

- experiences
- skills and knowledge
- approaches to learning
- personalities
- strengths and interests
- challenges

Allow yourself to wonder about the children in your classroom. Many of your questions will be answered by combining a systematic review of your data with thoughtful reflection. For example, you have noticed that Yolanda is very quiet. You wonder,

- Is she shy?
- Does she understand what is happening in the classroom?
- Is she unaccustomed to talking because her brothers are so assertive?

Look through the data to see whether there are answers to your questions.

Perhaps you wonder whether your group is ready to be introduced to initial consonant sounds. You examine all the evidence you have about children's letter knowledge and phonemic awareness to help answer your question.

Look for patterns in the data. As you study the data, you will notice patterns. For example, after reviewing your observation notes about Brandon, you notice that he periodically gets into conflicts with other children. You wonder why that behavior is occurring and how you can help him handle conflict in appropriate ways. You look at your data and notice that Brandon has most conflicts on Mondays. You make a note to observe Brandon carefully next Monday to see what happens. You may want to ask questions like these:

- Why is he involved in conflicts so frequently?
- Is it always with the same children?

If, after additional observation, you learn that Monday conflicts form a pattern, you can generate hypotheses about why he struggles on Mondays; what information you might need (for example, information from Brandon's family about his weekend activities); and what you might do to help him be more successful.

Focus on curricular goals and objectives. When you interpret data for planning purposes, you move from an open review of your data to a focused analysis. You examine the data to identify children's current needs, skills, and interests, and you use that information to guide your planning. You might focus on a specific developmental domain, particular children, the entire class, or classroom challenges. Systematic interpretation during planning helps you figure out

- whether or not you need more data and must determine when and where to collect it

- appropriate ideas for introducing curricular content and extending children's interests

- whether to move on or to provide more experiences related to certain objectives

- the appropriate instructional approach to support each child's development and learning

Notice how Deborah uses data as she plans for 4-year-old Tyrone.

> Deborah reviews the literacy checklist as she studies her data about Tyrone and finds that he loves books, shows little interest in writing, and has not yet made the link between written and spoken words. Deborah routinely points out words as she reads during story time, but after reviewing Tyrone's checklist she realizes that his awareness of print does not yet meet her state's standards for preschool. Her interpretation is that Tyrone may need a quieter, calmer setting in which to focus on print and gain some beginning alphabet awareness. This interpretation leads her to plan one-to-one time with Tyrone next week so they can read a story together.

Sometimes initial interpretations are wrong. As Deborah reads individually with Tyrone and supports his efforts to write, she observes for evidence that his awareness of print is developing. She continues to hypothesize other reasons for his not yet understanding the link. She also tries new strategies, such as writing his dictated captions for drawings and then reading them together. By reviewing the data regularly, she will be able to determine whether or not her interpretation was correct and whether she should explore additional reasons why his level of print awareness does not yet meet the state standard.

Evaluative Interpretation

Evaluative interpretation occurs several times a year and involves data collected over many weeks and months. Whether you are preparing progress reports or getting ready for family–teacher conferences, gathering and reviewing all the documentation you have for each child is a must. Give yourself plenty of uninterrupted time before reports are due or conferences begin so that you can think about each child, using your professional knowledge and expertise as you reflect.

As you begin, review all the information with an open mind. This helps you gain a fresh perspective and see each child holistically. Then pinpoint the information you need in order to complete your reports.

Evaluation always involves some form of comparison. When you want to know about the level of a child's current *performance*, you compare the information you have about a child against guidelines, developmental expectations, or standards. When you want to know whether or not a child has made *progress*, you have to compare the child's current and previous performances.

Comparing Data to Expectations

Determining how a child is doing in relation to expectations for performance requires a structured approach to thinking about the data:

1. Review the data.
2. Review the expectations for children of that grade or age.
3. Compare the two.

For example, your task might be to evaluate an infant's development. For each developmental domain, you would match what you know about that baby with the developmental expectations for babies that age. To make an accurate evaluation, either you must have a strong knowledge of child development or an assessment tool that clearly describes expected development. Similarly, when interpreting subject-area data (math, literacy, science, etc.), you need to understand subject-area expectations in order to draw conclusions about a child's level of performance in relation to the standards.

> Children have been in school 3 months, and Roni is preparing to evaluate her kindergarten students. She takes out her teacher file on Jasmine as well as Jasmine's portfolio. She uses her district's content and performance standards to help her complete the evaluation process. For each indicator on the report card, Roni studies her notes and the work samples in the portfolio. She compares her data to the standard and makes a rating. In some cases, Jasmine's performance is just as Roni expected. In math, however, Roni is surprised to see that Jasmine has many more skills than she assumed. She is pleased to have substantial documentation to support her evaluation.

Comparing the Child's Current Performance to an Earlier One

To evaluate progress, compare the same skill or evidence of performance on the same type of task at two points in time. For example, in October, Robin has two records of Teddy's (9 months) reacting strongly (crying, looking away, looking for his caregiver) when a new person entered the classroom. She also has a record of his looking intently at a classroom visitor several months later. Instead of crying, he continued his activity. She tentatively concludes that Teddy is learning to be more comfortable with strangers, but she also plans some further observations in this area to confirm her evaluation.

Interpreting Data Accurately

As you interpret, the goal is to acquire as accurate an understanding of children as possible so that you can support their learning most effectively. This can be a challenge. Interpretations may be inaccurate for many reasons. Let's look at two of the most common reasons: first impressions and who you are.

First Impressions

It is quite natural to form an impression when you see something for the first time. As teachers, our desire to understand children leads us to apply prior knowledge of and experiences with children to try to interpret and make sense of their behaviors. However, because each child is unique, it is critical to keep an open mind about the meaning of data until you have sufficient information to be confident about your interpretations. When you let first impressions determine your interpretations of children's actions, the result may be inaccurate. Consider this example.

> During Eryca's first day in kindergarten, she plays alone and whispers when talking with adults. Her teacher immediately forms the impression that Eryca is shy and needs help developing social skills. This belief leads Eryca's teacher to begin planning ways to help her participate in classroom activities. The teacher notes in her plan book that Eryca will need assistance with finding friends over the next week.

What are your reactions to this example? Can you think of reasons other than shyness that might explain why Eryca played alone on the first day of school?

Each time you observe, be open to information about a child that may not match your first impression. Perhaps Eryca needs time to get used to new situations and environments. Maybe she has never been in a school environment before. A teacher who strives to look at children openly will be able to see these changes in Eryca's behavior as they develop.

Who You Are Influences Your Interpretations

You are the second factor that affects the accuracy of interpretations! Who we are influences what we see and how we interpret information. Have you ever been with a person you know well and discovered that the two of you have entirely different views of the same event? It may be because you come from different cultural backgrounds, have different personalities, or have different kinds and depths of experiences and expertise. Let's explore how each of these can affect the way you interpret assessment data (Jablon et al., 2007).

Culture Our cultural backgrounds and family experiences filter our view of the world. Culture affects how we think and act, and what we value and believe. Culture influences our styles of communication, approaches to learning, social behavior and interactions, dress, eating habits, beliefs about health, and many other aspects of our everyday lives.

Consider this dramatic example of very different interpretations: When I, from a Western European culture, see a person having an epileptic seizure, I consider this to be a neurological problem. In contrast, someone from the Hmong culture may view a seizure as evidence that spirits inhabit the person (Fadiman, 1997).

Culture permeates many issues that engage early childhood teachers. It relates to beliefs about the importance of education, children's independence and interdependence, self-esteem, how children show respect for adults, child rearing practices, and communication styles. For example, in the United States, many cultural groups value independence. They encourage toddlers to feed themselves and preschoolers to dress themselves. Families with other backgrounds prefer to dress and feed their children past kindergarten age. Teachers who expect independence may misinterpret a child's lack of self-help skills as limited fine-motor abilities or a lack of motivation, although his behavior is accepted and expected by his own family.

Some families respond enthusiastically to children when they tell us about their successes ("Look at me! I'm on top of the slide!"). Both the child's announcement and adults' responses are influenced by culture. Some cultural groups foster interdependence rather than independence (Lynch & Hanson, 2004) and encourage children to help each other, to be part of the group, and not to draw attention to themselves as individuals. If you are assessing a child's social and emotional development, you might interpret a child's reluctance to draw attention to himself as poor self-esteem rather than as behavior her family encourages.

There are many other examples of cultural differences. As a teacher, it is important for you to recognize that your cultural filters affect your interpretations of children's behavior. Be aware of your cultural styles and values. Understand that having some basic knowledge of the family backgrounds of the children you teach can increase the accuracy of your interpretations.

- How do you define the cultural groups to which you belong?

- How does your culture affect your classroom interpretations?

- Think about the children in your classroom. Do you need to know more about any of their cultures or family backgrounds?

Reflect on Your Practice

Personality Who we are as individuals—our gut reactions and feelings, preferences, interests, and temperament—affects our role as assessors. Although it can be difficult for teachers to admit, we immediately like some children but find the behavior of others very challenging.

I will admit that, when I taught preschoolers, I tended to like children who acted out and tested limits. It was satisfying to me that, once they realized the limits were real and consistent, they relaxed into the routines of the classroom. Often their released energy—it does take energy to test every limit for days on end!—fueled active, engaged exploration of the environment. The transformation was remarkable.

I had a much harder time with children who constantly demanded my attention. One little girl, Molly, seemed to call my name or touch my arm or leg several times each minute of every day. Sometimes she would call my name, but she did not have anything to say when I responded. She habitually called to me for attention. Molly's vulnerability and neediness exasperated me. I had to acknowledge that my gut-level reaction was irritation; I had to work diligently to give her attention in positive ways.

It is not surprising that we respond differently to different children. However, we have to put safeguards in place to prevent our instinctive reactions from affecting our interpretations. I had to make sure that I did not pay more attention to and collect more data on challenging boys than I did on Molly. I had to be on the lookout for positive things Molly did, despite my feelings of exasperation. I had to interpret data cautiously so that my interpretations of boys' limit-testing behaviors were not unrealistically positive and my interpretations of Molly's behaviors were not overly negative.

Think about the children in your classroom.

- Are there some whom you felt instantly drawn to and others who made you feel uncomfortable? Can you identify why you reacted as you did?

- How can you prevent your initial reactions to children from affecting your interpretations of data?

Reflect on Your Practice

Some children share your interests or temperamental style. As a sports enthusiast, do you find yourself interacting more with the 5-year-olds who take the ball outside every day for their version of kick ball? If you are a neat and organized person, do you spend less time observing Charlie, who seems to create havoc wherever he goes? Our basic personality, our likes and dislikes, affect how much time we spend with children, what we notice about them, and how we interpret our assessment data.

As you become an experienced observer, you will develop an awareness of your own biases. You will realize that you have emotional reactions to certain children and that your personality affects your interpretations. Curtis and Carter (2000) recommend a "personal parking lot" where teachers can record their emotional reactions. They recount the story of a teacher who saw a toddler happily making lines on his belly with a marker. The teacher's first reaction centered on the mess and the parents' possible response rather than on the novelty the child was experiencing as he explored how the marker felt on his belly. Immediate responses can be parked so as not to limit our interpretations.

Experience and expertise Experience and expertise influence what you see, how much attention you devote to particular events, and how you interpret those events. Val, a speech pathologist in an elementary school, notices all aspects of children's linguistic development. After spending just a brief time with a child, she can describe his articulation, the quality of his voice, the length and sophistication of his sentences, and the level of his vocabulary in great detail—even when she is not intentionally assessing these skills. When interacting with children, it is difficult for her not to do this because her expertise is ingrained. We tend to devote more attention to what we understand best and have to remind ourselves to pay attention to areas about which we are less knowledgeable.

Think about your particular areas of expertise.
- **How do they affect what you observe?**
- **How might they have an impact on the way you interpret children's behavior?**

Reflect on Your Practice

We all have various lenses or mental filters through which we observe children's behavior and learning. It is impossible to observe without having our culture, personality, experience, and expertise play a role. The challenge is to prevent our unique perspectives from having an undue influence on our interpretations of the objective data we have collected.

Why Accuracy Is Extremely Important

When you interpret children's actions, you set off a chain of events based on those interpretations. When you interpret data and think you understand what is happening, you develop expectations or beliefs that are based on your interpretation. Our beliefs or expectations affect how we interact with children. Naturally, the quality of our interactions shapes our relationships with children and affects how they develop and learn.

Visualize the following choice-time scenario with Ahmed, a 4-year-old new to the classroom.

> Ahmed plays with small colored blocks at a table with three other children. He makes a flat, rectangular form with about 15 green and blue blocks, occasionally looking at the children at his table and around the room. He pushes his blocks to the middle of the table and walks quickly over to the pegboard where musical instruments are hanging. He picks up a tambourine, shakes it twice, puts it back, and runs over to the dramatic play area. For about 10 seconds, Ahmed watches a boy and a girl playing restaurant. Then he leaves to join a group of children working on a floor puzzle. He stays for about 2 minutes, until it is time to clean up. He begins taking the puzzle apart to put it away.

This description contains some facts about Ahmed's behavior during choice time. As you continue to learn about Ahmed, you will add many other facts to your knowledge base. You will observe him again during choice time and in many other situations before you feel as though you are starting to get to know him.

What if—instead of waiting and gathering more information—you immediately interpreted this observation and concluded that Ahmed is hyperactive? Your interpretation would lead you to expect certain behaviors of him. You might anticipate conflicts with other children or evidence of a short attention span. Once you have labeled him "hyperactive," you begin to act as though Ahmed *is* hyperactive, interpreting his actions as being the result of hyperactivity. The very act of labeling may convince you that you fully understand what you see. Your behavior with the child might change. You might structure his activities and direct his behavior more than you do for other children. You might intervene very quickly during social conflicts to solve the problem instead of facilitating Ahmed's ability to solve the problem by himself.

Expectations Guide Actions

Research shows that teachers act on their expectations of children (Good & Brophy, 2008). Expectations about children's achievement levels influence

- how long teachers wait for responses
- how much teachers interact with children
- the types of questions teachers ask
- the types of activities they offer
- the amount of praise and eye contact they use

In the previous example, Ahmed's teacher might think that overly active boys are low achievers who have trouble learning. Because of this belief, she may not give him as much time to respond to a question as she would give a child she thinks is a high achiever. She might answer questions for Ahmed, and smile at and praise him less than she would children she perceives as high achievers. Teacher expectations affect teacher behavior, which in turn affects children's learning.

Expectations guide perceptions as well as behavior. Once you form expectations or label a child, what you see tends to fit the expectations you already established. It is difficult to observe the child without being influenced, or biased, by your expectations. You begin to see what you expect rather than what is actually there. Your interpretations and subsequent expectations must be accurate because they affect your teaching.

Furthermore, expectations develop from sources other than interpretations of data. Teachers who have taught a child's older sibling, for instance, may expect the second child to be similar to the first. Teachers may accept stereotypes related to gender (i.e., think that boys are more active than girls and that girls are more verbal than boys) or poverty (e.g., think that all underprivileged children do poorly in school because they lack books at home). Expectations can be influenced by your relationship with a child's family, the child's degree of cleanliness, or her appearance. These and other factors have the potential to bias what teachers see when they observe and how they interpret their data.

Enhancing the Accuracy of Interpretations

What safeguards can you put in place to increase the accuracy of your interpretations? As a starting point, use these strategies:

Gather enough data. Wait until you have sufficient data before you draw conclusions. One instance of a behavior is not enough to make an interpretation. To determine whether or not you have enough information, ask yourself whether you have a complete picture of the child. Have you observed the child in a variety of situations and over time? The more information you have when assessing children's knowledge and skills, the greater the likelihood that the assessment results will be accurate.

Use multiple sources of information. Sometimes it is helpful to find out whether others' interpretations are similar to yours. Talk with other adults in the classroom to get their perspectives. Children's family members are also a great source of information, and most appreciate being consulted. Knowing that any event can be seen from multiple perspectives, make time to look at a child's behavior from the child's perspective. Sometimes considering what the child is getting from the behavior allows us to think more broadly when we interpret it.

Review your data regularly. Establish a regular time and place for review and have all the data you need ready. For example, you might review files every 2 weeks during planning time. Some teachers prefer to review data away from the classroom to get a fresh perspective, so they take home a few files at a time. If you are using an online system, you can access your documentation from your home computer. If you have more than one adult in your classroom, it is useful to review systematically as a team in addition to your daily, informal conversations. Whatever process you put into place, know that each time you look at a child's assessment data you will remember more precise details. That deepens your understanding of the child.

Keep expectations positive, current, and flexible. Keep in mind that our positive expectations tend to affect children positively. If you are in doubt about what to expect from a child, expect the most positive outcome that is realistic. Continue collecting data so that your interpretations will be based on current information. Try to keep your expectations flexible so that they change as you learn more about the child.

Develop several hypotheses. When you make interpretations, think of them as being tentative, as hypotheses rather than irrefutable conclusions. They may be true, or you might eventually learn that they are not. Continue gathering information to test your interpretations.

If possible, generate several interpretations based on your data. Sometimes we get stuck and cannot let go of one interpretation to allow for another. Consider the following situation:

> Tamara is a child with a moderate hearing impairment. Even with amplification, she still does not hear some sounds, especially in noisy environments. When it is story time, Tamara wanders around the classroom, never joining the group. Josh, her preschool teacher, has been very inconsistent about inviting her to join group activities. He assumes that she knows she will not be able to hear and that is why she does not want to participate. Jessica, the assistant in the classroom, wonders whether Tamara understands that everyone is expected to go to story time. When she initially mentions this to Josh, he is unresponsive. However, as time passes and Tamara never joins group activities, he wonders whether Jessica might be right. Maybe Tamara needs help learning how to participate in group activities. Maybe it has nothing to do with her hearing loss.

When you study data and immediately think you understand what it means, ask yourself whether there could be another interpretation of the same facts.

The best way to check on the accuracy of your hypotheses, or tentative interpretations, is to test them. In the previous example, if Josh decides that Tamara is not coming to group activities because she does not know that she is expected to or because she does not know how to participate in group activities, he will develop a plan to teach her the expectations for group activities. Perhaps he will invite her to join the group and seat her next to him. If she stays for part of the group time, he will continue this strategy. After a while, he might ask Jessica to invite Tamara to group and have Tamara sit next to Jessica. This gives Jessica a chance to model what children are expected to do as a participant during group time. However, if she comes to a group activity but leaves as soon as it starts, Josh should develop other hypotheses about Tamara's lack of participation.

Interpretation Paves the Way for Action

As a teacher, you have many demands on your time. Sometimes the immediate needs of children, families, and administrators require you to change plans flexibly and respond immediately to pressing issues. I can imagine that, when I suggest you need regular, quiet time to reflect, your first thought is, "You have to be kidding!"

I'm not kidding. Setting aside time for regular reflection allows for creative thinking about the children you care for and teach. It presents opportunities to develop new approaches to your teaching. It is also a way to bring your education and expertise to bear on the needs of your children and classroom. Isn't this a big part of why you became a teacher in the first place?

Reviewing and interpreting data prepares you to take action, which is the fourth phase of the assessment cycle. New curriculum ideas, teaching strategies, conversations to have with families, and resolutions to problems can all emerge from unhurried contemplation of the data you collect about children's learning.

Key Ideas to Remember

- Setting aside quiet time for reflection and interpretation is an essential part of using the assessment process to support children's learning.

- Your culture, family background, personality, and areas of expertise significantly influence your interpretation of what children say and do.

- Our interpretations of assessment data create beliefs about and expectations of children that affect our interactions with them.

- Reflecting regularly, making interpretations, and testing hypotheses and conclusions help us understand children and enhance our appreciation of each child's uniqueness.

References

Curtis, D., & Carter, M. (2000). *The art of awareness: How observation can transform your teaching.* St. Paul, MN: Redleaf Press.

Fadiman, A. (1997). *The spirit catches you and you fall down: A Hmong child, her American doctors, and the collision of two cultures.* New York: Farrar, Straus and Giroux.

Good, T. L., & Brophy, J. E. (2008). *Looking in classrooms* (10th ed.). Boston: Pearson.

Jablon, J. R., Dombro, A. L., & Dichtelmiller, M. L. (2007). *The power of observation* (2nd ed.). Washington, DC: Teaching Strategies, Inc.

Lynch, E. W., & Hanson, M. J. (2004). *Developing cross-cultural competence: A guide for working with children and their families* (3rd ed.). Baltimore, MD: Paul H. Brookes.

Taking Action

Taking action, the fourth phase of the assessment cycle, is the point at which you decide what to say and do on the basis of your interpretation. Sometimes you interpret quickly and act immediately. For instance, you might decide to question a child about a social studies concept, or you might change your planned transitional activity. At other times, you may have questions about a child's behavior, a developmental area, or a classroom problem, leading you to a more deliberate and extensive collection and interpretation of data. Your findings may encourage you to take a different approach to what you are teaching or prompt you to change your daily routines. You might also gain new insights about assessment that make you a more effective assessor.

Taking action is the culmination of the assessment cycle. The actions you take can directly benefit children and families. You take action to improve your teaching and help each child in your classroom learn.

As we have discussed, assessment is ongoing. The actions you take bring one full cycle to a close, and the sequence of steps begins again. You implement new strategies and observe the results to see how children respond to these approaches. Then you ask new questions. Taking action is the catalyst for beginning the cycle anew.

In this chapter, teachers describe the way they made and implemented plans based on their understanding of the data they collected. The stories show how teachers used data to

- benefit individual children
- improve the learning of groups of children
- solve classroom challenges

Taking Action to Help Individual Children

In this section, you will read stories that focus on teachers' questions and concerns about individual children and how collecting and interpreting data helped them respond more effectively.

Meeting the Needs of a Nonverbal Child

William Ryan teaches at an early learning center in the northeastern region of the United States. Most of the children in his class have Polish and Spanish backgrounds and come from families with low incomes. William describes Maria, a 5-year-old child whose native language is Polish. Before Maria came into his class, she was diagnosed as a *selective mute*, meaning that, although she has the ability to speak and has spoken in the past, she chooses not to speak.

William says,

> While talking with Maria's teacher from the previous year, I learned that Maria was anxious when she started school last year. It was hard for her to separate from her mother. She cried the entire day, all through the months of September, October, and November. During these months, however, Maria would say things when she cried, such as, "I want Mommy," or, "I go home." She cried, but she also spoke. She would even count with the assistant teacher at rest time to calm down. Then, one day, in December of 2007, Maria stopped speaking. Around the same time, she stopped crying and began to separate more easily from her mother.

> During that school year, her teacher worked with the intervention and referral team and the school social worker to try to help Maria speak. The only progress made was in the spring of 2008, when Maria began making some animal sounds while engaging in pretend play. In late spring, Maria said, "Good-bye," to her teacher at the end of the day, but only when holding her mother's hand and no one else was around.

> When Maria started school in my classroom this past September, she cried for about 3 weeks but then transitioned into school without a problem. However, she still did not speak.

Imagine that you are Maria's teacher. What would you want to know about Maria? William had many questions. Note how his questions led him to collect data and how his interpretations of that data helped him choose new strategies to use with Maria.

> **Asking questions.** I had several critical questions. First, I was trying to find out how to support Maria so she could participate in classroom activities that typically require verbal interactions. I had never had a child diagnosed as selective mute before, and I wanted to know what activities Maria would respond to positively and engage in willingly. How could I help her function successfully and independently in the classroom?
>
> Obviously, I wanted to understand why Maria wasn't talking and how I could increase her use of expressive language.
>
> In addition to questions about Maria, I also had to ask myself questions about how I would assess Maria's progress. I usually assess a child through verbal responses. For example, I would note, "The child said... while doing this," or, "The child responded to me by saying... " I knew I couldn't get data like that from Maria. I had to plan carefully and create activities in which Maria felt comfortable. I also had to figure out how to learn about her without relying on verbal responses.
>
> **Collecting data.** I routinely collected data for each child in my classroom, but I knew that I needed to collect more for Maria because of her special situation. I focused on her participation in classroom activities, what she was learning, and her expressive and receptive language skills.

The following pages show some examples of the data William collected to answer his questions.

9/25 Choice Time
Maria played alone, using a variety of manipulatives.

9/30 Transition
When I asked children the color of their shoes, Maria pointed to her shoes.

10/7 Transition to outside
Maria stood silently while the class counted the number of children in line. Her eyes moved from one child to the next.

11/14 Dramatic Play
Maria joined Jashana and Billy in the doctor's office. She grabbed the calendar from Billy's hands to find a date for Jashana's appointment. She scribbled a date.

11/24 Large Group
I called on Maria to answer a question about the calendar. She raised four fingers to show me which day of the month it was.

12/4 Outdoors
Maria pushed Emily aside to climb on the jungle gym.

12/12 Small Group
Maria worked on a puzzle next to Sarah. M pointed to the next piece Sarah needed.

12/15 Dramatic Play
In the "Grocery Store," Maria was working at the register. She tapped Katie on the shoulder, pointed to the cereal box and then to the register to indicate that Katie (the customer) should pay for the cereal before she took it.

11/1 Outside
Maria came up behind me and said, "Boo," trying to scare me.

11/12 Small Group
During a letter writing activity while we were studying mail and mail carriers, each child chose a classmate to write to. I gave Maria different sentences that she might like to write in her letter. She nodded "yes," indicating that she wanted to write, "I like to play with you." Then I told her, "I'll say it, and you write it." She wrote, "I like to play with u."

12/6 Children responded to a question from the 3-year-old class downstairs. They had asked what the rules of our classroom are. Maria copied our first rule from a list that hangs on the wall.

12/10 Study of frogs
Maria brought me paper, pointed to the stapler on my desk. I guessed she wanted me to create a book for her because we have done this before. After I stapled the paper for her, she worked for about 25 minutes in the Art area. The word "Frogs" was on our word wall, which Maria consulted as she wrote a title. We always talk about how authors/illustrators' names are on the covers of books, so Maria wrote her name on her cover.

Interpreting the data. I usually review data at school—mostly in the morning before the children arrive, in the afternoon at nap time, or at the end of the day. Often I adjust my plans for the day on the basis of new information I collected. I regularly shared observations with Maria's mother, the social worker, my assistants, the intervention team, and her former teacher. In return, I received plenty of ideas and strategies from all of them.

Even though Maria was not speaking, the data showed me that she was processing verbal information. She responded non verbally when I asked for a response during classroom routines and activities. If a verbal response was required, she remained silent. She knew who all the children were and could link them to their printed names.

Other data showed that, even though she wouldn't speak, she tried to control play scenarios and interactions with other children. I discovered this through my observations of her in the Dramatic Play area and during other times of the day while she was interacting with peers. I began to wonder whether Maria's inability to control being left by her mother at school led her to take control of something else: her expressive language.

Maria was making letter–sound connections and beginning to spell words by letter sounds! She had acquired some basic understandings about books and could express herself through drawing. She pointed to letters when I named them and could write most of them. I was pleased with Maria's literacy progress and surprised by how much information I was able to collect even though I couldn't rely on her spoken language.

William drew many conclusions about Maria's participation, language, and literacy skills from the data he collected. He also hypothesized that Maria needed some control over her world and exercised it by not speaking. Although it was natural for William to wonder why Maria wasn't speaking, his main purpose for assessment was to focus on Maria's learning rather than on proving or disproving that hypothesis.

Taking action. It seemed from observing her that Maria wanted to participate more, especially with other children. I introduced alphabet sign-language, and the children quickly learned to sign letters. I also taught them some words in sign language so Maria could communicate with her hands. I also created some nonverbal transitional activities in which all the children could participate. For example, when we got up from circle to wash our hands for lunch, the children counted the dots on a large die. They responded by showing me on their fingers, clapping, stomping, or in other ways that did not require words. For show-and-tell, Maria used a picture chart, indicating what she had, where she had gotten it, who got it for her, etc.

Since Maria had begun playing the "Boo" game with me on the playground, I decided that I needed to continue to do what we had been doing in terms of increasing her expressive language. My job was to provide her with a safe, secure, and interesting environment and to let her language emerge at her pace.

I had suspected that Maria knew more than I could easily assess, given that she wasn't speaking. However, I learned that Maria's literacy skills were strong, as were her skills in other areas. I planned to include her in the same literacy activities as other children and to be sure that she had some nonverbal ways to respond. I did collect more observation notes about Maria than about some other children, because I could not ask her questions that required spoken responses.

What happened next? Gradually, Maria became more comfortable and started participating with the other children. By November, Maria often said, "Boo!" on the playground, trying to startle me. She was able to function well throughout the day, which seemed to build her confidence.

In December, Maria's mother brought in a tape recording of Maria reciting the alphabet, counting numbers, and answering questions about her favorite things. I asked Maria each day whether we could listen to the tape together. She shook her head, "No," until one day in mid-December, when she nodded, "Yes." I was so excited!

Maria and I went into the hallway, and I pressed the play button. I finally heard the voice of this little girl who had been in my room for over 6 hours a day, 5 days a week, for the past 4 months. She spoke beautifully. Maria smiled the entire time we listened.

That afternoon when Mom came to pick her up, she held her mother's hand; turned to me as she was leaving; and said, "Good-bye, Mr. Ryan." I smiled from ear to ear for the rest of the day.

By using the assessment cycle, I learned a great deal about Maria. One, she was participating in most classroom activities. Two, she was learning a lot. It was an eye-opening experience for me because I realized that listening to what a child says isn't the only way to assess the child's understanding of, say, phonetics and letter–sound correspondence.

Maria brought some interesting challenges to William's classroom. Because Maria did not speak, William needed to find ways for her to participate in classroom activities with the other children, and he needed to expand his assessment methods to capture her learning through nonverbal means. At the same time, he wanted to help Maria express herself through language. Through continued observation and repeated review of his data, William was able to craft teaching and assessment strategies that benefited Maria. By the end of the year, she was talking!

Supporting a Child Who Is Acquiring English

Karla Flanders teaches at a preschool that serves the children of students, faculty, and staff members of a large university. The center has a diverse population, and household incomes range from medium to high. At least one-third of the children speak a language other than English as their first language. Karla is concerned about 3½-year-old Amanda, who speaks Chinese. At the beginning of the school year, Amanda is using only a few English words.

Asking questions. In preparing to complete a checklist on Amanda, I reviewed the anecdotal notes that were collected over the past few months. Little was recorded under the domain of mathematical thinking. I began to reflect on why this was so. I wondered about the following questions:

- Was she not participating in activities that would show her mathematical thinking? Was she more interested in other activities?
- Were we not looking for evidence of her math skills?
- Was language a barrier for me to document what she knows?
- Were there not enough opportunities and materials available for her to explore mathematical problems?

Collecting data. We began observing Amanda more closely during choice time. I also took time to reread previous observation notes in all domains.

I wanted to try some different methods of collecting data. I decided to tally the times I observed Amanda interacting with children other than Joy, the only other Chinese-speaking child in our class. I kept a pad of sticky notes in my pocket, marked whenever I saw this happen, and noted the situation.

I also tracked how she spent her choice time. I had a list of open centers for each day and just tallied when Amanda visited each one, not worrying about how long she stayed in each place.

Observing Amanda carefully for a few days, I found that her time was spent mainly in the Dramatic Play and Art Areas of the classroom. During those 3 days, she never visited the math or literacy centers and only went to the reading nook once. She played mostly with Joy. The two girls spoke Chinese when they played together. Amanda followed Joy around inside, outside, and to lunch.

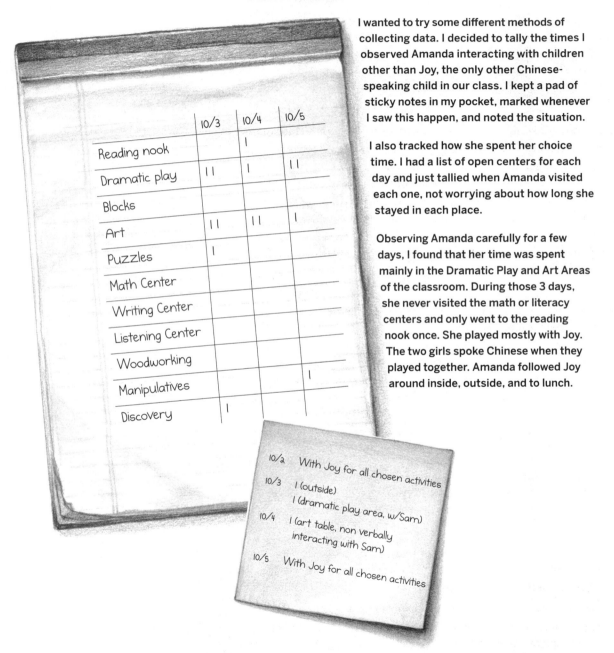

	10/3	10/4	10/5
Reading nook		I	
Dramatic play	I I	I	I I
Blocks			
Art	I I	I I	I
Puzzles	I		
Math Center			
Writing Center			
Listening Center			
Woodworking			
Manipulatives			I
Discovery	I		

10/2   With Joy for all chosen activities
10/3   I (outside)
        I (dramatic play area, w/Sam)
10/4   I (art table, non verbally interacting with Sam)
10/5   With Joy for all chosen activities

Looking at my observation notes, I found that most of them related to physical development, the arts, and personal/social development. Most of the observations focused on Amanda's actions, and little language was included.

I also found that a few notes containing information related to mathematical thinking had been categorized under a different domain. For example, the following note was categorized under physical development. When I re-read it, I saw evidence of a math skill.

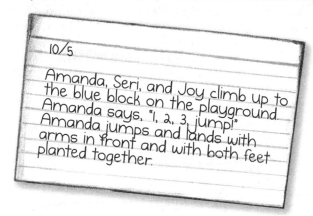

10/5

Amanda, Seri, and Joy climb up to the blue block on the playground. Amanda says, "1, 2, 3, jump!" Amanda jumps and lands with arms in front and with both feet planted together.

Interpreting the data. Amanda spent most of her time with Joy and the two girls spoke Chinese to each other, so it was difficult for the teachers (none speaks Chinese) to understand their conversations or interactions. Also, since Amanda never visited the math center, we did not have the chance to observe her use of math manipulatives. It is difficult to know about Amanda's mathematical skills because we have not been able to observe them carefully.

Taking action. I organized a few small-group activities for Amanda and purposely did not include Joy. (Children typically choose the activities in which they participate.) Some of these small-group activities took place outside the classroom, either in the hall, outdoors, or in the multi-purpose room. I wanted to limit the distractions for children so that I could really listen and watch to find evidence of problem solving and other thinking skills.

I became much more aware of how to study and organize my observation notes in order to look for information about all domains. I know that one observation note can provide information about several domains, but I had been neglecting to look for evidence of math learning in notes that I had organized in other domains.

What happened next? When Amanda was with English-speaking peers, I could see that she understood many English words and could actively participate in small-group activities. She worked with a group of children to put together a bug-counting puzzle. She was able to recognize many of the numerals and count the bugs in the picture. She also did some patterning and categorization with shells and buttons (big shell, little shell, big shell, little shell, etc; blue button, red button, red button, blue button, etc.). Now that I have a better idea of Amanda's skills, I want to know more about other math skills and how she uses English. I realize I'm starting another assessment cycle, and I have more information as I begin again.

William and Karla describe the challenges of collecting data about children who, for different reasons, have difficulty expressing themselves verbally. By collecting data, considering possible interpretations, and taking actions based on those interpretations, both teachers help children interact more fully in the classroom and support their learning with appropriate activities.

William's and Karla's stories also illustrate how they had to modify the ways they collect and think about data in order really to learn about children. William had to learn to watch Maria's actions rather than rely exclusively on language. Karla had to discover a way of looking at observation notes from many perspectives. Both teachers adapted activities in order to be able to learn about children.

- To meet the needs of an individual child, how have you based action on the thoughtful interpretation of collected evidence?

- When did you last interpret evidence quickly and act immediately to respond to an individual child? What happened?

Reflect on Your Practice

Taking Action to Help Groups of Children

In the previous section you read about how teachers use data to meet the needs of individual children. The stories that follow highlight how teachers enhance the learning experiences of children in groups. Basing their plans on assessment data, the teachers are able to focus on different areas of learning and development.

Monitoring Preschoolers' Gross-Motor Development

Jasmine Little is a new preschool teacher at a child care center on the campus of a large mid western university. It is early in the school year, and she is using observational assessment to learn about her children's gross-motor skills. Her classroom has access to a gym and an outdoor play yard. The class includes children from the local community as well as those of university employees and students. Of the ten girls and eight boys in the group, about half are Caucasian from a variety of family backgrounds. The others are Hispanic, Asian, and African American.

Asking questions. During the first few weeks of school, I've been busily collecting data on each child and in all developmental areas. My focus has been mostly on their social and emotional behavior and literacy skills, so I decided to make a more conscious effort to learn about other areas. My first questions were "What gross-motor skills do they have? Are they developing as expected in this area?" My state identifies two early learning standards related to gross-motor development (Michigan State Board of Education, 2005):

1. Children experience growth in gross-motor development and use large muscles to improve a variety of gross-motor skills in both structured and unstructured settings.

2. Children increase their ability to understand and control their bodies and learn that regular physical activity can enhance their overall physical, social, and cognitive development.

Collecting data. To answer my questions, I first spent 2 days observing how children moved around the room. Did they move quickly or slowly? Did they bump into things or people? What was their affect as they moved? Were they eager and happy to move, or were they content to stay in one place?

I made some checklists of typical gross-motor skills (jumping, hopping, skipping, balancing on a beam, throwing, catching, kicking, etc.). Over the next few weeks, when we were in the gym or outside, I set up various activities and obstacle courses so children could practice gross-motor skills.

Observing children as they made choices outside and in the gym, I took brief notes on what they did and how they did it.

Here are some examples of the data that Jasmine gathered:

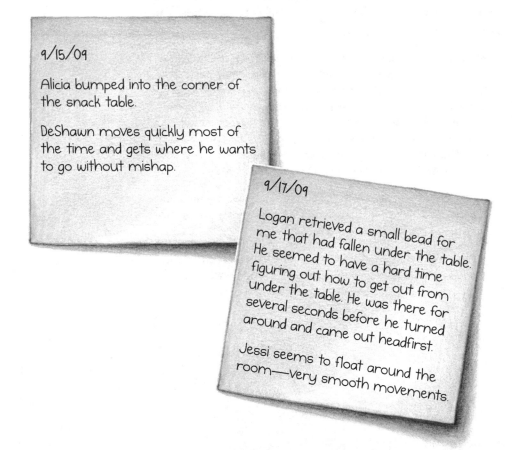

9/15/09

Alicia bumped into the corner of the snack table.

DeShawn moves quickly most of the time and gets where he wants to go without mishap.

9/17/09

Logan retrieved a small bead for me that had fallen under the table. He seemed to have a hard time figuring out how to get out from under the table. He was there for several seconds before he turned around and came out headfirst.

Jessi seems to float around the room—very smooth movements.

Gross-Motor Skills Observation Matrix

✔ demonstrates skill
- does not demo skill
+/- sometimes, not consistently

9/20 9/30	Hopping 10x on each ft	Balance beam	Stop & start on signal	Alternates feet on stairs up/down	
Logan	R: 4, L: 1	✔	Hard time stopping, slow to start	+/-	-
Sonali	R:10, L:10	✔	✔		
Jessi	R:10, L:10	✔ Enjoyed, graceful	✔	✔	✔
Marie	R:10, L:10	✔	✔	✔	✔
Lily	R: 5, L: 4, appears unsure? Nervous?	Refused, fearful?	✔ appears to be concentrating	-	+/- last step only
Dwayne	R:10, L:10	✔	✔		
Alicia	R: 2, L: 7	✔ shaky	✔	✔	✔
DeShawn	R:10+, L:101	✔ con dent	+/- tried hard	-	-
Julio	R: 6, L: 4	✔	✔	✔	✔
Jennifer	R:10, L:10	✔	✔	✔	- quickly
		✔ rapidly, afraid of falling if she slows down?	✔	✔	✔

Brief Notes— Gross-Motor Observations

	9/21	9/25	9/29
Logan	Tossed beanbags. Throws too hard. bb went beyond box.	Held rail of loft steps, alternated going up entire way.	Tried rock climbing wall outside. Took 3 steps, couldn't seem to find next step.
Sonali	Rides a tricycle on the path outside.		Walked around the edge of the sandbox 3 times.
Jessi	Moving around the classroom gracefully while pretending to fly.	Loped down the gym floor, stopped, spun on one foot, saying, "I'm a ballerina. I'm a ballerina."	Climbs the rock wall on the playground.
Marie	Used the "big slide" and swung from bar to bar (2x) on the suspended "ladder"		Walked the length of the balance beam (4') while holding objects and without falling.
Lily	Wandered around the playground, joined Mae at the beanbag toss.	Ran in and out of the outdoor playhouse, played in the sandbox making food.	Walked around the hula hoops on the gym floor, did not try to use them.
Dwayne	Successfully jumped from a tall mat to a short mat in the gym.	Walks up and down the loft stairs without holding on.	Had three successful turns with the hula hoops.
Alicia	Threw beanbags into a box. Moved to within 3 feet of the box to get bean bags in.	Tried to use the swings, requires significant support to get on and swing.	Runs from one end of the playground to the other with a group of children, stumbled 4 times, fell once.
DeShawn	Successfully jumped from a tall mat to a short mat in the gym.	Walks the length of the balance beam (4') while holding objects and without falling.	Hopped in the Moon Bounce, alternating feet three times.
Julio		Walked up and down the stairs to the loft without holding the rail.	
Jennifer	Took several turns at the beanbag toss. Made it in 3 of 4 times.	Ran from one end of the playground to the other several times.	Played in the sandbox, then joined 2 children in a chase game around the playhouse.

Interpreting the data. I reviewed my data at the end of 2 weeks. Most of the children's gross-motor skills meet the state standards. They seem to enjoy unstructured time—both outside and in the gym—and the games, obstacle courses, and challenges I set up for them. Using my knowledge of developmental expectations, I have some questions about Jennifer, Logan, Lily, and Alicia.

Overall, Jennifer's skills seem strong, except for the balance beam. Perhaps she is nervous or fearful of its height. Does she use the big slide outside? Climb the rock wall?

Logan seems to have difficulty coordinating more complex movements. He loves to run around, but his movements are not very rhythmic. They seem bumpy or jerky.

Lily had trouble hopping, refused to walk on the balance beam, and stumbled on the stairs. She can roll the ball easily, grab it when it comes to her, and even throw it. She also runs with agility, easily stopping on a signal. I know she is an only child, is very well behaved, and spends a lot of time with her grandmother. I wonder whether she just doesn't have a great deal of experience with large-motor activities.

Alicia had difficulty with most of the tasks I presented. Her physical development does not seem to be typical for a 4-year-old.

Taking action. I will continue to offer a variety of structured and unstructured gross-motor experiences to the class, since most children are responding well to them. I'm going to collect more specific information about Logan, Lily, Alicia, and Jennifer. I don't want them to feel incompetent, so I'm going to make sure that I offer challenges at different levels: walking on a balance beam but also walking on a tape line because that would be easier. I'll try to offer an easier and harder option whenever I can.

What happened next? Now that I'm focusing on movement skills, the children are much more aware of their own abilities and are having a lot of fun. I'm continuing to collect data on all the children but focusing intentionally on Jennifer, Lily, Alicia, and Logan. Just as I suspected, Jennifer has good skills except climbing or balancing off the ground. I'm gently encouraging her to try these skills; she is making some progress.

Lily seems to be slowly making progress. These days, she even smiles when we're running around outside. I talked with her mom and grandmother about how much experience Lily has with gross-motor skills. They said she doesn't have much. They live in an apartment without a fenced playground area. I talked about how much I learned from being involved in sports in school and how important it is to develop in all areas at this age. Yesterday, Mom said she had seen a sign for a Saturday morning soccer club that Lily could join. Things seem to be moving for Lily.

As I get to know Alicia better, I'm finding that she seems to have delays in many areas, not just gross-motor development. I'm going to take more time to document her skills and then talk to my director about her and what we should do next.

Logan is a puzzle to me right now, so I'm paying close attention to him. His fine-motor skills are also awkward. He knows many things and is fascinated by motorcycles and race cars. His math and language skills are just where they should be for a 4-year-old. However, he has difficulty recognizing many letters and writing his name. I'm gathering more information.

I'm getting better at providing activities at different levels of difficulty. When I give children challenges, I try to make them open-ended. For example: How can you get to the other side of the playground without walking or running? In obstacle courses, I'll put the big and little tunnels out right next to each other, so Logan can choose the one he can crawl through successfully.

I'm learning about children's gross-motor skills, but I don't have information about whether they understand that regular physical activity can enhance their overall physical, social, and mental development. I have to think about what that understanding means for preschoolers, and how to teach and assess it, because a state standard requires me to promote it.

Jasmine, a very competent first-year teacher, is developing strategies to collect and manage data on her children. At this point, she is gathering basic information and being careful to check that she is assembling enough data to get a complete picture of each child. She is making sure she has evidence of how the children are performing with regard to her state's standards, and she uses the evidence and the standards to guide her teaching.

Investigating Mathematical Thinking

Anne Barnard is a full-day kindergarten teacher in a public school
located in an upper-middle class community in Maryland. She
has 23 students in her classroom, including 2 English-language
learners. She also has one child who is being evaluated to determine
his eligibility for special education services because of behavioral
issues and possible learning disabilities. Fifty-six percent of the
children are Caucasian, 32 percent are Asian American, and about
8 percent are African American or Hispanic.

Anne's school's professional development plan this year includes a
focus on teaching children mathematical process skills. Anne
thought that she had a good grasp on assessing her students' basic
math skills and knowledge (shapes, counting, quantity, graphing,
etc.), but she does not feel particularly successful in her attempts to
capture and analyze her students' mathematical thinking.
Specifically, she wants to find out how her students use words and
representations to express mathematical ideas. Here's what she says:

> Since my math activities involve extensive hands-on use of materials,
> I am easily able to see children's concrete representation of their
> concepts, but I needed to focus on their ability to use words to
> convey their ideas. My earliest data collection showed that the
> same few students consistently offered comments and minimal
> explanations during math lessons, but the majority of the class
> appeared either unable or unwilling to explain their thinking verbally.

Anne had already completed the assessment cycle and had data
that led her to realize that "the majority of the class appeared either
unable or unwilling to explain their thinking." This interpretation
led to more questions.

> **Asking questions.** I wondered, "Do the children lack the
> vocabulary or the expressive ability to explain their thoughts? Are
> they unsure of themselves and afraid to take a risk in front of their
> peers? How can I encourage them to share their thinking?"

> **Collecting data.** I collected data for another few weeks, and the
> same few children volunteered their thinking. Their explanations
> were often simple and not related to math processes.

Number and Quantity: One-to-One Correspondence Strategies

ZL	ST	CC	CS
When you line them up, you can see how many. You won't make a mistake.	Playing w/ manips., no obvious counting	Look at mine. They're marching in a circle.	I have a strategy to tell the kids... You put them in lines.
JM	KO	AS	AR
Shrugged in response to "How did you know to do that?"		Ms. B, I don't have 10. I need more.	Looks away, does not respond
DD	AL	MS	ET
	I already know it, I knew it last year.	Well, 5 + 5 = 10. I know it!	I can count it and see it. It looks like four.

Interpreting the data. I decided that perhaps the children did not share their thinking because they did not know how to verbalize it or because they did not know it was important to do so.

Taking action. During our upcoming unit on number and quantity, I decided to model my thinking strategies and celebrate children's descriptions of their strategies. During our whole-group minilesson at the beginning of math time, I used some of the math materials while the students handled them, and I explained my thinking. I wanted children to follow my lead and get comfortable contributing ideas. At one point during the lesson, for example, I said, "I have a strategy! I can tell this group has four without counting, because I see two and two. I know two and two is four." I gave very specific responses to each student's contribution. When I saw Yuki working with the bears, I said, "Wow, Yuki, you're thinking like a mathematician! It looks like your strategy was to arrange the bears as you've seen on a domino to show five. And then I called the other children's attention to Yuki's idea by saying, "If you had the same idea, show me the sign for 'same idea' and give yourself a pat on the back! Who has another strategy to share?"

What happened next? Many students showed more enthusiasm for volunteering ideas. I noticed that more children were participating.

I struggled with recording children's specific statements during the whole-group mini lessons. I made a concerted effort to have conversations with children as they worked in small groups or engaged in math-center activities. Strategic placement of sticky notes helped me capture children's comments. I gave my para educator a few simple tips for recording observations, and she became an invaluable resource.

After a while, children were eagerly contributing their thoughts. I repeatedly heard, "Ms. Barnard, look what I did! I have a strategy to tell the others!" Those who initially appeared reluctant seemed better able to respond in a small group or when informally talking with an adult. My repeated use of mathematical vocabulary led to a richer use of language in student comments: "I can tell that the groups are unequal because, when I line them up, they don't have a matching partner."

I also started to use a matrix for each major mathematical concept. This refined my data collection.

During a unit on graphing, Anne collected the following data about how each child expressed mathematical thinking.

Graphing 1-27-09

I - Independently   W - With assistance   N - Not apparent

Names	Make Graph	Explain equal/ most/least	Comments
Johnny	I	I	Red is the most, my yellow has less.
Ava	I	I	These 2 have the same.
Collin	I	I	Most is red. These are the equal ones.
Juliana	I	I	There's 3 more blue than red. I can see it.
Drew	I	I	I have 3 equals.
Clementine	I	I	It's easy to see the most, it's the tallest.
Balan	W	I	This is my most, this is my least one.
Amira	I	I	My least is zero. You can't have any less.
Keegan	I	W	Needed prompting
Matthew	I	I	Look at mine. I have 2 equals: blue and red, and yellow and white. How do I color the white?
Yuki	I	I	Ms. Barnard, I want to tell a strategy. If you just look for the ones that are the same, they're equal.
Abraham	I	I	I don't have any equal ones.
Julian	I	W	I don't know.
Sarina	W	W	No response
Alia	I	I	2 colors are equal. See they're the same size.
Ariana	W	W	w/adult help only
Cesar	I	I	The least is my blue ones.
Zino	W	N	Would not talk
Avery	W	W	What is equal?
Vinh	I	I	It's easy. This is most, this is equal.
Amber	I	W	Didn't understand "least," w/help "equal"
Kieran	I	W	W/help
Emily	I	W	Would only point w/teacher questions

Although the data showed a positive change in the students' willingness to explain their thinking, I am constantly seeking ways to reinforce and improve their mathematical explanations. I recognize that it is a "work in progress." As I contemplate next steps, new questions arise.

- **How can I continue to refine my system so that I promote each child's language development and metacognition?**
- **What are other ways that the students can show their thinking?**
- **How can I support them to further expand and elaborate on their ideas?"**

Jasmine's and Anne's stories illustrate how teachers can gather data on the entire class as they focus on curriculum standards. In order for both teachers to develop new approaches to teaching and data collection, it was critical for them to take time to reflect carefully on the information they had gathered. As each teacher studied the data, they not only learned about children but also discovered how they could more effectively assess children's skill levels.

These two stories also illustrate how providing children with more experience enables teachers to collect data about abstract learning. In her first year, Jasmine was figuring out how to effectively manage assessment of each child's gross-motor skills. Anne had developed strategies for collecting information on specific math skills (e.g., rote counting) but was grappling with how to collect data on children's mathematical thinking and expression. Becoming an efficient and effective assessor requires skills that develop over time.

- How have you adjusted your curriculum or instruction according to what you learned from data?

- Give an example of when you took action to enhance the learning of the entire class or a group of children.

Reflect on Your Practice

Taking Action to Resolve Classroom Challenges

Using the assessment cycle effectively helps you discover what actions to take when things are not going as smoothly in your classroom as you would like. For instance, assessment will help you decide how to handle a conflict that occurs regularly among several children, a classroom that feels chaotic or disorderly, or situations when children show little interest in a certain area of the classroom. (See chapter 3 for Cindy's story about her children's use of the art area).

Keeping the Classroom Safe for All Children

Rochelle Peterson is the head teacher in an infant–toddler room at a private child care center in a middle-class suburb. Her families are mostly Caucasian, and about 20 percent are Hispanic. In this program, teachers stay with a group of four infants (their family group) until the children are ready to move to the preschool classroom. At this time, Rochelle's four children (David, Curt, Brooke, and Julio) range in age from 23 to 26 months. They occupy a classroom with another toddler family group of slightly younger children. For the past month, Rochelle has noticed that the children are sometimes aggressive. One child in particular, David, has started biting other children. Now other children have started biting as well. She uses careful assessment to help her solve this problem.

> **Asking questions.** I wanted to know when David was biting and in what situations it occurred. Is David hungry, thirsty, or tired when he bites? Does he bite the same children repeatedly? How often are other children biting? When and what else is happening when the biting occurs?

> **Collecting data.** I decided to keep a log of each biting incident. I wrote the date, time, biter, victim, setting, and what else was happening at the time. I also requested another adult (sometimes a substitute teacher and at other times a resource person) to come into the room so I could shadow David for a few days. I wanted to determine the triggers for his biting and intervene to help him and other children.

Date	Time	Biter	Victim	Setting	What Happened?
5/1	9:30	David	Julio	Lg. play room	David dropped his ball, and Julio picked it up for him.
5/1	10:45	David	Julio	Lg. play room	Julio playing w/ball, and David was next to him.
5/1	10:55	David	Lora	Lg. play room	????
5/6	10:10	David	Julio	Dramatic play	Julio playing w/a spatula, and David wanted it. Julio walked away, and David bit his right shoulder.
5/11	10:30	David	Hal	Near sink	Hunter walked by D. at sink, D bit him on shoulder.
5/11	11:10	David	Lora	Dramatic play	Fought over doll, bit R on shoulder.
5/15	9:30	David	Curt	Large-motor room	Curt pushed David to go up small slide. After sliding, David bit him on back.
5/15	10:35	David	Julio	Large-motor room	David bit Julio on shoulder, several children around
5/15	2:30	David	Marc	Dramatic play area	On couch playing together. Marc climbing on David.
5/15	3:00	Marc	Lora	Pushing toy vacuum on carpeted area	Lora tried to take toy from Marc. He bit her shoulder.
5/17	11:30	Zeke	David	At table, eating	Zeke bit D on hand.
5/23	9:45	David	Ally	Near ball-storage area	Ally walking w/ball. Two other children near. A walked close to D. Bit her left shoulder.
5/23	10:00	Curt	Hal	Large cardboard blocks	Fought over toys. Knocked down blocks.
5/23	10:10	David	Curt	Large cardboard blocks	Fought over toys. Knocked down blocks.
5/26	11:00	David	Manny	Outside	Manny on large riding car. David wanted it. M refused. D bit elbow.

Interpreting the data. From the observation data, I saw that most of the biting occurred in the morning between 9:30 AM and 11:00 AM. It often seemed to be related to space or toys. David (and others) perceived someone as being too close to him, or there was conflict over a desired toy. Some of the younger children liked to climb on David, and it seemed that David could only tolerate this for a few minutes before he bit. Children start the day quite early, so I wondered whether hunger might have something to do with the occurrence. Even as I carefully observed and stayed close to David, his biting was becoming contagious. Other children began biting, too.

Taking action. The first thing I did was change the toys that were available. I put out more duplicates of toys so that we had three of the large riding buses, duplicates of kitchen utensils, etc. Whenever there was toddler "roughhousing" and several children were close together in one area, I made sure I was there to talk about what was happening. I kept a close watch over the situation.

I also started to introduce or announce when children were entering a space. For example, I might say, "Hi, Curt. Are you coming to play with the blocks on the shelf near David?" This seemed to alert David (and others) that someone was near and that a teacher was also there.

We also started making an extra morning snack available at about 10:00 AM. Although we respond to children's physical needs on demand, I wasn't sure that 2-year-olds could recognize when they are hungry or thirsty, or whether they could reliably ask for what they needed.

What happened next? After several weeks of implementing these changes, the biting incidents with David and others slowly tapered off. We haven't had a biting incident for the past month! The children seem happier, families are happy, and I'm ecstatic!

Sometimes a problem in the classroom is acute and must be dealt with quickly. Rochelle took immediate steps to shadow David and to collect data about the increased aggression of toddlers in her classroom. Her data lead her to several ideas, or hypotheses, about why the biting occurred. She responded to each of her ideas with an action. She thought, for instance, that David might be uncomfortable when he felt his space was invaded, so she was extra vigilant when several children were close together. She also watched what happened when a new child entered a play area. Her data-based strategies worked!

Involving Everyone in Cleanup

Shakira Nelson is a preschool teacher in a Head Start program in a large urban area. Her children all meet the federal income guidelines for enrollment in Head Start and are diverse in terms of ethnicity (60 percent African American, 25 percent recent Eastern European immigrants, and 15 percent Caucasian). It is the end of October, and overall she has been pleased with how the year is going. However, she notices that positive engagement drops off as soon as it is time for the children to clean up after an hour-long choice time. She explained the situation in the following way:

> I've been teaching for 4 years in this program, and I love it. However, I've never been great at getting children to clean up. I clean up a lot, and my teaching assistant does, too. Otherwise, we'd never get to the next activity. But this group really doesn't like to clean up. They keep playing, get into conflicts with each other, and turn cleanup into my least favorite part of the day.
>
> **Asking questions.** I want to know what's going on during cleanup. Why do they keep playing, even after we think we have given clear directions? Is anyone cleaning up? What are they doing instead? Do they not know how to clean up? Are our expectations not clear? Are some children cleaning up independently?
>
> **Collecting data.** My teaching assistant, Kari, and I decided that each day this week one of us will stay out of the action during cleanup and take notes on what is happening. Next week we're going to code what each child does when we announce cleanup, and then we'll code it again once or twice during the actual cleanup period. Maybe by stepping back we can understand what is happening.

The data that Shakira and Kari collected are shown on the next two pages.

Day	Observations
Monday 11/2	Kari gave 5-minute warning. Then clapped hands and announced cleanup time. Tonya, Maurice, Maria, and Nate in grocery store started putting food away. DaShondra left and wandered over to the puzzles. Ramon kept building w/unit blocks. Matthew and Willette in conflict over who gets to put the lid on the Bingo game box. Shakira intervenes. Jasmine, Darryl, and Eddie moving (drifting) from one area to another.
Tuesday 11/3	Shakira gave warning and announced. Amber and Ebony immediately dumped their partially completed puzzles on the table and restarted them. Ramon kept working on fitting the train tracks together. Jasmine put the money in the cash register in the grocery store. Darryl and Eddie walking from one area to another. Tonya and Maurice finished their puzzles, put them away, and stood in the puzzle area. Tyrone stood with the can of scissors in front of the art shelf, looking for their spot. Darryl and Eddie began tossing a beanbag to each other.
Wednesday 11/4	Kari warned and announced. Maria and Nate in block area began putting unit blocks away. Ramon did not stop building, but Tyrone, who was building with him, stopped but did not start cleaning up. Jason put books away on the shelf. Maurice and Tonya washed paintbrushes in the sink after suggestion from Kari. Turned into a splashing game after Kari left. Ally, Amber, Jasmine, and Ebony wandering around. Matthew putting large hollow blocks away. Julia had head down on table.
Thursday 11/5	At the signal, Jason and Willette began running around the room until Shakira asked them to put blocks away. Ramon traced around blocks in art area and did not stop. DaShondra left grocery store and sat next to Ramon, watching. Jason and Willette argued over who got to put the arch-shaped blocks away. Eddie and Darryl went to the trucks and pushed the big trucks around. Ally, Maria, Tonya, and Maurice put food and money away in the store. Amber and Ebony wandered from one area to another, did not put anything away. Jasmine and Matthew got books and sat down to read.

Behavior During Cleanup

11/9

Code:

✔ cleaning

W wandering   C conflict   P playing w/same or new toy

Name	Announce + stopped - kept playing L left area, not cleaning	2 min.	4 min.	6 min.
Ally	+	✔	W	W
Amber	L	W	P	W
DaShondra	L	W	W	W
Darryl	L	P	P	W
Ebony	-	W	W	W
Eddie	L	P	P	W
Jasmine	+	✔	✔	W
Jason	+	✔	C	W
Julia	+	✔	W	?
Maria	+	✔	✔	✔
Matthew	+	W	✔	✔
Maurice	+	✔	✔	✔
Nate	+	✔	✔	✔
Ramon	-	P	P	P
Tonya	+	✔	✔	✔
Tyrone	+	✔	✔	W
Willette	L	W	C	C

Interpreting the data. I think we have a much clearer picture of things that are going on during cleanup. First of all, some children don't pay any attention to the cleanup signal. Every day that we observed them, Ebony and Ramon kept playing. I think Ramon gets so involved in his play that it is actually hard for him to stop. He needs help to make the transition.

Some children immediately leave the area they've been playing in when it's cleanup time. Do they not know what to do? Do they need to be assigned a job? Do they think that by being in an area where they did not play they won't have to clean up? Maybe we just need to say that, at cleanup time, you stay where you've been playing and work there until it's clean before moving anywhere else.

Some children go somewhere else and start playing in the new area. Do they not understand the term *cleanup*? Are transitions hard for them?

There's a fair amount of wandering around. It looks aimless to me. I'm not sure what it's about. Are the wandering children trying to look busy? Maybe they're not sure where they should go when they're done cleaning up.

I have more questions, but at least I now have a handle on what is happening during cleanup time. I also know that some kids are actually cleaning up. I think we have to keep collecting data, but we also have to take action.

Taking action. Kari and I have a few ideas about next steps. First, we'll have a class meeting about cleaning up. Kari and I will dramatize what happens when we don't keep the room clean. We'll trip over toys, try to use hardened paintbrushes and dried-up markers without caps. We'll demonstrate how long it takes and how frustrating it is when you can't find the dollars for our grocery store. Our goal is to model for children why cleanup matters and hopefully get them motivated to put things away. We can show a photo of a pretty, tidy space and one that looks like a tornado hit it.

Then, the next day, we'll introduce a new signal and make sure every child responds by raising his or her hands. Maybe having to take their hands off what they've been playing with will help them get the idea to stop playing and put materials where they are stored.

We'll also generate some rules for cleanup. We'll get some input from the children, but we're currently thinking about the following rules:

- Stay where you play.
- If you don't know what to do, ask.
- If you don't know where something goes, ask.
- When you're done, get a book and read it on the rug.

We're going to give Ramon two warnings, one 10 minutes before cleanup and one 5 minutes before. Again, I think he gets so involved in his play that it is hard for him to stop when he's not finished with his current activity. We'll see whether two warnings help.

What happened next? Let's see what Shakira has to say.

Well, cleanup isn't perfect, but it's much better. We realized some of our children are not expected to clean up at home, so we have to look at this as a learning opportunity, not a behavioral issue. We also have to remember that what's clear to us as teachers isn't always clear to children. We've had to add more labels to the shelves and actually teach children what the labels tell them.

After Kari and I dramatized the importance of cleanup, the children talked a lot about it. We talked about "our room" and how we want it to be organized so we can find things. We want our room to look nice and be welcoming all the time. It was a real community-building discussion.

"Stay where you play" is a very important rule for the children. Gradually, the children are becoming interested in having a clean and orderly room.

Many classroom challenges can be resolved when teachers utilize the assessment cycle as a tool to obtain a clear picture of what is happening. Sometimes teachers think of assessment only in terms of documenting children's learning, but, as Rochelle's and Shakira's stories indicate, assessment can also guide teachers when they are faced with difficult or puzzling classroom situations.

Think about your classroom or a classroom you know well.

Describe a classroom situation that you found challenging or puzzling. How did you use your evidence and interpretations to resolve the challenge?

Reflect on Your Practice

Taking Action: The Long and Short of It

Some of the stories in this chapter involve extensive data collection over time. However, because you understand child development and have a repertoire of teaching strategies, actions based on assessment information can be simple and immediate. The toddler teacher who realizes that children are suddenly very interested in trucks decides to put cracker crumbs and small trucks on the sensory table. She bases her actions on her interpretation of assessment information.

Key Ideas to Remember

- The most important reason for using the assessment cycle is to take action that benefits children.

- After taking action, teachers often recognize that they need to make changes in how they collect or review their assessment data.

- As a result of interpreting data, teachers can take a variety of steps, such as developing new curricular ideas, modifying instruction, creating plans for individual children, or changing routines and schedules.

- Sometimes teachers take action after thoughtfully reviewing data. Other times, teachers take action in the moment, interpreting what they observe and deciding what to do next as they interact with children.

Reference

Michigan State Board of Education (2005). *Early childhood standards of quality for prekindergarten.* Lansing, MI: Michigan Department of Education.

CHAPTER 12

Evaluating the Quality of Assessment Systems

Until now, our focus has been on how to use the assessment process in your classroom. Now we turn our attention to the characteristics of high-quality assessment methods and tools. In order to evaluate, select, and use assessment systems effectively, it is important to understand how to judge quality.

Early childhood professional organizations have described features of child assessment systems that indicate acceptable quality (Meisels & Fenichel, 1996; Meisels & Provence, 1989; NAEYC & NAECS/SDE, 2003; Shephard, Kagan, & Wurtz, 1998; Snow & Van Hemel, 2008). Numerous textbooks on assessment also discuss criteria for judging the value of an assessment instrument (Bagnato, 2007; McMillan, 2007; Puckett & Black, 2008; Stiggins, 2005). Taken together, this work presents a clear picture of the features of high-quality tools for assessing children from birth through age 5.

This chapter defines the characteristics of exemplary assessment systems. Such systems

- are developmentally appropriate
- respect families and children
- meet technical and ethical standards of quality
- help teachers teach
- benefit children

High-Quality Assessment Is Developmentally Appropriate

Like developmentally appropriate curricula, developmentally appropriate assessment tools and methods consider a child's

- developmental level
- cultural and linguistic background
- individual strengths and needs

Let's examine how these three dimensions affect assessment.

Developmental Level

Developmental characteristics of a young child affect the assessment process. For example, it may take longer to use a standardized assessment tool with a very young child than with an older child, because the younger child's pace may be slower or the child may become distracted. The following developmental factors affect the quality of the assessment process and its results:

Attention span For assessment information to be accurate, it must be tailored to the length of time the child can attend to a task or activity.

- **Infants and toddlers** How long babies pay attention to something depends on their interest and other circumstances. Have you ever seen a baby staring at moving shadows or a family pet? Did it seem as though the baby sustained attention for a long time? However, when an adult tried to focus the baby's attention on a particular task, the infant's attention may have seemed fleeting!

- **Preschoolers and kindergartners** Like infants and toddlers, preschoolers sometimes have short attentions spans, especially when they are not interested in the activity. When they are not fully engaged in what they are doing, they may be distracted by other activity in the room. Who just walked in the door? Was that Robin's garage that just toppled over in the block area? Many 5-year-olds have longer attention spans than younger children, but their interest in the task has a significant impact on the length of time they remain engaged.

Environmental factors Environmental factors (temperature of the room, time of day, noise level, etc.) influence the quality of assessment results. If the room is too hot or cold, for example, the behavior you see may not be the way that child typically responds.

Familiarity of the assessor Young children's behavior is affected by the degree to which they are familiar with the adult. For instance, a stranger in the room can change a baby's behavior if he is in the throes of stranger anxiety.

Language and communication Most assessment instruments rely on the child's understanding and use of language, so the child's ability to respond in assessment situations is affected by age, experience, home language, and the language(s) used during the assessment process.

- **Infants and toddlers** Babies cannot answer our questions verbally. Instead, adults must read their nonverbal cues (sounds, movements, and facial expressions), which can be subtle.

- **Preschoolers and kindergartners** Although most preschoolers and kindergartners have more sophisticated language skills than infants, the potential for misunderstanding remains strong because young children are concrete thinkers.

  I saw this firsthand in my classroom when Josie, a 5-year-old with a language delay, was being evaluated by Patty, a physical therapist. When they returned to the classroom, Patty asked Josie to show me how she could stand on one foot. Josie promptly moved both of her feet to stand on top of one of the therapist's feet. She did indeed "stand on one foot"—just not her own!

Pace and autonomy Most young children perform best when they can do so at their own paces and in their own ways. Frequently, this means a slower pace than an adult's and with a different sense of time. For example, Denise asks Féfé, a 3-year-old, to quickly finish his drawing about the story she just read. However, he is busy finding exactly the right shade of blue in the crayon box, and that could take several minutes.

Assessment is most effective when the child's developmental levels are considered during the selection of assessment methods and tools. When teachers want to find out what children know, how they think, and what they can do, it is best to follow their lead. Teachers should watch them in situations in which children feel comfortable and provide interesting materials so they can observe how children use them. In fact, many of the challenges of assessing young children disappear when we let them show us what they know. That's why we recommend using authentic assessment methods to capture young children's development and learning.

Cultural and Linguistic Background

Knowing about the cultural and linguistic backgrounds of the children you are assessing is as vital for assessment as it is for teaching (NAEYC, 2005; NAEYC & NAECS, 2003; Puckett & Black, 2008). Children's cultural and linguistic backgrounds affect their responses and therefore the accuracy of assessment results.

Culture Each culture has unique values and expectations, and there may be significant variation within each cultural group. Keep in mind that the tasks you ask a child to do for assessment purposes must make sense within the child's cultural framework. For example, many early childhood programs value children's growing independence, so children are encouraged to do tasks by and for themselves. Teachers celebrate each new skill a child acquires, from putting on a sock and pulling up a zipper to putting on boots and snow pants without help. However, family members from some cultural groups do these tasks for children well into first or second grade as a sign of love and caring. Assessing a 4-year-old's fine-motor development by observing dressing skills might be inappropriate if the child never attempted to dress him- or herself. The teacher would probably not get a true picture of the child's small-muscle development. Perhaps fine-motor skills could be more accurately assessed by watching how the child manipulates pegs in a pegboard. Unless you are aware of the practices of the children's families, you may inadvertently misinterpret evidence of the children's skills and knowledge.

What to Avoid

Infants and young children are likely to resist approaches that use on-demand tasks in which an examiner provides a material, asks the child to complete a task with it, removes the first material, and replaces it with something new. For example, an examiner might give a child a crayon and ask her to draw a circle on a piece of paper. Then the examiner might take the crayon away and provide blocks to stack. More tasks would be presented with different materials.

Assessment strategies used with older children are usually stressful for young children. Paper-and-pencil tests and standardized tests administered to groups (usually by following rigid procedures and time frames) often yield inaccurate assessment results.

Language A child's primary language influences the accuracy of assessment results. Most assessment instruments rely on the child's ability to understand and use language. A child who is learning English as a second language may have difficulty comprehending directions given in English, responding in English, and communicating needs and ideas in English. Moreover, caregivers and teachers who do not speak the child's language may find it challenging to build a positive relationship with the child. As we have discussed, familiarity and comfort with the assessor also affects the quality of the results. When assessing English-language learners, be sure that the gathered information reflects more than the fact that the child has limited English skills.

For recommendations regarding the appropriate assessment of young English-language learners, see the National Association for the Education of Young Children's positions statements *Screening and Assessment of Young English-Language Learners* (2005) and *Responding to Linguistic and Cultural Diversity Recommendations in Early Childhood Education* (1995).

Individuality

The third component of developmentally appropriate practice asks teachers to honor each child's individuality by planning learning experiences with individual differences in mind. One important aspect of children's individuality is that they learn and express themselves in different ways (see chapter 4). Researchers describe children's different ways of learning in these ways:

- approaches to learning (Kagan, Moore, & Bredekamp, 1995)
- working approaches (Chen & McNamee, 2007)
- types of intelligence (Gardner, 1999)

Some children, for example, have to move to learn, while others rely on visual cues. Some children rush to begin projects while others pause and watch before getting started. Understanding that children engage in the learning process and express their learning in different ways is important for assessment.

High-Quality Assessment Respects Families and Children

Assessing children effectively means understanding them in the context of their families. It also means encouraging family involvement in the assessment process as well as helping children become more aware of their own learning.

A Meaningful Role for Families

Family involvement is vital to children's performance in school. Research studies indicate that children whose family members are involved with their center or school achieve at higher levels and stay in school longer than children whose families are less involved (Henderson & Mapp, 2002; Hidalgo, N., Siu, S-F., & Epstein, J. L., 2003; Sheldon, 2003; Sheldon & Epstein, 2002).

Families have important information to contribute, so high-quality assessment systems incorporate ways to involve family members to increase the accuracy of assessment information. The assessment process is designed so that teachers communicate regularly with families, not just at conference times. Teachers invite family members to share observations, anecdotes, and stories, and to express concerns. Because the family has a unique relationship with their child, and views the child through a special lens, family members bring a singular and valuable perspective about the child. The teacher who partners with families to expand his or her understanding of the child reaps huge benefits. Refer to chapter 9 for further discussion of the family's role in the assessment process.

A Meaningful Role for Children

In chapter 8, you read about how assessment that involves children actively helps them begin to reflect on their own work and learning. When children have some input and access to their portfolios, they see how their skills change. Even 4-year-olds notice how their ability to write their names has improved. Young children can talk about what they are good at, what is hard to do, and what they like doing best. Discussions help children develop their concept of self—of who they are. This sets the stage for being able to set personal goals. You may be surprised that children as young as 3 and 4 can learn about assessment and participate actively.

High-Quality Assessment Meets Technical and Ethical Standards

To evaluate the quality of assessment tools and practices, you must understand four basic concepts:

- validity
- reliability
- fairness
- ethical use

These concepts must be considered regardless of whether you are using formal instruments or more informal assessment practices.

Validity

Validity concerns the accuracy of the assessment instrument and its results: whether or not the instrument actually measures what it claims to measure. For example, does a tool meant to assess literacy skills accurately measure the child's literacy skills? Does the child actually have the literacy skills the results say he has? Do you trust the results enough to base decisions about children on them?

Several issues related to validity are important to understand and will help you judge the quality of a particular assessment tool.

Content validity Content validity is a type of validity that is especially important to teachers who are selecting assessment instruments. They need to understand what the tool measures so they can decide whether its content reflects their objectives. Consider this example from Ms. Dawson, a kindergarten teacher who was looking for a math checklist to help her evaluate children's mathematical thinking and prepare progress reports:

> I studied one math checklist and found that it addressed rote counting, one-to-one correspondence, and shape recognition. However, the checklist did not include items about size, measurement, probability, or geometry (except naming shapes) —all of which are important to what I teach. So many math concepts were left out of this checklist, I decided that it would not be a comprehensive way to assess my children's mathematical understanding and skills. It didn't match what I teach.

In this example, Ms. Dawson found that the content of the checklist she was considering did not match the objectives for the children's learning. Moreover, the checklist items required only lower levels of cognition. When Ms. Dawson teaches math, she asks children to apply math concepts to real-life situations and to solve problems. The checklist items were simple, only requiring children to memorize and name things rather than apply knowledge to solve problems. For Ms. Dawson's approach to math, this checklist proved inadequate. Although it was valid for measuring some math skills, it was not sufficient for assessing what Ms. Dawson taught.

Threats to validity Factors that negatively influence the accuracy of assessment findings are called *threats to validity*. Consider these potential threats to validity in early childhood assessment:

- **The way directions are given** Imagine that you observed children's gross-motor skills over the last few weeks. You observed in the classroom, outdoors, and in the motor room. To get all the information you need, you asked children to perform particular tasks. If you gave directions verbally, without demonstrating what you wanted the children to do, you might find that you inadvertently assessed how well children understood your directions, rather than their motor skills. How would you know whether a child simply could not hop or whether he just did not understand what the word *hop* means? Perhaps you asked children to climb over a hurdle. Did Joachim crawl under it because he did not know the word *over* or because he did not have the physical ability to climb over the obstacle? In this example, your assessment of motor skills might be invalid—you might not be able to trust the results to accurately reflect children's large-muscle skills rather than their understanding of language. When children do not understand the directions used during assessment, the teacher may not be able to interpret the results.

- **Children's individual differences** Children learn and express their learning in various ways. Children differ in their cultural backgrounds, the presence or absence of disabilities, their languages, their approaches to learning, and their life experiences. A child with delayed language skills, for example, may have difficulty verbally expressing the main events of a story. However, she might be able to show that she understands the story by illustrating the main events. To obtain valid information about her story comprehension, her teacher must focus on what is being measured and provide her with an appropriate way to demonstrate her knowledge.

- **The purpose of the assessment** Assessment results are not valid when the tool is used for something other than its intended purpose. For example, when a screening instrument, such as the widely used *Ages and Stages Questionnaires* (Squires & Bricker, 2009), is used as a pre- and post-test of achievement or to plan curriculum, that use is invalid. (See chapter 2 for more information about the purpose of screening tools.) If a teacher encourages 5-year-olds to use invented spelling as they write creatively in journals, it is not valid to use their journal pages to measure their ability to spell words correctly. To assess effectively, you must be clear about why you are assessing, stay focused on what you are hoping to learn, and use the results of the assessment instrument for the purpose intended by the tool's developers.

Think about the validity of assessment findings in your program.

- Did you ever use an assessment tool, only to find out that you did not gather the information you hoped to collect?

- Have you had experiences in which a child's language, culture, or disability affected assessment results?

- Did you ever use an assessment instrument that claimed to measure one set of skills but actually measured something else?

Reflect on Your Practice

Reliability

Reliability refers to the consistency of assessment results. High-quality assessment tools provide consistent results as long as they are administered properly. When you assess a child's skills, does his performance on that day and in that setting reflect lasting characteristics of his performance (Puckett & Black, 2008)?

All assessment involves *sampling*, which means that you look at a small part of something in order to make generalizations about the whole. For instance, when you want to learn about a child's language skills, you might use a checklist of language skills as you observe the child at certain times and in particular situations. From this data, you would draw conclusions about the child's language that you would expect to be true in other situations and at other times. Your assumption is that the language sample provides accurate information about the child's language skills in general. You use the information to make general statements to the child's family, for example, that the child's language skills exceed expectations for his age-group or that the child is still in the process of developing vocabulary typical of children his age.

Sometimes the behavioral sample is atypical for the child, that is, not representative of the child's skills. That does not mean that the tool is invalid or unreliable. Perhaps environmental factors interfered with the child's performance. Maybe the room was hot or noisy, or perhaps the child was tired or getting sick. Consider this example:

Estera, a kindergarten teacher, observed Joni tying her shoes. Can Joni always tie her shoes, or was she only able to tie them then because Kim, a college student volunteer, was cheering her on and giving lots of directions? Can Joni repeat this skill independently tomorrow morning when Kim is not working in the classroom? Is the result dependable or just a fluke due to a particular set of circumstances?

Reliable assessment information enables you to draw conclusions from your data and apply them to other situations. If an assessment tool is reliable and used appropriately, the results should not change even with changes in the location, materials, or adults involved in the assessment process. These seven strategies will enhance the reliability of the data you collect:

Minimize distractions. Think about the child's ability to focus. For example, assessing children's interactions on a holiday or the day after is unlikely to give you accurate results.

Be aware of environmental factors that may affect children's behavior. Is the room too hot or cold? Is there more noise than usual? Is the phone ringing repeatedly because school is going to be closed early due to a snowstorm?

Pay attention to children's emotional and physical well-being. Is Ian upset because his mother just returned to active duty in the Army? Are some children coming down with sore throats? Is Jana wandering around the room, frustrated because she cannot find her favorite book? If children are under stress, either physically or emotionally, the data may not be useful.

Gather assessment data in different contexts. Try to assess children in many different contexts: during varied activities, at different times of day, on various days of the week, in small- and large-group activities, while alone, and while interacting with others. When you give children a variety of opportunities to demonstrate what they know, you go a long way toward making sure your assessment results will be reliable.

Gather assessment data from different sources. Having families and other team members involved in classroom assessment enhances the range of information you collect. The child who is very quiet in your classroom may talk nonstop at home or in a one-to-one situation with your assistant. With more people collecting data, you obtain a larger and more representative sample of the child's skills and behaviors.

Use multiple methods and tools to gather assessment data.
Using various assessment methods gives children different ways to express their learning. Observe, use checklists, take photographs, use video and audio recordings, study children's work, and conduct interviews to gather data about children's learning. When the information gathered by using several different assessment approaches is consistent, you can be more confident of your findings. Beware of making decisions or relying entirely on a single type of data. Especially when using assessment for *high-stakes decisions* that are irreversible or have lasting consequences, using the results from more than one source of information is critical (Brookhart, 2009).

Ask yourself whether the findings are representative of what the child typically does. Consider assessment results in the context of the rich knowledge about the child you garnered through many interactions over time. Occasionally, assessment results contradict your view of a child. There might be discrepancies between assessment data and your other experiences with the child, between your perspective and another team member's, between your perspective and a family member's, or between the results of two different assessment instruments. These call your attention to your need to collaborate with others to observe the child, study the data, and figure out what the child knows and can do.

Think about reliability and your own experience with assessing children's skills.

- Have you ever observed something one day, only to find out the child could not perform the same task or behavior the next?

- Were you ever excited because a child finally wrote his name independently but, when you asked him to show your teaching assistant, he needed help?

- Did you ever think you understood a child but then observed her at home and realized your observations at school were not consistent with her behavior at home?

- Did you and a colleague ever observe the same child at the same time but notice different skills? How might a reliable tool help you maintain the same focus as you observe children?

Reflect on Your Practice

Fairness

High-quality assessments are fair. Test developers talk about fairness as the absence of bias. A biased test is one that offends or unfairly discriminates against a particular group of people. In discussions of fairness, the group is typically distinguished by characteristics such as gender, age, race, ethnicity, disability, primary language, or socioeconomic class.

Think about a group of children in a rural school district. Imagine that they are taking a math test created by their new teacher, Ms. Carpenter, who recently moved from a large city to their community. Ms. Carpenter includes story problems that involve street cleaners, subway stops, and street vendors. This may be a biased test for this group of children who may have no experience with city life. Their performance on the math test may not show what they know about math because they did not have the background to understand the story problems. Similarly, consider an older female student who becomes angry during a test because all the doctors and lawyers in the examples are men and all the low-paid workers are women. Her emotional reaction may influence her test performance.

Bias comes in many different forms. Sometimes it is related to groups of students. In an early childhood classroom, a teacher may have extended conversations with children in the dramatic play area but have simpler verbal exchanges with children who build roads and ramps for toy car races in the block area. The teacher ends up with many examples of some children's language skills and far fewer examples of other children's. In effect, the teacher has less data by which to evaluate the language skills of children who frequent the block area.

Other times, we allow our assumptions, beliefs, and expectations of individual children to influence how we interact with, teach, and assess them. Were you ever surprised because the sibling of a child you taught 2 years ago was totally different from his older brother? Before you figured this out, did you assume that the younger child's skills would be the same as his brother's were at that age? When we teach two children from the same family, we have to be careful that we do not assume that they are similar just because they are related. Sometimes individual children develop halos in our minds. Suppose that Jennifer excels in language, literacy, and math skills. Do you automatically expect her to excel socially as well?

We must be aware of bias and assumptions because our expectations of children affect the way we interact with them. Do you find yourself asking a child like Raymond, who has an articulation problem, only *yes–no* questions because it is difficult to figure out what he is saying? He may be a great problem solver, but, because of his speech problem, his strengths might be overlooked. Do you tend to pay less attention to Lucy because she smells unwashed? The frequency and quality of our interactions with children affect how well we get to know and understand them.

How does the issue of fairness affect your work as an early childhood teacher who is not testing her children? In chapter 5, we explored how important it is to observe and to record objectively what you see and hear. Fairness is also affected by our personal biases. They can influence a teacher's behavior and the opportunities provided for children to learn and demonstrate their knowledge.

- Think about examples of biases that may affect observations, judgments, and decisions about children.
- Which biases do you personally have to be aware of as you assess young children?

Reflect on Your Practice

Three strategies will enhance the fairness of the assessment practices you develop:

Be aware of your own biases. Learn what you bring to your work with children. How do your age, gender, culture, race, socioeconomic background, and religion affect your perspective on teaching and your interactions with children?

Try to look at children from a fresh perspective each day. Leave your assumptions and beliefs about individual children behind and try to see clearly what each child does each day.

Record what you see and hear as objectively as you can. By recording facts and waiting until you have more evidence by which to interpret children's behavior, you will be more likely to acquire a deep and accurate understanding of each child.

By using these strategies, you become more able to discover each child's unique combination of skills, knowledge, personality, and interests.

Ethical Use of Assessment Information

Early childhood teachers engaged in assessment activities must use them responsibly. The NAEYC *Code of Ethical Conduct and Statement of Commitment* (2005) and the *Code of Professional Responsibilities in Educational Measurement* (1995) prepared by the National Council on Measurement in Education (NCME) can guide ethical decision making. These comprehensive documents address what it means to work responsibly with young children, including in the area of assessment. Here are six important guidelines:

Maintain confidentiality about the children and families with whom you work. Families have a right to privacy. Be careful not to talk about children in public places. Keep confidential information in locked file drawers.

Inform families before making any major decisions about their children. Families should be involved in any changes made to their child's program.

Explain your assessment strategies to families in clear language they can understand. Part of your job is to help parents understand how you assess children, what the results mean, and how they will be used. (See chapter 9.)

Stay informed about laws related to assessment. Through professional reading and conferences, stay current with families' rights related to assessment and with changes in relevant laws.

Recognize the limits of your expertise and be careful not to diagnose children. Teachers can develop a high degree of expertise in classroom assessment, but they are not qualified to make diagnoses or determine children's eligibility for special services.

Use appropriate assessment processes and tools, and only for their intended purposes. Assessment is not valid if the instruments are not used for the function for which they were designed. Teachers must carefully select instruments to accomplish their goals. (See chapter 2 for more information about the purposes of various types of assessments and for a discussion of screening-tool misuse).

High-Quality Assessment Helps Teachers Teach

You now know that high-quality assessment must be developmentally appropriate, involve children and families, and meet technical requirements. Assuming the assessment system actually meets these criteria, what else should you consider when examining how an assessment method or tool is used? Look for these characteristics in an assessment system:

- efficient and practical
- designed to yield formative information
- aligned with your curriculum
- authentic

Efficiency and Practicality

In order for teachers to have full lives—go to movies, have hobbies, play with their own children, and occasionally take a weekend off—the assessment systems they use must be practical. If you have input into the selection of an assessment system, make sure that the amount of information you need to collect and analyze, and the amount of time needed to do so, are reasonable.

As you learn about various assessment instruments, keep in mind the purpose of formative assessment, which is to help you get to know children in order to adjust your teaching. Be sure that you put your energy into meeting that purpose, rather than into irrelevant tasks. All too often, teachers spend a great deal of time copying observation notes to make them more legible or doing other unnecessary paperwork. Although it takes time to put a new approach to assessment into place, most teachers devise efficient methods and integrate assessment activities into their teaching. Then they can reap the benefits of assessment for learning.

Formative Information

Some evidence indicates that teachers use assessment primarily for summative, not formative, purposes (McNair, Bhargava, Adams, Edgerton, & Kypros, 2003). (The differences among types of assessment are discussed in chapter 2.) Teachers focus on collecting data about children's learning to complete progress reports and share information with families. Consequently, they spend less time using what they learn about children to influence the instructional experiences they plan.

Because young children grow and change rapidly, assessment should be ongoing and used to guide daily decision making, not just to summarize a child's development and learning at a particular point. Formative assessment enables teachers to give feedback to children about what they are learning and how they can improve.

A growing body of research documents that formative assessment can improve children's learning (Black & Wiliam, 1998; Meisels et al., 2003; Stiggins, 2007). When an assessment instrument is designed solely for completing progress reports, I strongly recommend that you look for another tool.

Alignment With Curriculum

When evaluating an assessment tool, determine whether it aligns with your curriculum (Bricker, 1996; Gullo, 2005; Meisels, 1996). Ask these questions:

- Does it align closely with state standards as well as with program and classroom goals and objectives?

- Can you easily take what you learn by using the assessment tool and use the information to decide which learning opportunities to offer children?

Assessment and curriculum go hand-in-hand. Assessment information should guide your decisions about what to teach and how to teach it. The closer your assessment tool aligns with your curriculum, the more meaningful it will be. (Refer to chapter 4 for more information on deciding what to assess.)

Authenticity

Authenticity has two meanings related to early childhood assessment: 1) how information is gathered and 2) what information is collected (the content of the assessment).

How information is gathered Are the methods used to assess young children authentic or artificial? For a true picture of what a young child can do, children should be assessed in authentic situations. The child must feel comfortable with the people, location, materials, and methods. As discussed earlier, in unfamiliar situations the child might be distracted, so it is very difficult to get a true picture of his or her skills and knowledge. Does this story of my early teaching experience ring true for you?

> When I was first teaching young children with special needs, I was very excited when I found out that the school psychologist was coming to evaluate a child. I was certain that, after a thorough assessment, I would have the key to the child— the one that would open the door, allowing the child's previously hidden abilities to emerge.
>
> Dr. Dixon, the school psychologist, spent about 10 minutes in the classroom, developing rapport with the child. Then she took the child down the hall to her office (a former closet) and administered a battery of standardized tests. It took two sessions to complete the evaluation. A week or so later, our team met to hear the results. What did I find out? Nothing new. This happened a few times with different children. I felt disappointed each time, until I realized that my daily observations and assessment information gave me more useful information about the child than Dr. Dixon's work.

Why do you think this was so? Consider what we asked the child to do:

Go to a strange room.
Spend time with an unfamiliar adult.
Work on unfamiliar tasks.

This is not the ideal situation for a young child to reveal her skills, knowledge, and personality. Instead, young children should be assessed more authentically in natural settings—at home or in the classroom—where they are comfortable.

Content of the assessment What are you assessing? Is it clearly defined? Is it significant? Is what you are assessing meaningful to the child? What you assess (chapter 4) warrants careful thought (Chappuis, Chappuis, & Stiggins, 2009). To understand how the content of assessment can be authentic, consider another example from my classroom.

> While I was reviewing different assessment tools during my second year of teaching, I noticed that many included a particular task. I thought I would try it. Diligently, I checked to see whether all of my children could touch each finger to their thumbs in sequence, first with the right hand and then the left. I had no clear idea about why this was important. I suspected that not being able to do it might indicate a neurological problem, but of course I was not a neurologist. Some children had fun doing it. Aside from that, however, the task had no meaning for the children or me. In retrospect, I wonder why I was assessing them on this task. If they could not do it, was I supposed to teach them how?

This example exemplifies inauthentic assessment. The assessment has no meaning for the children and does not help the teacher know what or how to teach. High-quality assessment measures things that are educationally significant for children and teachers.

High-Quality Assessment Benefits Children

In 1990, NAEYC's first position statement about assessment, *Guidelines for Appropriate Curriculum Content and Assessment in Programs Serving Children Ages 3 through 8*, included this guideline: "Assessment results in benefits to the child, such as needed adjustments in the curriculum or more individualized instruction and improvements in the program" (NAEYC, 1990; p. 23). I strongly believe that this is the essential feature of high-quality assessment.

Children should benefit from assessment through improved teaching that enhances their learning. Assessment can benefit children in several ways:

When assessment is ongoing, children can be given feedback about their learning. Teachers and children can talk about skills that are hard and easy. Children can begin to appreciate their own strengths and to feel competent as they experience the joy of learning and acquiring new skills.

Assessment helps teachers get to know and form positive relationships with children. Assessment should be viewed as a context for interaction between teachers and children. When teachers learn more about children—their strengths, needs, approaches to learning, and interests—this information can be used to promote meaningful interactions, build a relationship between the child and teacher, and scaffold each child's individual learning.

Teachers can communicate accurately with family members about the child. Families value teachers whose knowledge and appreciation of their child is apparent during conferences. When teachers share stories and show photos along with ratings on a progress report, they demonstrate appreciation for and a strong connection with the child.

If your assessment practices, methods, and results do not benefit children, it is time to change what you are doing.

Key Ideas to Remember

- Effective assessment requires you to pay attention to each child's developmental levels, individuality, and cultural background.

- Children and families have important roles in assessment. Encourage their involvement through open and shared communication.

- If you are going to base decisions on assessment results, the tools and methods you use must be valid, reliable, and fair to all children.

- The major purpose of classroom assessment is to help children learn and help teachers teach.

- On an ongoing basis, gather meaningful information that aligns with your curriculum. Then you will be able to provide feedback to children and modify your teaching according to what you have learned.

References

Bagnato, S. J. (2007). *Authentic assessment for early childhood intervention: Best practices.* New York: Guilford Press.

Black, P., & Wiliam, D. (1998). Assessment and classroom learning. *Assessment in Education, 5,* 7–74.

Brookhart, S. M. (2009). The many meanings of "multiple measures." *Educational Leadership, 67*(3), 6–12.

Bricker, D. (1996). Assessment for IFSP development and intervention planning. In S. J. Meisels, & E. Fenichel (Eds.), *New visions for the developmental assessment of infants and young children* (pp. 169–192). Washington, DC: ZERO TO THREE.

Chappuis, S., Chappuis, J., & Stiggins, R. (2009). The quest for quality. *Educational Leadership, 67*(3), 14–19.

Chen, J. Q., & McNamee, G. D. (2007). *Bridging: Assessment for teaching and learning in early childhood classrooms, PreK–3.* Thousand Oaks, CA: Corwin Press.

Gardner, H. (1999). *Intelligence reframed: Multiple intelligences for the 21st century.* New York: Basic Books.

Gullo, D. F. (2005). *Understanding assessment and evaluation in early childhood education.* New York: Teachers College Press.

Henderson, A. T., & Mapp, K. L. (2002). *A new wave of evidence: The impact of school, family, and community connections on student achievement.* Austin, TX: Southwest Educational Development Laboratory.

Hidalgo, N., Siu, S.-F., & Epstein, J. L. (2003). Research on families, schools, and communities: A multicultural perspective. In J. Banks (Ed.), *Handbook of Research on Multicultural Education* (2nd ed., pp. 631–655). New York: Macmillan.

References, *continued*

Kagan, S. L., Moore, E., & Bredekamp, S. (1995). *Reconsidering children's early development and learning: Toward common views and vocabulary* (Goal 1 Tech. Planning Group Rep. No. 95–03). Washington, DC: National Education Goals Panel.

McMillan, J. H. (2007). *Classroom assessment: Principles and practice for effective standards-based instruction* (4th ed). Boston: Pearson.

McNair, S., Bhargava, A., Adams, L., Edgerton, S., & Kypros, B. (2003). Teachers speak out on assessment practices. *Early Childhood Education Journal, 31*(1), 23–31.

Meisels, S. J. (1996). Charting the continuum of assessment and intervention. In S. J. Meisels, & E. Fenichel (Eds.), *New visions for the developmental assessment of infants and young children* (pp. 27–52). Washington, DC: ZERO TO THREE.

Meisels, S. J., & Fenichel, E. (1996). *New visions for the developmental assessment of infants and young children.* Washington, DC: ZERO TO THREE.

Meisels, S. J., & Provence, S. (1989). *Screening and assessment: guidelines for identifying young disabled and developmentally vulnerable children and their families.* Arlington, VA: ZERO TO THREE.

National Association for the Education of Young Children. (1990). *Guidelines for Appropriate Curriculum Content and Assessment in Programs Serving Children Ages 3 through 8.* Washington, DC: Author.

National Association for the Education of Young Children. (2005). *Code of ethical conduct and statement of commitment.* Washington, DC: Author. Retrieved January 25, 2006, from http://www.naeyc.org/positionstatements/ethical_conduct

National Association for the Education of Young Children. (2005). *Screening and assessment of young English-language learners.* Washington, DC: Author. Retrieved June 15, 2008, from http://www.naeyc.org/about/positions/ELL_Supplement.asp

National Association for the Education of Young Children, & National Association of Early Childhood Specialists in State Departments of Education. (2003). *Early childhood curriculum, assessment, and program evaluation: Building an effective, accountable system in programs for children birth through age 8.* Washington, DC: Author.

National Association for the Education of Young Children. (1995). *Responding to linguistic and cultural diversity recommendations in early childhood education.* Washington, DC: Author. Retrieved March 19, 2010, from http://www.naeyc.org/about/positions/pdf/PSDIV98.PDF

National Council on Measurement in Education (1995). *Code of professional responsibilities in educational measurement.* Retrieved March 19, 2010, from http://www.ncme.org/about/documents.cfm

Puckett, M. B., & Black, J. K. (2008). *Meaningful assessment of the young child* (3rd ed.). Upper Saddle River, NJ: Pearson Education.

Sheldon, S. B. (2003). Linking school-family-community partnerships in urban elementary schools to student achievement on state tests. *Urban Review, 35*(2), 149–165.

Sheldon, S. B., & Epstein, J. L. (2002). Improving student behavior and discipline with family and community involvement. *Education in Urban Society, 35*(1), 4–26.

Shephard, L. A., Kagan, S. L., & Wurtz, E. (1998). Goal 1 Early Childhood Assessments Resource Group recommendations. *Young Children, 53*(3), 52–54.

References, *continued*

Snow, C. E., & Van Hemel, S. B. (Eds.). (2008). *Early childhood assessment: Why, what, and how.* Washington, DC: The National Academies Press.

Squires, J., & Bricker, D. (2009). *Ages & stages questionnaires* (3rd ed.). Baltimore, MD: Brookes Publishing.

Stiggins, R. J. (2007). Conquering the formative assessment frontier. In J. H. McMillan (Ed.), *Formative classroom assessment*, (pp. 8–28). New York: Teachers College Press.

Stiggins, R. J. (2005). *Student-involved assessment for learning* (4th ed.). Upper Saddle River, NJ: Pearson.

U. S. Department of Health and Human Services, Administration for Children and Families, Office of Head Start. (2009). *Head Start program performance standards: 45 CFR Chapter XIII* (10-1-09 ed.). Retrieved February 20, 2011, from http://eclkc. ohs.acf.hhs.gov/hslc/Head%20Start%20Program/Program%20 Design%20and%20Management/Head%20Start%20 Requirements/Head%20Start%20Requirements/45%20 CFR%20Chapter%20XIII/45%20CFR%20Chap%20XIII_ ENG.pdf

CHAPTER 13

Snapshots of High-Quality Assessment Systems

Teachers are frequently asked to participate in decisions about classroom assessment, so this chapter discusses several widely used early childhood assessment systems that exemplify characteristics of high-quality assessment. Descriptions of the systems are brief, but the chapter provides basic information to help you identify assessment systems you would like to investigate further.

The systems are presented by identifying their primary components and how they work together. You will also read about teachers' experiences with using the assessment systems in the classroom. I highlight how each system exemplifies one or more of the features of high-quality assessment discussed in chapter 12.

These assessment systems are described:

- The *Child Observation Record for Infants and Toddlers* (also known as the *Infant-Toddler Child Observation Record*) and the *Preschool Child Observation Record*

- *Teaching Strategies GOLD®*

- *The Work Sampling System®* and *The Ounce Scale™*

Child Observation Record

The *Infant-Toddler Child Observation Record* (*Infant-Toddler COR*) and the *Preschool Child Observation Record* (*Preschool COR*), developed by the HighScope Educational Research Foundation (2002; 2003), are observational assessment tools. The *Infant-Toddler COR* is used to assess children from 6 weeks to 3 years of age, and the *Preschool COR* is used to assess children from 2½ to 6 years of age. Both versions of the *COR* are closely aligned with the HighScope curriculum, but they may be used with any developmentally appropriate early childhood curriculum. The *COR* is also aligned with the 2010 *Head Start Child Development and Early Learning Framework*, and it has been used to assess children with special needs. There are three versions: paper, CD-ROM, and online (*OnlineCOR*). *COR Information for Decision Makers* and the user guides for the *Preschool COR* and *Infant-Toddler COR* present information about the development and validation of the tools.

The *Infant-Toddler COR* and the *Preschool COR* are organized by six categories of development:

Infant-Toddler COR	Preschool COR
Sense of self	Initiative
Social relations	Social Relations
Creative representation	Creative Representation
Movement	Movement and Music
Communication and language	Language and Literacy
Exploration and early logic	Mathematics and Science

In the six categories, the *Infant-Toddler COR* has 28 items, and the *Preschool COR* has 32 items. Each item has five developmental levels that range from simple (1) to more complex (5) behavior. For example, Social Relations has four items:

- Relating to adults
- Relating to other children
- Resolving interpersonal conflict
- Understanding and expressing feelings

The following excerpt from the preschool *COR Observation Items* shows the five developmental levels for the item "Relating to other children."

| Initiative | SOCIAL RELATIONS | Creative Representation | Movement & Music | Language & Literacy | Mathematics & Science |

E.   **Relating to adults**

F.   Relating to other children

G.   **Resolving interpersonal conflict**

H.   **Understanding and expressing feelings**

The relationships preschoolers build with their peers provide substantial benefits: emotional support in unfamiliar settings, the opportunity to play with a partner, and experiences in leading, following, making suggestions, trying out ideas, negotiating, and compromising. All future relationships are built on these social skills.

Level 1. Child responds when another child initiates an interaction.

The child responds verbally or nonverbally when another child starts the exchange.

- *1/15 At work time in the toy area, when Samantha says that she needs another bead, Trey responds with "Here one" and hands her a bead. [Trey's anecdote]*
- *10/10 During the transition to small group, when a classmate calls to Jared, "Sit by me!" Jared sits next to him.*

Level 2. Child initiates an interaction with another child.

The child at this level is able to initiate (verbally or nonverbally) conversation or another exchange with another child.

- *3/19 At greeting time Haydon hands Maria a puzzle piece to put in his puzzle.*
- *2/15 At large group, Joey tells Haley, "Hey Haley, you sat by Marquise and I did, too."*

Level 3. Child sustains an interaction with another child.

The child interacts (verbally or nonverbally) with another child for an extended period of time. A conversation at this level consists of five or more exchanges.

- *4/15 At cleanup time in the house area, Beth and Dawn carry a tub of dishes and silverware to the shelf and put them away together. [Beth or Dawn's anecdote]*
- *4/28 At work time in the house area, Patricia [the teacher] takes out the cups and asks Anthony, "Are you thirsty? You need a drink?" Anthony says he is thirsty for chocolate milk. Ari says, "We don't have chocolate milk." Anthony and Ari then discuss*

what they like to drink and don't like to drink, with Ari stating, "I hate that nasty juice that my Mama drinks" and Anthony concluding, "Chocolate milk is my best one." [Anthony or Ari's anecdote]

Level 4. Child invites another child to play.

The child makes a decision about whom he or she wants to play with. Inviting another child to play is evidence that the child recognizes it can sometimes be more fun to have a playmate than to play alone.

- *5/13 At work time in the block area, Brooklyn says to Joy, "Come sit on my bus. I'm driving the kids to school."*
- *4/25 During greeting time, Hannah asks Kate, "You want to go read with me?"*

Level 5. Child shows loyalty to another child.

This level applies when the child demonstrates friendship and support to another child over time. For example, a child might regularly save a spot for a friend next to him or her at the table or on the floor; two children might repeatedly make plans to play together during work time; two children might play together during outside time several days in a row; or a child might express disappointment at a classmate's absence.

- *6/1 At small-group time Miranda saves the seat next to her for Ruth. She also does this at planning time and at snack time.*
- *7/7 Outside, when B. J. goes inside to use the bathroom, Asia waits by the school door until he comes back out. Then they run to continue their play under the climber. [Asia's anecdote]*
- *8/4 For over a week, Bo and Allen plan every day to work on the "space station and space ships and aliens" that they are making, using most of the Legos and some of the really small blocks.*

Social Relations   **11**

The teacher regularly records observation notes and sorts them into categories, as shown below. Then the teacher assigns a level to each observation note according to the best match with one of the five levels. Given that the *COR* uses a developmental approach, the five levels of each item illustrate the continuum of development for each indicator rather than correspond to specific ages.

Samples

Sample Page From the Preschool COR *Child Anecdotes Booklet*

Language and Literacy	Language and Literacy	Language and Literacy
/6/16 *(Circle one)* Item → Q ®️ S T U V W X Date SG *(Circle one)* Level→ 1 2 ③ 4 5 Observer	/6/20 *(Circle one)* Item → ⓠ R S T U V W X Date CB *(Circle one)* Level→ 1 ② 3 4 5 Observer	/7/1 *(Circle one)* Item → Q R S T ⓤ V W X Date SG *(Circle one)* Level→ 1 ② 3 4 5 Observer
At work time in the house area, Asia used an empty cake mix box, a cake pan, and a mixer. She told Sue (teacher) "Hey, look, I'm using the mixer to make a cake for my mom!"	At greeting time, Asia listened to Paul's dad read "The Very Hungry Caterpillar." When Paul's dad read "and on Tuesday he ate through two ____," Asia said, "Pears!"	During work time in the book area, Asia sat on the beanbag chair and looked at all the pictures in "Flower Garden," turning the pages from right to left.
/7/13 *(Circle one)* Item → Q R S ⓣ U V W X Date CB *(Circle one)* Level→ 1 ② ③ 4 5 Observer	/ / *(Circle one)* Item → Q R S T U V W X Date *(Circle one)* Level→ 1 2 3 4 5 Observer	/ / *(Circle one)* Item → Q R S T U V W X Date *(Circle one)* Level→ 1 2 3 4 5 Observer
At small-group time, working with the finger paints, Asia said, "The paint feels icky sticky."		

Letter Recognition Record: Circle the letters child identifies and names (Item V).

Ⓐ B C D E F G H I J K L Ⓜ N O P Q R Ⓢ T U V W X Y Z

20   www.highscope.org

Teachers use the same methods to rate the *Infant-Toddler COR* as they use for the *Preschool COR*.

Corresponding Items on the Infant-Toddler and Preschool CORs

Infant-Toddler COR

Sense of self
A. Expressing initiative
C. Solving problems
D. Developing self-help skills
No direct correspondence: *B. Distinguishing self from others*

Social relations
F. Relating to unfamiliar adults
G. Relating to another child
H. Expressing emotion
I. Responding to the feelings of others
J. Playing with others
No direct correspondence: *E. Forming an attachment to a primary caregiver*

Creative representation
K. Pretending
L. Exploring building and art materials

No direct correspondence: *M. Responding to and identifying pictures and photographs*

Movement
N. Moving parts of the body
O. Moving the whole body
P. Moving with objects
Q. Moving to music

Communication and language
R. Listening and responding
T. Participating in give-and-take communication
U. Speaking

V. Exploring picture books
W. Showing interest in stories, rhymes, and songs

No direct correspondence: *S. Communicating interest nonverbally*

Exploration and early logic
X. Exploring objects
Y. Exploring categories
Z. Developing number understanding
AA. Exploring space
BB. Exploring time

Preschool COR

Initiative
A. Making choices and plans
B. Solving problems with materials
D. Taking care of personal needs

Social relations
E. Relating to adults
F. Relating to other children
H. Understanding and expressing feelings
H. Understanding and expressing feelings
C. Initiating play (from Initiative category)
No direct correspondence: *G. Resolving interpersonal conflict*

Creative representation
K. Pretending
I. Making and building models & J. Drawing and painting pictures

Movement and music
L. Moving in various ways & M. Moving with objects
L. Moving in various ways
M. Moving with objects
O. Moving to music
No direct correspondence: *N. Feeling and expressing steady beat; P. Singing*

Language and literacy
Q. Listening to and understanding speech
Q. Listening to and understanding speech
R. Using vocabulary & S. Using complex patterns of speech
U. Demonstrating knowledge about books
T. Showing awareness of sounds in words & U. Demonstrating knowledge about books
No direct correspondence: *V. Using letter names and sounds; W. Reading; X. Writing*

Mathematics and science
Y. Sorting objects
Z. Identifying patterns
BB. Counting
CC. Identifying position and direction
DD. Identifying sequence, change, and causality
No direct correspondence: *AA. Comparing properties; EE. Identifying materials and properties; FF. Identifying natural and living things*

From *COR User Guide*, by HighScope Educational Research Foundation. Copyright 2003 by HighScope Educational Research Foundation. Reprinted with permission of HighScope Press, Ypsilanti, MI.

Using the *Child Observation Record*

Trisha, a teacher of 3-year-olds, describes how she uses the *Preschool COR*.

My program started using the *COR* 3 years ago, after trainers from HighScope came to our site and taught us how to use it. It took me some time to get to know the indicators and levels, but now I find it easy to use. Here's what I do.

Each day I observe the children in my class. Sometimes I focus on certain indicators; other times I focus on certain children. When I observe during the day, I write brief notes, highlighting who did what, when, and where. Then, during nap time or for half an hour or so at the end of the day, I expand the brief notes that I wrote during class. That way, I'll remember more clearly the details of what happened.

After I write the expanded anecdote, I have to decide where it fits among the six categories. Then I put it in the *Child Anecdotes* booklet under the proper category and item, being careful to remember to date it. Once I've decided where to put it, I score it, deciding which of the five levels this child is demonstrating. This helps me really think about the skills the child has demonstrated and what might develop in the near future.

As I'm writing anecdotes, I also pay attention to what my children were interested in that day and the skills they were demonstrating. When planning, I ask three questions from the *COR User Guide* (HighScope Educational Research Foundation, 2003, p. 9):

- What did we see children doing today?

- What do their actions tell us about them?

- How can we provide materials and interact with children to support their play and learning tomorrow?

The *COR User Guide* describes different planning scenarios. For example, I might focus on a child or a developmental area, observe in an area for which I don't have many anecdotes, or find ideas for large or small groups. These scenarios make it easy to take my assessment data and turn it into curriculum. I use ideas from the planning guide (*What's Next: Planning Children's Activities Around COR Observations*) and then modify my plans for the next day.

We summarize our observations and prepare reports to families three times a year in my program, although I know some programs only do it twice. I use the *Family Report* form, where I use the indicators to summarize the child's development in each category, add an anecdote or two, and sometimes add another story that the family tells me when we talk during conferences. Parents love these glimpses into their child's activities and behaviors at school!

II. Social Relations
Relaciones Sociales

Developmental summary:
Resumen del Desarrollo:

Supporting anecdotes:
Anécdotas que lo complementan:

Parent observations:
Observaciones del padre o madre:

From *COR Family Report*, by HighScope Educational Research Foundation. Copyright 2003 by HighScope Educational Research Foundation. Reprinted with permission of HighScope Press, Ypsilanti, MI.

My friend, who teaches in a Head Start program, uses an additional form, the *Child Information and Developmental Summary* form, because her program collects data on how all the children are progressing. She uses the online version that can print different reports about how children are doing.

Preschool Child Observation Record
2nd Edition

Child Information and Developmental Summary

Child's Developmental Summary

Record the highest level number you assigned to the anecdotes related to each of the COR items below. Calculate the child's average level of development for each COR category by adding the item levels and dividing by the number of items completed. (For example, if the child has levels of 3, 2, and 4 in the Creative Representation Category, you would calculate as follows: 3 + 2 + 4 = 9; (9 ÷ 3 = 3.)

Sex: _____   Date of Birth: ___ / ___ / ___

	Time 1	Time 2	Time 3	
I. Initiative	___	___	___	A. Making choices and plans
	___	___	___	B. Solving problems with materials
	___	___	___	C. Initiating play
	___	___	___	D. Taking care of personal needs
				Category average *(Divide only by the number of items completed.)*
II. Social Relations	___	___	___	E. Relating to adults
	___	___	___	F. Relating to other children
	___	___	___	G. Resolving interpersonal conflict
	___	___	___	H. Understanding and expressing feelings
				Category average *(Divide only by the number of items completed.)*
III. Creative Representation	___	___	___	I. Making and building models
	___	___	___	J. Drawing and painting pictures
	___	___	___	K. Pretending
				Category average *(Divide only by the number of items completed.)*
IV. Movement and Music	___	___	___	L. Moving in various ways
	___	___	___	M. Moving with objects
	___	___	___	N. Feeling and expressing steady beat
	___	___	___	O. Moving to music
	___	___	___	P. Singing
				Category average *(Divide only by the number of items completed.)*
V. Language and Literacy	___	___	___	Q. Listening to and understanding speech
	___	___	___	R. Using vocabulary
	___	___	___	S. Using complex patterns of speech
	___	___	___	T. Showing awareness of sounds in word
	___	___	___	U. Demonstrating knowledge about books
	___	___	___	V. Using letter names and sounds
	___	___	___	W. Reading
	___	___	___	X. Writing
				Category average *(Divide only by the number of items completed.)*
VI. Science and Mathematics	___	___	___	Y. Sorting objects
	___	___	___	Z. Identifying patterns
	___	___	___	AA. Comparing properties
	___	___	___	BB. Counting
	___	___	___	CC. Identifying position and direction
	___	___	___	DD. Identifying sequence, change, and causality
	___	___	___	EE. Identifying materials and properties
	___	___	___	FF. Identifying natural and living things
				Category average *(Divide only by the number of items completed.)*

___ ___ ___ TOTAL
(Sum of all completed items A to FF divided by number of completed items. **Do not include category averages.**)

Include scores on ESL items here.
___ ___ ___ Child's understanding of English
___ ___ ___ Child's ability to speak English

Observation Record (COR)
...sences, or a late start date, for example. Complete only as needed.)

...n whose home language is not English.

Speaking English
1. Child speaks own language only.
2. Child names some things in English.
3. Child uses some English phrases.
4. Child uses some English sentences.
5. Child participates in conversation in English.

...ween ___ / ___ / ___ and ___ / ___ / ___.
...een ___ / ___ / ___ and ___ / ___ / ___.

...ational Research Foundation

P1214   © 2003 High/Scope Educational Research Foundation   ISBN 1-57379-194-6

The *COR* as a High-Quality Assessment Tool

The *COR* is based on the same developmental framework as the HighScope curriculum. The indicators are not tied to age levels, but they represent the continuum of development in an area. Teachers share information with families and incorporate input from the family on the *COR Family Report*. The technical properties of the *COR* have been investigated, and it meets basic levels of validity and reliability (HighScope, 2003).

A strength of the *COR* is its emphasis on using assessment information on a daily and weekly basis for planning. This is emphasized in the *User Guide* and in an additional planning guide, *What's Next: Planning Children's Activities Around Preschool COR Observations*. The suggested strategies are explained clearly, and the *Guide* presents many developmentally appropriate curriculum ideas. The *COR* makes it easy for teachers to base action on their assessment data and to plan emergent curriculum based on clear evidence of children's interests and skills.

Teaching Strategies GOLD®

Teaching Strategies GOLD® (Heroman et al., 2010) combines authentic observational assessment with performance tasks for selected objectives in literacy and numeracy. It can be used with any developmentally appropriate early childhood curriculum and is available in toolkit form or online. The online version can aggregate data for groups of children at the class, program, site, or district level. It is aligned with the 2010 *Head Start Child Development and Early Learning Framework.* According to a newly released *Technical Manual*, the system has been found to yield highly reliable scores and teachers are able to make valid ratings of the developmental progress of children (Lambert, R.G., Kim, D.H., Taylor, H., & McGee, 2010).

Teaching Strategies GOLD® has five components:

- *Objectives for Development & Learning: Birth Through Kindergarten*
- *Child Assessment Portfolio*
- *Assessment Opportunity Cards*™
- *On-the-Spot Observation Recording Tool*
- *Family Conference Form*

Objectives for Development & Learning anchors the system and explains how to use the various components together. It presents the research foundation for each of the 36 objectives, which were selected because they are most predictive of school success or are part of most states' early learning standards. The objectives are organized into nine areas of development and learning:

- Social–Emotional
- Physical
- Language
- Cognitive
- Literacy
- Mathematics
- Science and Technology
- Social Studies
- The Arts

A tenth area, English language acquisition, has two objectives. A "Home Language Survey" is used to determine whether or not a child is an English-language learner. If so, the English language acquisition objectives are used to assess the child's receptive and expressive language skills.

Objectives for Development & Learning shows expectations for age-groups and for classes/grades; strategies that promote learning in relation to each objective; and dimensions, or more specific aspects, of each objective. For example, in the area of Language, Objective 10, "Uses appropriate conversational and other communication skills," has two dimensions:

10a. Engages in conversations
10b. Uses social rules of language

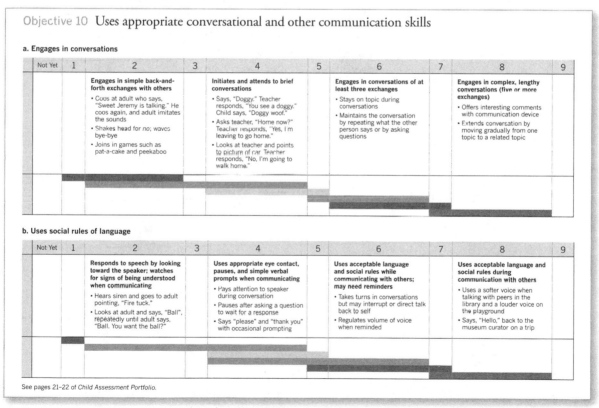

Objective 10 Uses appropriate conversational and other communication skills

a. Engages in conversations

Not Yet	1	2	3	4	5	6	7	8	9
		Engages in simple back-and-forth exchanges with others • Coos at adult who says, "Sweet Jeremy is talking." He coos again, and adult imitates the sounds • Shakes head for no; waves bye-bye • Joins in games such as pat-a-cake and peekaboo		**Initiates and attends to brief conversations** • Says, "Doggy." Teacher responds, "You see a doggy." Child says, "Doggy woof." • Asks teacher, "Home now?" Teacher responds, "Yes, I'm leaving to go home." • Looks at teacher and points to picture of car. Teacher responds, "No, I'm going to walk home."		**Engages in conversations of at least three exchanges** • Stays on topic during conversations • Maintains the conversation by repeating what the other person says or by asking questions		**Engages in complex, lengthy conversations (five or more exchanges)** • Offers interesting comments with communication device • Extends conversation by moving gradually from one topic to a related topic	

b. Uses social rules of language

Not Yet	1	2	3	4	5	6	7	8	9
		Responds to speech by looking toward the speaker; watches for signs of being understood when communicating • Hears siren and goes to adult pointing, "Fire truck." • Looks at adult and says, "Ball," repeatedly until adult says, "Ball. You want the ball?"		**Uses appropriate eye contact, pauses, and simple verbal prompts when communicating** • Pays attention to speaker during conversation • Pauses after asking a question to wait for a response • Says "please" and "thank you" with occasional prompting		**Uses acceptable language and social rules while communicating with others; may need reminders** • Takes turns in conversations but may interrupt or direct talk back to self • Regulates volume of voice when reminded		**Uses acceptable language and social rules during communication with others** • Uses a softer voice when talking with peers in the library and a louder voice on the playground • Says, "Hello," back to the museum curator on a trip	

See pages 21–22 of *Child Assessment Portfolio.*

A progression of development and learning is shown for each objective and dimension in these areas: social–emotional, physical, language, cognitive, literacy, mathematics, and English language acquisition. Colored bands show widely held expectations for development and learning. They indicate where most children of a particular age or class/grade are likely to be at the beginning and end of the program year. The rating scale at the top assigns values to children's places (levels) on the progression.

Another part of *Teaching Strategies GOLD®* is the *Child Assessment Portfolio*. Each child has a *Child Assessment Portfolio* where evidence of learning related to each objective (observation notes, photographs, work samples, audio and video clips, writing samples, etc.) can be stored. (In the online system, everything can be stored in an online portfolio.) One page is devoted to each dimension, and it includes a tracking form for teachers to record the child's level for each progression at three or four points during the year. Objective 18, "Comprehends and responds to books and other texts," Dimension a, "Interacts during read-alouds and book conversations," is illustrated below.

Objective 18 Comprehends and responds to books and other texts

a. Interacts during read-alouds and book conversations

	Not Yet	Level 1	Level 2	Level 3	Level 4	Level 5	Level 6	Level 7	Level 8	Level 9
			Contributes particular language from the book at the appropriate time		Asks and answers questions about the text; refers to pictures		Identifies story-related problems, events, and resolutions during conversations with an adult		Reconstructs story, using pictures, text, and props; begins to make inferences and draw conclusions	
Checkpoints:										
First	☐	☐	☐	☐	☐	☐	☐	☐	☐	☐
Second	☐	☐	☐	☐	☐	☐	☐	☐	☐	☐
Third	☐	☐	☐	☐	☐	☐	☐	☐	☐	☐
Fourth	☐	☐	☐	☐	☐	☐	☐	☐	☐	☐

Checkpoint				Not observed because:
1st	2nd	3rd	4th	
☐	☐	☐	☐	Recently enrolled
☐	☐	☐	☐	Excessive absences
☐	☐	☐	☐	Other: _____

See page 95 of *Objectives for Development & Learning: Birth Through Kindergarten.*

From *Teaching Strategies GOLD® Child Assessment Portfolio*, by Teaching Strategies, Inc. Copyright 2010 by Teaching Strategies, Inc. Reprinted with permission of Teaching Strategies, Inc., Washington, DC.

Ten *Assessment Opportunity Cards*™ offer literacy and mathematics activities that provide structured opportunities for children to demonstrate what they know and can do in relation to particular literacy and math objectives. Knowledge, skills, and behaviors related to those objectives are sometimes difficult to capture through children's spontaneous play activities. The cards describe small-group or individual activities, suggesting materials, directions, adaptations for children with special needs of any type, and links to other objectives.

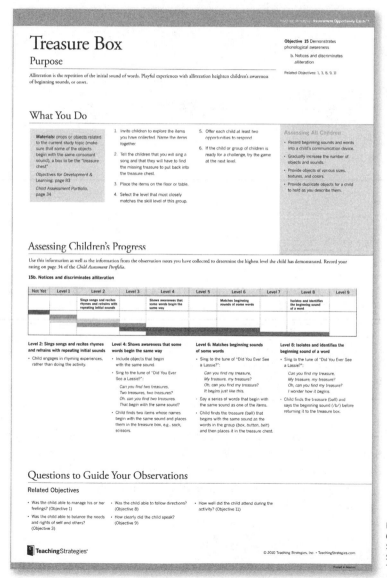

From *Teaching Strategies Assessment Opportunity Cards™: Treasure Box*, by Teaching Strategies, Inc. Copyright 2010 by Teaching Strategies, Inc. Reprinted with permission of Teaching Strategies, Inc., Washington, DC.

The *On-the-Spot Observation Recording Tool* is a checklist for collecting information about selected objectives in physical development, literacy, and mathematics. It is a quick way to record information, including the date you observed the specified behavior.

Objective 20   Uses number concepts and operations

a. Counts

Children		Not Yet	Level 1	Level 2	Level 3	Level 4	Level 5	Level 6	Level 7	Level 8	Level 9
				Verbally counts (not always in the correct order)		Verbally counts to 10; counts up to five objects accurately, using one number name for each object		Verbally counts to 20; counts 10–20 objects accurately; knows the last number states how many in all; tells what number (1–10) comes next in order by counting		Uses number names while counting to 100; counts 30 objects accurately; tells what number comes before and after a specified number up to 20	
1. Alicia	1.										
2. Alya	2.										
3. Bryson	3.										
4. Connor	4.										
5. DeShawn	5.										
6. Dwayne	6.										
7. Jessi	7.										
8. Julia	8.										
9. Julio	9.										
10. Lily	10.										
11.	11.										
12.	12.										
13.	13.										
14.	14.										
15.	15.										
16.	16.										
17.	17.										
18.	18.										
19.	19.										
20.	20.										
21.	21.										
22.	22.										
23.	23.										
24.	24.										
25.	25.										

On-the-Spot Recording Tool, by Teaching Strategies, Inc. Copyright 2010 by Teaching Strategies, Inc. Reprinted with permission of Teaching Strategies, Inc., Washington, DC.

Three or four times a year, after teachers record ratings in the *Child Assessment Portfolio*, they complete the "Family Conference Form." Teachers describe children's strengths in nine areas of development and learning, and they suggest goals for further development. They elicit information from the family and add family goals to the report.

Using *Teaching Strategies GOLD®*

Melissa, a teacher of 4-year-olds, describes her experience with this new assessment system.

We first started using *Teaching Strategies GOLD®* in October. Going into the training, I was a bit intimidated, but after the first day I realized how it was going to make my life a lot easier. Before, I struggled with knowing where to place each child developmentally, but *GOLD®* has made the assessment process much more efficient.

I have several ways of gathering documentation daily. Sometimes I take pictures throughout the day and have quick photo documentation that I can enter into the computer later on. Or my assistant teacher and I might do a 5-minute observation on a child a couple of times a week or once every 2 weeks as a way to get more of an in-depth observation. But most of the time I just carry my little pad of paper around and try to get a 30-second to 1-minute observation on a child during an activity.

After the children leave for the day, I go to my computer and enter my notes into *GOLD®* online. That is the part that I think is so fabulous because it's easy to type in what I want to say. Then I just click a few buttons to match the observations up with the learning objectives and dimensions. I love it! I can go back and easily view my past observations (from last week or a few weeks ago) and use them to set up my weekly planning forms for the upcoming week.

I use the preliminary checkpoints for ongoing assessment. The thing that I love most about the checkpoints is that, when I go in to complete them, I can actually see where (with which objective) I put my observations. Before, when I just had my observations on paper, I would have to sit down with my binder and flip through it a million times to find notes for a particular child and a particular goal. Now, when I log in, I can see each child's observation notes and when they were taken. I'm busy all day, and I know I'm not going to remember to which dimension a child's skills relate. With *Teaching Strategies GOLD®* online, I have all the information at my fingertips.

Because I can easily see the information on *GOLD®* for each child, I notice when I haven't observed a particular objective. Sometimes I'll look at my documentation and think, "Oh, I know that this child can do this skill, but I haven't documented it yet." *Teaching Strategies GOLD®* is great for pointing out areas that I might have missed, too, and it helps guide me on what to observe next.

I'm currently preparing for my family conferences. Before when I would fill out the information, sometimes I felt like I wasn't writing exactly what I wanted to say. With *GOLD®*, I can print out a conference form, and it says everything so much better than I might write it. But I can also add my own notes. *Teaching Strategies GOLD®* has made assessment so much easier.

Teaching Strategies GOLD® as a High-Quality Assessment Tool

Teaching Strategies GOLD® is a developmentally appropriate assessment system that combines curriculum-embedded assessment with interesting performance tasks that can be done as small-group activities. Careful attention has been paid to the selection of objectives, dimensions, indicators, and examples. The descriptions, progressions, and research summaries detailed in *Objectives for Development & Learning* combine to provide an in-depth explanation of child development. Teachers report assessment information to families three or four times a year, focusing on children's current skills, sharing evidence of learning, and establishing goals for the future.

Unlike the other assessment systems described in this chapter, *Teaching Strategies GOLD®* uses the same materials and procedures to assess children from birth through kindergarten. For programs that serve infants, toddlers, preschoolers, and kindergartners, it is teacher-friendly for all staff members to use the same tool.

Moreover, throughout the assessment materials, assessing all children—regardless of cultural, language, or ability differences—is highlighted. *Teaching Strategies GOLD®* not only includes two objectives for children who are learning English, but it also provides a way (the "Home Language Survey") for teachers to determine whether or not those objectives should be used to assess a particular child's language skills. The entire product is now available in Spanish as well as English, and it will become available in Arabic in 2012.

The Work Sampling System®

The Work Sampling System® *(WSS)* is a curriculum-embedded performance assessment instrument for children from preschool 3 through grade six (Meisels, Jablon, Dichtelmiller, Marsden, & Dorfman, 2001). It is designed to accompany any developmentally appropriate curriculum. It consists of three elements: developmental guidelines and checklists, a structured method of portfolio collection, and summary reports. It is available as a paper version (preschool 3–grade 6) or an online version (preschool 3–grade 5), which was revised in 2011. Information about its development and validation is available from several reliability and validity studies (Meisels, Bickel, Nicholson, Xue, & Atkins-Burnett, 2001; Meisels, Liaw, Dorfman, & Nelson, 1995; Meisels, Wen, Beachy-Quick, 2010; Meisels, Xue, & Shamblott, 2008). A version of *The Work Sampling System*® was also developed for Head Start (Dichtelmiller, Jablon, Meisels, & Marsden, 2001) with indicators modified to align with the *Head Start Child Outcomes Framework*.

The Work Sampling System® addresses seven developmental domains based on child development research and on national and state curriculum standards:

- Personal and Social Development
- Language and Literacy
- Mathematical Thinking
- Scientific Thinking
- Social Studies
- The Arts
- Physical Development and Health

Each domain is divided into several functional components. For example, Mathematical Thinking consists of

- Mathematical processes
- Number and operations
- Patterns, relationships, and functions
- Geometry and spatial relations
- Measurement
- Data collection and probability

Each component has several indicators that provide the focus for teacher observation. For example, at the kindergarten level, Geometry and Spatial Relations has two performance indicators:

1. Sorts objects into subgroups, classifying and comparing according to a rule
2. Recognizes, duplicates, and extends patterns.

The *Developmental Guidelines* and *Omnibus Guidelines* provide age/grade-level expectations for each indicator in single grade and multigrade formats, respectively. A mathematical thinking indicator from the *Omnibus Guidelines* is shown below.

The Work Sampling System
III Mathematical Thinking
B Number and operations

Preschool-3

1 Shows curiosity and interest in counting and numbers.

Most three year olds are interested in numbers and counting. They may ask, "How many?" and begin to say numbers in order, counting verbally up to three, six, or even ten with help. They can count small sets of one, two, or three objects with one-to-one correspondence. Most three year olds can identify a group of one, two, or three objects without counting, visually recognize whether two sets have the same or one has more, and make sets of up to three items. Examples include:

- following directions for getting "just two jars of paint" for the easel;
- recognizing that they have the same number of cars as a friend does;
- counting out loud to themselves while occupied at an activity;
- commenting that there are two cookies left on the plate without counting;
- being actively involved in reading a counting book;
- commenting that everyone at snack has two crackers and one cup of juice;
- singing counting songs and enjoying fingerplays about counting.

Preschool-4

1 Shows beginning understanding of number and quantity.

Four year olds can count five to ten objects meaningfully using one-to-one correspondence, and some can count verbally up to 20 or 30. Most four year olds understand that the last number named in the collection represents the last object as well as the total number of objects. They are just learning that the next number in the counting sequence is one more than the number just named and continue to explore the meaning of "more" and "less." Examples include:

- pointing to each object they count and assigning the appropriate number to it;
- recognizing that there are four blocks without counting them;
- commenting that there are more cars than tow trucks in the block area;
- telling a friend who is first in line, "I am second";
- adding a friend's two yellow beads to their own two yellow beads and saying, "I have four beads";
- filling in the next number when the teacher says "4, 5, 6, …";
- counting footsteps, jumps, or repetitions of exercises.

Kindergarten

1 Shows understanding of number and quantity.

Kindergarten children can count objects to at least 20; many learn to count verbally (that is, by rote) to 100. They can count using one-to-one correspondence reliably, use objects to represent numbers, and use numerals to represent quantities. With experience, they can begin to understand that a set of objects equals the same number regardless of the position, shape, or order of the objects. They continue to learn about ordinal numbers (first through tenth) and understand that the last number named in a collection represents not only the last object, but the total number of objects as well. Examples include:

- explaining that there are 17 people at the circle today, after counting them aloud with their classmates;
- associating the correct numeral with sets of up to ten objects;
- using number words to show understanding of the common numerical property among nine children, nine cups, nine trucks, and nine blocks;
- continuing counting pennies to ten after a friend stopped at 6 (… "7, 8, 9, 10").

76

From *The Work Sampling System® Omnibus Guidelines: Preschool Through Third Grade* (4th ed.), by M. L. Dichtelmiller, J. R. Jablon, D. B. Marsden, and S. J. Meisels. Copyright 2001 by NCS Pearson, Inc. Reprinted with permission of Pearson PsychCorp™, San Antonio, TX.

First Grade

1 Shows understanding of number and quantity.

Six year olds can count, read, model, and write whole numbers to 100 or more. It is essential that first graders understand that numbers can be represented in many ways (for example, 10, ten, two sets of five stars). Their understanding of number includes knowing the value of coins. Examples of how six year olds demonstrate their understanding include:

- looking at a set of six objects and instantly recognizing it as six;
- recognizing equivalent forms of the same number (for example, knowing that 30 is the same quantity if it is 30 horses or 30 M&Ms or 15 + 15 red dots);
- counting the number of objects in a group with understanding and writing the correct numeral to describe the set (for example, writing the numeral 30 to match 30 cubes);
- looking at a set of coins and identifying the value of each coin.

Second Grade

1 Shows understanding of number, quantities, and their relationships.

Seven year olds can count, read, write, model, order, and compare whole numbers to at least 999. They can express quantities in different ways (for example, 30 as 15 + 15 or 3 tens) and they can group numbers into hundreds, tens, and ones, identifying the place value for each digit. Their understanding of quantity includes modeling, representing, and solving problems involving money (pennies, nickels, dimes, quarters, and dollar bills). They demonstrate their understanding by:

- reading and writing two- and three-digit numerals purposefully, such as recording card game scores;
- describing the comparative relationship of numbers using the symbols >, <, = (for example, 234 > 150);
- counting by 3s and 4s to 100 and by 10s or in multiples of 10s beginning at different numbers (for example, from 20, 55, or 120);
- switching among different counts (for example 100, 200, 300, 310, 320, 330, 331, 332, 333, etc.);
- identifying the value of a group of coins (5 dimes, 3 nickels, and 3 pennies equal 68¢).

Third Grade

1 Shows understanding of number, quantities, and their relationships.

By third grade, students demonstrate their comprehension of the meaning of four- and five-digit whole numbers by modeling, ordering, and comparing numbers to at least 10,000. They show understanding of place value by calculating addition and subtraction algorithms accurately, using models to explain place value, and representing four- and five-digit numbers using expanded notation. They begin to explore numbers less than zero using a number line. Examples include:

- ordering numbers by relative size (640 comes before 1200 because it is smaller by about half);
- representing comparisons of large numbers or quantities using equations with the symbols <, >, =, ≠;
- rounding numbers to the nearest ten, hundred, and thousand when solving problems where an approximate answer is sufficient;
- representing a five-digit number in different ways (5,432 is the same as five thousands, four hundreds, three tens, and two ones, or 5000 + 400 + 30 + 2).

III Mathematical Thinking

77

271

The indicators provide a focus for ongoing classroom observation. *WSS* offers teachers the opportunity to record and organize observational data in any way that suits their working styles, and it suggests several options. The form shown below provides a way to record data for individuals and for groups of children.

The Work Sampling System				
I Personal & Social Development A Self concept B Self control C Approaches to learning D Interaction with others E Social problem-solving				
II Language & Literacy A Listening B Speaking C Reading D Writing E Research (3-5)				
III Mathematical Thinking A Mathematical processes B Number and operations C Patterns, relationships, and functions D Geometry and spatial relations E Measurement F Data collection & prob. (K-5)				
IV Scientific Thinking A Inquiry B Physical science (K-5) C Life science (K-5) D Earth science (K-5)				
V Social Studies A People, past and present B Human interdependence C Citizenship and government D People and where they live				
VI The Arts A Expression and representation B Understanding and appreciation				
VII Physical Development & Health A Gross motor development B Fine motor development C Personal health and safety				

Domain Process Notes

From *The Work Sampling System®
Reproducible Masters, Domain Process
Notes* (4th ed.),. Copyright 2001 by
NCS Pearson, Inc. Reprinted with permission
of Pearson PsychCorp™, San Antonio, TX.

On the basis of their observations, teachers complete a *Developmental Checklist* for each child three times per year, making ratings of "Not yet," "In process," and "Proficient."

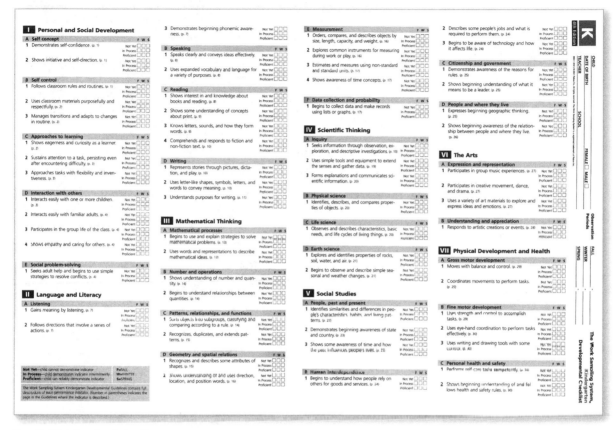

From *The Work Sampling System® Kindergarten Developmental Checklist* (4th ed.). Copyright by NCS Pearson, Inc. Reprinted with permission of Pearson PsychCorp™, San Antonio, TX.

In addition to completing a *Developmental Checklist* for each child, teachers and children develop portfolios to provide additional evidence of the child's performance in the seven domains. The approach to portfolios is very structured. Each portfolio is designed to capture the child's progress within domains, as well as his or her individual strengths, interests, and abilities across all domains.

The third element of the system is the *Summary Report*, a progress report completed three times per year and shared with families. There are three versions. One includes ratings of performance and progress with brief narratives. A second is entirely narrative. The third, designed for Head Start, includes space to record the family's comments, individual learning goals for the child, and activities to support the child's learning at home.

Using *The Work Sampling System*®

Alicia, a teacher of 3-year olds, describes her experience with this assessment system.

My program chose to use *The Work Sampling System*® (*WSS*) a year and a half ago. We had never used a structured, commercially available assessment tool in the past, but we thought *WSS* might be an effective tool for us. We are currently using the online version, which provides teachers with a way to organize anecdotal observations notes by domain and shows age-appropriate expectations.

I usually take observation notes throughout the day. Most often I pick up a clipboard, sit in an area of my classroom, and begin taking a few brief anecdotal notes. Depending on the day, I may be focusing on a specific domain or on a certain child, or I might record what I see at a particular time. I often document group interaction while writing brief notes about each child. Sometimes I take a photograph that captures the observation.

During my planning time, I flesh out the notes using *Work Sampling Online*. The program allows me to select the date and child (or children) I observed. Next, I type in the anecdotal observation note. Once the note is elaborated, I categorize the observation by domain and performance indicator. As time goes on, I am able to view all the observation notes about each child and begin to focus my note taking on areas I have not documented in the past.

The Work Sampling System® is organized around three collection periods during the year. We are working to implement the full program but are not there yet. After each collection period, we complete the *Developmental Checklist* that gives us an overall picture of the child's development by domains. The observations that the teacher documented over time are used to make decisions about the child's performance. The online version makes this very easy because, when I am working on a child's checklist, I can click on an icon that reveals all of the observation notes about the child that we categorized under that indicator. The anecdotal notes and children's work provide evidence about the child's performance in that area.

Once the *Developmental Checklist* is finished, using *Work Sampling Online*, we write a narrative report that includes a few of the observations from that collection period. The narrative report provides the families with an understanding of the child's progress in the various areas of learning, strengths, and areas of concerns. I find it very helpful to be able to give parents concrete examples of how their child is demonstrating a specific skill. As we begin incorporating the portfolio component of *WSS*, parents will be able to see concrete evidence of their child's development over time.

As a teacher, I also take advantage of *The Work Sampling System®* to guide my curriculum planning. The online checklist allows me to run group reports by indicators to see how the group is performing. I may see that a number of children are still "In process" in fine-motor development. I will then be sure to plan activities that provide them with opportunities to develop this skill. It is a great tool not only for sharing information with families, but also for guiding my planning.

The Work Sampling System® as a High-Quality Assessment Tool

The Work Sampling System® is a developmentally appropriate assessment system in terms of content and process. Its checklist items are based on child development research as well as state and national standards. The reliability and validity of the system is strong (Meisels, Bickel, Nicholson, Xue, & Atkins-Burnett, 2001; Meisels, Xue, & Shamblott, 2008; Meisels, Liaw, Dorfman, & Nelson, 1995).

The Work Sampling System® is available for preschool through sixth grade and therefore enables teachers to see the progression of development. Using the *Omnibus Guidelines*, teachers can look at an earlier age or grade level if a child is having difficulty. Similarly, they can look at higher grade levels to anticipate skills that will develop next. Moreover, it is relevant to instruction. Children are assessed during regular classroom activities, and *WSS* provides many examples of developmentally appropriate curriculum for each indicator. It also includes a portfolio method through which children can gradually acquire skills to assess and direct their own learning.

The greatest strength of *The Work Sampling System®* is that it is structured but flexible. For example, the portfolio approach limits the number and types of items, but it allows teachers to determine which items to collect. Similarly, teachers must collect evidence of each child's performance on particular indicators, but they have great flexibility in terms of the methods they use for collecting and organizing data. Its flexibility is also reflected by the opportunity to create a gradual implementation plan for teachers to whom to the system is new.

The Ounce Scale™

The Ounce Scale™ (Meisels, Dombro, Marsden, Weston, & Jewkes, 2003) is an observational assessment instrument for infants and toddlers from birth to 3½ years. There are paper and online versions. *The Ounce Scale*™ focuses on six areas of development:

- Personal Connections: How children show trust
- Feelings About Self: How children express who they are
- Relationships with Other Children: How children act around other children
- Understanding and Communicating: How children understand and communicate
- Exploration and Problem Solving: How children explore and figure things out
- Movement and Coordination: How children move their bodies and use their hands

The Ounce Scale™ has three parts. Caregivers use the *Observation Record* to guide the observation process and store observation notes. Each area of development has two or three questions that focus the caregiver's observations.

Babies III
8-12 months

IV. Understanding and Communicating: Baby Talk

How babies understand and communicate

How does the baby show his understanding of gestures and words?

Babies show they understand what's being said to them by responding to the gestures and words they see and hear most often. As routines become established, babies demonstrate they are beginning to feel comfortable with things happening in predictable ways.

The baby might do one or more of the following:

- **Answer you**—point to the banana on his tray when you ask, "Where is your banana?"
- **Look forward to what's next**—giggle even before "This Little Piggy" is finished because he knows what will happen at the end.
- **Show you**—put a block in a cup, then take it out when you point and ask, "Where did the block go?"
- **Connect to books**—put his hand right beside yours when you are pointing to the picture you are reading about.
- **React to you**—start to cry, or turn away when you say, "It's time for bed."

How does *this* baby show understanding of tone and gestures? (Indicate dates.)

_____

_____

_____

_____

_____

How does the baby use gestures and sounds to communicate?

At this stage, babies begin to make consistent sounds and use them to communicate. They often use their own wordlike sounds to label familiar people or objects. They continue to express feelings and desires through sounds, facial expressions, and gestures.

The baby might do one or more of the following:

- **Let you know it's no go**—shake his head or turn away when he sees the washcloth in your hand.
- **Show it's playtime**—start a game of peekaboo or "Where's Baby?" by hiding his face in his bib or his hands.
- **Indicate satisfaction**—push his cup away when he's finished drinking.
- **Invite a conversation**—babble away when someone is nearby, as though talking to him or her.
- **Motion to get down**—lift his arms toward you when he wants to get down from his high chair.

In what ways does *this* baby use sounds to communicate? (Include dates.)

_____

_____

_____

_____

_____

5

From *The Ounce Scale*™: *Babies III: 8–12 months: Observation Record*, by S. J. Meisels, A. L. Dombro, D. B. Marsden, D. R. Wetson, and A. M. Jewkes. Copyright 2003 by NCS Pearson. Reprinted with permission of Pearson PsychCorp™, San Antonio, TX.

Caregivers and families work together on the *Family Album*, a place to collect observations, photos, and mementos of a child's growth and development.

I. It's About Trust

How your baby shows trust

How does your baby let you know he wants to be with you?

As your baby gets to know and trust you, he wants to be with you more and more. He may smile or laugh to get your attention. He does this because he knows you will help him get what he wants and needs. To show you he wants to be with you, your baby might:

- put out his arms and smile as you come near his crib or bouncy seat
- bounce on your lap so you'll go on playing horsie
- make loud sounds when you're in another room

How does *your* baby let you know he wants you?

_____

_____

_____

_____

_____

Your expressions, the sound of your voice, and what you say and do mean a lot to your baby. That's because you are so important to him.

2

The *Family Album* also suggests ways for families to help their babies develop.

Try this and see what happens!

Here are some things you can do to help your baby trust you.

Watch and listen.

As he grows, your baby's signals about what he wants and needs become clearer. Keep letting him know that you understand him by responding to his actions.

Wait for a response.

When you get ready to pick up your baby, say, "I'm going to pick you up. It's time for your bath." Then wait until he looks at you or holds up his arms before you lift him.

Let him know what's happening.

Tell your baby what will happen next. For example, tell him when you're leaving, even if he fusses. You'll teach him that he can depend on you to let him know what's going on.

Help your baby meet new people.

Be there to pick up, hold, and comfort your baby when he meets and gets to know a new adult. Being there helps him feel safe and secure.

Take care of yourself too!

Spend a few minutes each day doing something you enjoy. When you are feeling happy, you'll be better able to respond to your baby.

From *The Ounce Scale™ Family Album: Your Baby's Life: Watch Wonder Enjoy! Babies II: 4–8 months*, by S. J. Meisels, A. L. Dombro, D. B. Marsden, D. R. Wetson, and A. M. Jewkes. Copyright 2003 by NCS Pearson. Reprinted with permission of Pearson PsychCorp™, San Antonio, TX.

The *Developmental Profiles* are ratings scales used to evaluate children's growth and development at the end of each of eight age levels. The *Standards* are used with the *Developmental Profiles* to explain each item on the rating scales, as illustrated below.

The Ounce Scale Toddlers 1
Developmental Profile

Child _____
Date of birth _____ Age _____
Teacher/Home _____
Assessment con _____
Today's date _____

24 Months

SOCIAL and EMOTIONAL

I. Personal Connections: It's About Trust
- Seeks support of familiar adults to try things (p. 42)
- Acts cautiously around unfamiliar adults (p. 43)

II. Feelings About Self: Learning About Me
- Expresses own ideas, interests, and feelings (p. 43)
- Tries to manage own behavior (p. 44)

III. Relationships With Other Children: Child to Child
- Watches and plays briefly with other children (p. 45)
- Shows awareness of other children's feelings (p. 46)

COMMUNICATION and LANGUAGE

IV. Understanding and Communicating: Toddler Talk
- Follows simple directions and suggestions consistently (p. 46)
- Uses a growing number of words and puts several words together (p. 47)
- Pays attention to and tries to participate in conversations (p. 47)

COGNITIVE DEVELOPMENT

V. Exploration and Problem Solving: Toddler Discoveries
- Explores the environment and learns how things work (p. 48)
- Shows increasing memory for details and routines (p. 49)
- Expects specific results when playing with toys and other objects (p. 50)

PHYSICAL DEVELOPMENT

VI. Movement and Coordination: Toddlers in Motion
- Shows increasing coordination and balance, and combines actions to participate in play activities (p. 50)
- Uses hands and eyes to accomplish a variety of tasks (p. 51)
- Participates in self-help activities (p. 52)

Parent signature _____

The Developmental Profiles should be used in conjunction with obs Records and matched to the age-level descriptions (page numbers ap

© 2003 Regents of the University of Michigan. Published and distributed by New York 10036.

COMMUNICATION and LANGUAGE

IV. Understanding and Communicating: Toddler Talk
- Follows simple directions and suggestions consistently (p. 46)
- Uses a growing number of words and puts several words together (p. 47)
- Pays attention to and tries to participate in conversations (p. 47)

Use a growing number of words and put several words together

Toddlers move at their own pace in how and when they use words and language. Children this age display a wide span of development in their production of words, ranging from just beginning to label objects to talking in sentences. The words toddlers do use can usually be understood, but some words still run together. Toddlers' vocabulary develops from their daily experiences so that in different cultures and different settings children use the words and phrases they hear spoken to them. As toddlers' language abilities develop, they move from simple labels to using words that show intent, such as, "No!" or "Mine!" For example, they might:

Developing as Expected:
- name pictures in their picture book
- jabber to themselves as they make different shapes with the play dough
- say their word for shirt as they pick out one that is red
- put several words together, such as, "More cookie" or "Go out now"
- use language with increasing specificity to ask for what they want
- start asking questions related to the story you are reading or the things they see as you go on walks together
- respond to something that just happened, such as, "Kitty gone?"
- look at Daddy getting ready to go out and say, "Juan go?"

Needs Development:
- continue to use gestures rather than words to communicate
- cry or stamp their feet when you don't understand what they want
- try to tell you about something, but their babbling sounds don't make sense
- point to the juice but use sounds that are not distinguishable as words

Pay attention and try to participate in conversations

Toddlers are now attempting to participate in conversations with the people around them. They have enough language ability that they can understand what grown-ups and older children are talking about, and they want to be a part of the action. They use the language they hear most often and can be encouraged to use the social conventions of the culture in which they are living. For example, they might:

Standards for the Developmental Profiles 47

From *The Ounce Scale™ Developmental Profile: Toddlers I*. Pearson Early Learning. Copyright 2003 by NCS Pearson. Reprinted with permission of Pearson PsychCorp™, San Antonio, TX.

From *The Ounce Scale™ Standards for Developmental Profiles: Birth–42 months*, by S. J. Meisels, A. L. Dombro, D. B. Marsden, D. R. Wetson, and A. M. Jewkes. Copyright 2003 by NCS Pearson. Reprinted with permission of Pearson PsychCorp™, San Antonio, TX.

The Ounce Scale™ includes eight age levels:

- Babies I: Birth–4 months
- Babies II: 4–8 months
- Babies III: 8–12 months
- Babies IV: 12–18 months
- Toddlers I: 18–24 months
- Toddlers II: 24–30 months
- Toddlers III: 30–36 months
- Preschoolers: 36–42 months

Each age level has its own *Observation Record*, *Family Album*, and *Developmental Profile*.

To use *The Ounce Scale*™, the caregiver observes the child during everyday activities and regularly records observations for the six areas of development. In each area, the family explores two or three questions with the caregiver's help, by working on the *Family Album*. Finally, at the end of each age level, the caregiver uses the collected data to evaluate the child's development in terms of the expectations described in the *Standards*. After completing a *Developmental Profile*, the caregiver and family meet to discuss the child's development and set goals.

Using *The Ounce Scale*™

Cora, a family childcare provider who works with infants and toddlers, describes her experience with this assessment system.

I have been using *The Ounce Scale*™ in my family childcare home for the past 4 years. My original goal for learning *The Ounce Scale*™ was to have a format to use when conferencing with my families. Because I use *The Ounce Scale*™ in the world where my infants and toddlers are comfortable—my home and theirs—the parents and I think we can trust what we learn from it. It includes questions about children's everyday experiences of trust, self, child-to-child relationships, language, discoveries, and movement. The questions help me focus on specific skills and behaviors.

Because I usually work alone, I have to be creative in catching and noting my observations of the children I care for. Each day I capture tidbits of information and jot them down on sticky notes. My cupboards are adorned with short anecdotes about various children. I don't have a specific time to observe, but I do it casually, incorporating it into my daily schedule. Since it is so important to assess growth over time, I try to observe several times a week during the 4 to 6 months preceding my work on each child's *Developmental Profile*.

A typical day might involve observing as Scottlynn crawls across the carpet to reach her favorite ball. I delight in watching her movements and discoveries and in learning more about her personality. To observe a child intentionally brings watching to an entirely different level. As I gather evidence about the various observation questions, I transfer the information to her *Observation Record*.

The Ounce Scale™ provides me with a vehicle to develop a deeper bond with Scottlynn and her family. After I have evidence in Scottlynn's *Observation Record*, I complete the *Summary Report*, which pulls all the information I have about Scottlynn together. Then I set some goals for Scottlynn and share them with her family. I give Scottlynn's parents the option to meet in their home, which gives me additional insights about their family. Scottlynn's parents come to the meeting with information from their *Family Album*. Its format mirrors my *Observation Record*. They seem to feel empowered because they have information to share, too. It is exciting to share information and gain some new insights, set appropriate goals, and discuss the wonder of childhood with each other.

I appreciate how *The Ounce Scale*™ accentuates Scottlynn's accomplishments but also reveals any areas needing extra support. The *Standards* book and my awareness of her successes and limitations assist me in setting realistic goals and offering appropriate experiences for her.

The Ounce Scale™ has made me feel more professional in my business. My conferences are successful because they enhance communication with families. Ultimately, I feel more connected to my families, and I can provide positive learning experiences based on evidence from *The Ounce*. Most importantly, I have come to appreciate deeply the opportunity to watch my children develop and grow.

The Ounce Scale™ as a High-Quality Assessment Tool

The Ounce Scale™ is a developmentally appropriate assessment system based on child development research and expectations for infant and toddler development. Its reliability and validity are being studied (Meisels, Wen & Beachy-Quick, 2010, in preparation.)

It is family-friendly; it helps teachers build positive relationships with families by giving them a meaningful role in the assessment process. The language is simple and clear, and the materials are inviting. Family participation is tailored to the needs of individual families, who can share their own observations and participate as actively as they would like through the *Family Album*. Depending on program requirements, summarized information can be shared with families through the more formal *Developmental Profiles* or the friendlier *Summary Report*.

Finally, *The Ounce Scale*™ has been used successfully in center-based, home visiting, Early Head Start, and family support programs. The *User Guide* addresses how *The Ounce Scale*™ can be used and provides specific strategies for use in each type of program.

Conclusion

Early childhood teachers can choose from many good, commercially available options for classroom-based assessment, including others not described in this chapter. The assessment tools in this chapter share many features. They are all based on a foundation of current child development research and early learning guidelines. Each of these assessment systems can be used easily with any developmentally appropriate early childhood curriculum. Each approach can be described as curriculum-embedded assessment; children are assessed as they interact in a familiar setting during regular classroom activities. All report information to families and provide teachers with formative assessment information that they can quickly use to inform their teaching. The technical properties of each approach have been studied.

Nevertheless, the systems are different. How do you go about selecting one? Here are some strategies for further research:

1. Talk with people who have used the system.
2. Examine the materials.
3. Attend a conference presentation about the approach you are considering.

Once the important criteria for high-quality assessment have been met, you can base your decision on how well the particular tool aligns with your program objectives and the styles and preferences of the teachers in your program.

No matter which system you choose, you will need training. Although professional development support comes with a cost, in the long run trained teachers will be able to use the system as its developers intended and with less frustration than teachers who lack training.

Key Ideas to Remember

- Several developmentally appropriate, classroom-based assessment systems meet the criteria for high-quality assessment.

- Most assessment systems require some training in order to be able to use them reliably and as intended.

- It is important to see the materials and talk with knowledgeable people before making the decision to purchase a commercially available assessment system.

References

Dichtelmiller, M. L., Jablon, J. R., Marsden, D. B., & Meisels, S. J. (2001). *The Work Sampling System® omnibus guidelines: Preschool through third grade* (4th ed.), San Antonio, TX: Pearson PsychCorp™

Dichtelmiller, M. L., Jablon, J. R., Meisels, S. J., & Marsden, D. B. (2001). *The Work Sampling System for Head Start.* NY: Pearson Early Learning.

Heroman, C., Burts, D. C., Berke, K., & Bickart, T. S. (2010). *Teaching Strategies GOLD® objectives for development & learning: Birth through kindergarten.* Washington, DC: Teaching Strategies, Inc.

HighScope Educational Research Foundation. (2002). *Infant-toddler child observation record.* Ypsilanti, MI: HighScope Press.

HighScope Educational Research Foundation. (2003). *COR information for decision makers* [Electronic version]. Ypsilanti, MI: HighScope Press.

HighScope Educational Research Foundation. (2003). *Preschool child observation record* (2nd ed.). Ypsilanti, MI: HighScope Press.

References, *continued*

HighScope Educational Research Foundation. (2003). *Preschool child observation record: Child information and developmental summary.* Ypsilanti, MI: HighScope Press.

HighScope Educational Research Foundation. (2003). *Preschool child observation record: Family report.* Ypsilanti, MI: HighScope Press.

HighScope Educational Research Foundation. (2003). *Preschool child observation record: Observation items.* Ypsilanti, MI: HighScope Press.

HighScope Educational Research Foundation. (2003). *Preschool child observation record: User guide* (2nd ed.). Ypsilanti, MI: HighScope Press.

Lambert, R. G., Kim, D.-H., Taylor, H. McGee, J. R. (2010). *Technical manual for the Teaching Strategies GOLD® assessment system.* Charlotte, NC: University of North Carolina Charlotte.

Meisels, S. J., Bickel, D. D., Nicholson, J., Xue, Y., & Atkins-Burnett, S. (2001). Trusting teachers' judgments: A validity study of a curriculum-embedded performance assessment in kindergarten to grade 3. *American Educational Research Journal, 38*(1), 73–95.

Meisels, S. J., Dombro, A. L., Marsden, D. B., Wetson, D. R., & Jewkes, A. M. (2003). *The Ounce Scale™: Babies II: 4–8 months: Family album: Your baby's life: Watch wonder enjoy!.* New York, NY: Pearson Early Learning.

Meisels, S. J., Dombro, A. L., Marsden, D. B., Wetson, D. R., & Jewkes, A. M. (2003). *The Ounce Scale™: Babies III: 8–12 months: Observation record.* New York, NY: Pearson Early Learning.

Meisels, S. J., Dombro, A. L., Marsden, D. B., Wetson, D. R., & Jewkes, A. M. (2003). *The Ounce Scale™ developmental profile: Toddlers I.* New York, NY: Pearson Early Learning.

Meisels, S. J., Dombro, A. L., Marsden, D. B., Wetson, D. R., & Jewkes, A. M. (2003). *The Ounce Scale™ standards for developmental profiles: Birth–42 months.* New York, NY: Pearson Early Learning.

Meisels, S. J., Jablon, J. R., Dichtelmiller, M. L., Marsden, D. B., & Dorfman, A. B. (2001). *The Work Sampling System®* (4th ed.). NY: Pearson Early Learning.

Meisels, S. J., Liaw, F-R., Dorfman, A., & Nelson, R. (1995). *The Work Sampling System*: Reliability and validity of a performance assessment for young children. *Early Childhood Research Quarterly, 10*(3), 277–296.

Meisels, S. J., Wen, X., & Beachy-Quick, K. (2010). Authentic assessment for infants and toddlers: Exploring the reliability and validity of *The Ounce Scale. Applied Developmental Science, 14*(2), 55–71.

Meisels, S. J., Xue, Y., & Shamblott, M. (2008). Assessing language, literacy, and mathematics skills with Work Sampling for Head Start. *Early Education and Development, 19*(6), 963–981.

Teaching Strategies, Inc. (2010). *Teaching Strategies Assessment Opportunity Cards™*. Washington, DC: Author.

Teaching Strategies, Inc. (2010). *Teaching Strategies family conference form* Washington, DC: Author.

Teaching Strategies, Inc. (2010). *Teaching Strategies GOLD® child assessment portfolio*. Washington, DC: Author.

Teaching Strategies, Inc. (2010). *Teaching Strategies GOLD® on-the-spot recording tool*. Washington, DC: Author.

Work Sampling For Head Start Family Report (2001). New York: NY: Pearson.

The Work Sampling System® kindergarten developmental checklist (4th ed.) (n.d.). New York, NY: Pearson.

The Work Sampling System® reproducible masters, domain process notes (4th ed.) (n.d.). New York, NY: Pearson.

CHAPTER 14

Testing Young Children

We have all been tested at some point in our lives. What do you think about when you hear the words *test* and *testing*? If you are anything like me, you may think that tests do not paint an accurate portrait of what you understand or are capable of doing. If this is so, your experiences with tests may strengthen your appreciation of the mismatch between the demands of standardized tests and the characteristics of young children.

Testing is on the rise in the United States (McAfee & Leong, 2007). The No Child Left Behind Act (a reauthorization of the Elementary and Secondary Education Act) mandates that testing begin in third grade. Despite serious concerns in our field about the problems inherent in testing young children and the (hopefully) minor role of tests in our work, basic knowledge about testing is essential to communicating with other professionals and families. This chapter presents

- basic concepts related to standardized testing
- issues related to testing young children
- recommendations for using tests appropriately

- What experiences have you had with standardized tests, whether administered individually or in group settings?
- What assumptions or beliefs do you bring to the discussion of tests and testing young children?

Reflect on Your Practice

Basic Concepts Related to Standardized Testing

In chapter 2, you read about various types of assessment that are used for different purposes. Considered to be formal assessment instruments, tests can serve some of those purposes. For example, there are screening, readiness, diagnostic, and achievement tests. This chapter addresses five important topics related to testing:

- individual or group administration
- standardization
- interpreting test data by making comparisons
- accountability
- test selection

Individual or Group Administration

Tests can be administered either one-to-one or in groups. Screening and diagnostic tests are typically administered individually. In contrast, most readiness and achievement tests are administered to groups of children, beginning as early as kindergarten. Whether a test is administered individually or in a group setting makes a significant difference to a young child. One-to-one administration provides more support to the child, who is functioning in the context of a relationship with an adult. For example, an experienced examiner would notice when a child is beginning to lose interest and might suggest a short walk to get a drink of water. In contrast, group testing lacks that kind of support and requires the independent use of a young child's limited test-taking skills. As you think about using tests, it is important to distinguish between different types of administration.

Standardization

McAfee and Leong (2007) wisely differentiate *standardized procedures* from *standardized tests*.

Standardized procedures When procedures are standardized, the assessment instrument is administered identically to each person. The conditions of the test, including the tasks, materials, directions, time allowed, and assistance given, are the same for each test taker. As you read each of the following examples, consider the effects of nonstandardized procedures in informal assessment.

In February, Rashan's teacher assessed his balance skills by watching him walk across the outdoor balance beam. At the time, Rashan was wearing boots. In May, when she assessed him again, he was barefoot and walked across the balance beam in the gym. Given the changed assessment conditions, what conclusions can his teacher form about his progress with balance?

A group of children created collages at the art table. They used a variety of scissors to cut pieces from newsprint, scrap paper, wallpaper, construction paper, and poster board. For example, Zak used the last of the old, dull metal scissors to cut poster board and wallpaper. What can the teacher conclude about each child's cutting skills, given the different conditions (different types of scissors and paper) each child experienced?

When assessing children, paying attention to procedures will make you more confident about the results. Using nonstandardized procedures may inadvertently obscure the meaning of the results or make it difficult to compare results from one time period to another. Be aware that many teachers have negative attitudes about "standardized" assessment that may be unwarranted when one considers the advantages of standardized procedures.

Standardized tests These tests have standardized procedures and are created in accordance with guidelines set forth in *Standards for Educational and Psychological Testing* (American Educational Research Association, American Psychological Association, & National Council on Measurement in Education, 1999). The same procedures are used for each test taker when the tests are administered, scored, and interpreted.

Standardized tests are designed to have certain properties necessary for accurate measurement, and they must be reliable and valid (see chapter 12). Furthermore, a test manual must be included that explains

- how the test is constructed
- how reliability and validity were determined
- the population used to develop and pilot the test
- the scoring system

For more information about the development of standardized tests, see McAfee & Leong (2007) and Popham (2011).

Interpreting Test Data by Making Comparisons

All assessment, including standardized testing, involves some type of comparison (see chapter 10). We compare children's actions, behavior, or performances to expectations for their age or to mastery of particular learning objectives. Standardized tests use two different comparisons: to norms or to criteria.

Norm-referenced tests These tests compare a child's score, or performance, to the scores of other children who took the test previously. The original test-takers are known as the *norming group*. The characteristics of the norming group should be similar to the characteristics of the ultimate test-takers. For example, if a test of motor development was normed with a group of boys, it may not give accurate information about girls' motor development.

Overall, the goal of norm-referenced tests is to differentiate among children or, stated differently, to rank children's performance. Norm-referenced tests describe a child's performance in comparison with that of the norming group. The percentile scores show this comparison. For example, if a child receives a percentile rank of 92, it means that 92 percent of the children taking the test scored at or below that child's level.

Criterion-referenced tests When instruments compare a child's performance on the test to a set of criteria, they are called criterion-referenced tests. Rather than compare a child's performance with the performance of a norming group, criterion-referenced tests compare a child's performance to standards, a set of specific skills, or benchmarks. How well other children do has no influence on a particular child's score. Because criterion-referenced tests describe how well a child has mastered particular content, the test results can be used to guide instruction. Many state achievement tests, which are based on a state's standards, are criterion-referenced.

Accountability

The need for accountability is often cited to justify the use of standardized tests. A program's constituents, such as parents, funders, state departments of education, and sometimes the federal government, want to know whether or not a program is effective. Is it accomplishing its goals and fulfilling the purposes for which it was established? Are children learning? Because standardized tests produce numerical scores that *appear* objective, they are perceived as providing data that is easy to understand, interpret, and communicate to others.

As demand for accountability increases, tests are frequently used to demonstrate program effectiveness to parents and policy makers. Many early childhood programs—dependent on funding from foundations or the government—are required to report outcomes that standardized tests are purported to measure. Unfortunately, legislators and funders encourage the use of tests because they perceive them to be inexpensive and easy to understand (Goodwin & Goodwin, 1997). In fact, Hills (1992, p. 44) refers to standardized tests as the "fast food" of assessment.

Test Selection

If you are responsible for selecting a standardized test, be sure to read several critiques of the tests you are considering. Although test publishers provide information about the technical properties of the test, it is essential to read objective evaluations of tests before making selection decisions. Reviews can be accessed online from the Buros Institute's *Test Reviews Online* for a small fee. Additionally, many college and university libraries provide free online access to the Buros Institute's *Mental Measurements Yearbooks* reviews.

Issues Related to Testing Young Children

Early childhood professional organizations urge extreme caution in—or even denounce—using standardized tests with children before third or fourth grade (NAEYC, 1987; NAEYC & NAECS/SDE, 2003; Solley, 2007). Standardized tests are a poor fit for young children for three primary reasons:

- It is difficult to obtain accurate information by testing children under the ages of 7 or 8 years because of the way young children perform in the test environment.

- There is a disconnection between the way tests work and the knowledge underlying developmentally appropriate practice.

- Research shows that standardized tests frequently have negative effects on children, teachers, curricula, and programs.

Young Children Are Not Good Test-Takers

Some characteristics of young children affect test performance negatively (Gullo, 2005; McAfee & Leong, 2007; Puckett & Black, 2008). Young children

- have limited language skills and may misinterpret verbal directions

- have limited auditory memory and may therefore be unable to follow test directions

- have short attention spans (especially for adult-directed activities) and can be distracted easily

- do not understand why they are being asked to perform in a testing situation or play games with a stranger

- may feel uncertain when their teacher's behavior changes in order to correctly administer a standardized test by using only specified directions and prompts

- are just beginning to develop the necessary eye–hand coordination to manipulate small objects or fill in answer bubbles

- are concrete thinkers who most easily demonstrate what they know through manipulation of objects, whereas tests generally use pictures and symbols

In addition, children in high-quality, developmentally appropriate programs may find the discrepancy between the everyday routines of their classrooms and the peculiarities of the testing situation confusing. They may react to the demands of the test by behaving in a way that is not typical for them.

- Have you ever administered or observed the administration of a standardized test to young children?

- How did the children respond to the testing situation?

Reflect on Your Practice

Developmentally Appropriate Assessment Practices

Standardized test results frequently do not capture the information that early childhood educators need in order to make decisions about children. Many standardized tests use multiple choice, true/false, and fill-in-the-blank items because they are easy to decipher and score. While such test items can measure some knowledge and rote recall, they less easily measure the critical thinking and problem-solving skills that are far more important to a child's overall learning and cognitive development.

Standardized tests have many features that do not align with our knowledge about developmentally appropriate assessment practices:

- Standardized tests assume that all children learn and demonstrate their knowledge at the same pace and in the same way (Gullo, 2005).

- When a child responds to a test item, we learn about the child's specific knowledge related to a particular question, but anything else the child knows about the question is not "counted" or considered relevant. As Puckett and Black state (2008; p. 65), "Each test can address only a limited universe and cannot tell us what else a child knows and can do."

- Skills are tested in isolation. Children may not understand why, for example, they are being asked to hop on one foot or draw a circle when doing so is not in a meaningful context.

- Children only receive credit for skills they can perform independently; those they can accomplish with minimal help are not counted.

Some standardized tests are unfair to certain ethnic, cultural, racial, gender, language, age, ability, and socioeconomic groups (Goodwin & Goodwin, 1997; McAfee & Leong, 2007). Many early childhood programs have diverse populations whose achievement is not reflected accurately by standardized test scores. Remember, the comparison used by norm-referenced tests is to the norming group. If the demographics of the norming group do not match the demographics of the group of children in your classroom, the conclusions drawn from the test may not be valid. A test normed on a group of middle-class children, for example, may not be appropriate for use in a Head Start program where children have very different life experiences.

Negative Effects of Standardized Tests

Using standardized tests in early childhood programs can have negative effects on children, curricula, teachers, and programs.

On children Standardized tests have a major negative impact on young children because the results of the tests can be inaccurate. When teachers use the results as the basis for decisions, they run the risk of making poor decisions. In addition to the mismatch between how young children function and the requirements of a testing situation, test results can also be inaccurate because young children's behavior—and therefore their test performance—varies from day to day. A test given on one day does not capture variation in children's development over time and sometimes does not even measure what a child knows and can do on the day of the test. Basing curricular decisions on misleading test results can negatively impact children's learning. Moreover, teachers may perceive and treat children differently because of their test scores, focusing less on individual strengths that may not be tapped by the test. Ongoing, informal methods of assessment are more effective for measuring children's actual growth and development.

Many children are asked each year to spend significant amounts of time and energy on test-preparation activities and standardized test-taking rather than on meaningful learning. Young children may experience testing as stressful, particularly when standardized tests require their teachers to interact with them in ways that are different from typical classroom situations (see chapter 12).

On teachers and the curriculum A major concern about the growing use of standardized tests is that their use results in a narrowing of the curriculum to focus primarily on the content of the test. Rather than teaching a rich curriculum, teachers "teach to the test." Teachers have less autonomy in developing learning experiences that match children's interests and skills, indirectly giving test developers greater control over the curriculum. Teachers of young children feel pushed to emphasize inappropriate academic skills and knowledge at younger ages to help "prepare" children for tests in later grades.

On programs Programs using standardized tests must spend a portion of their limited financial resources on test materials and scoring costs. Money and time are also on spent training teachers to administer the tests. Despite this investment, tests of young children are likely to deliver information that is of little use.

Misuses of Standardized Tests
Misusing a test means using the assessment instrument for a purpose that its authors did not intend. For instance, using tests of student achievement to evaluate teachers and to compare schools or districts are clear misuses of the tests. Similarly, using a screening test to assess whether or not children have made progress during the program year is misusing the test. Additionally, when tests are used with children who differ from the norming group, their results are often misleading.

Tests are often used to make "high stakes" decisions—decisions that affect a child's life. Readiness tests have been used to deny kindergarten entrance and to place children in 2-year programs before first grade. This is done despite research that shows that retention has a negative impact on development, motivation, and self-esteem (Owings & Magliaro, 1998; Marshall, 2003). Misuses of standardized tests argue against even limited use in early childhood education.

Recommendations for Using Tests Appropriately

The following six recommendations are compiled from the position statements of the National Association for the Education of Young Children (NAEYC), National Association of Early Childhood Specialists in State Departments of Education (NAECS/SDE), and Association for Childhood Education International (ACEI). They counteract some of the potentially negative effects of standardized tests (NAEYC & NAECS/SDE, 2003; Solley, 2007; NAEYC, 1987).

- Only use the test only for its intended purpose.

- Carefully review the test manual before using the test, making sure that the test has adequate reliability and validity. For norm-referenced tests, make sure the characteristics of the norming group are similar to the characteristics of the group of children you will be testing.

- Never use a single test to make important decisions, such as those concerning enrollment, retention, or eligibility for special education services. Evaluate a child's test score by comparing it with other evidence of the child's development and learning.

- Do not use group-administered, standardized tests until third or fourth grade.

- Do not use the results of standardized tests to delay entry into kindergarten or to retain children in other ways. Research on retention clearly shows that it is not an effective strategy for promoting development and learning.

- Administer the test in the language with which the child is most comfortable.

Key Ideas to Remember

- An assessment instrument can require standardized procedures without being a standardized test.

- Standardized tests use standardized procedures and meet particular technical standards related to validity, reliability, and absence of bias.

- Standardized tests can be norm-referenced or criterion-referenced.

- Group administration of standardized tests does not align well with the values and beliefs of developmentally appropriate practice for young children.

- A single standardized test should never be used to make an important decision, such as whether or not to retain a child.

- Early childhood professional organizations that have established positions on standardized testing do not recommend standardized tests for children before third or fourth grade.

References

American Educational Research Association, American Psychological Association, & National Council on Measurement in Education. (1999). *Standards for educational and psychological testing.* Washington, DC: American Psychological Association.

Goodwin, W. L., & Goodwin, L. D. (1997). Using standardized measures for evaluating young children's learning. In B. Spodek & O. N. Saracho (Eds.), *Issues in early childhood educational assessment and evaluation* (pp. 92–107). New York: Teachers College Press.

Gullo, D. F. (2005). *Understanding assessment and evaluation in early childhood education* (2nd ed.). New York: Teachers College Press.

References, *continued*

Hills, T. (1992). Reaching potentials through appropriate assessment. In S. Bredekamp & T. Rosegrant (Eds.), *Reaching potentials: Appropriate curriculum and assessment for young children* (Vol. 1, pp. 43–63). Washington, DC: National Association for the Education of Young Children.

Marshall, H. H. (2003). Opportunity deferred or opportunity taken? An updated look at delaying kindergarten entry. *Young Children, 58*(5), 84–93.

McAfee, O., & Leong, D. J. (2007). *Assessing and guiding young children's development and learning* (3rd ed.). Boston: Allyn & Bacon.

National Association for the Education of Young Children. (1987). *Standardized testing of young children 3 through 8 years of age: A position statement of the National Association for the Education of Young Children.* Washington, DC: Author.

National Association for the Education of Young Children, & National Association of Early Childhood Specialists in State Departments of Education. (2003). *Early childhood curriculum, assessment, and program evaluation: Building an effective, accountable system in programs for children birth through age 8.* Washington, DC: Authors.

Owings, W. A., & Magliaro, S. (1998). Grade retention: A history of failure. *Educational Leadership, 56*(1), 86–88.

Popham, W. J. (2011). *Classroom assessment: What teachers need to know* (6th ed.). Boston: Pearson Education.

Puckett, M. B., & Black, J. K. (2008). *Meaningful assessments of the young child* (3rd ed.). Upper Saddle River, NJ: Pearson Education.

Solley, B. A. (2007). On standardized testing: An ACEI position paper. *Childhood Education, 84*(1), 31–37.

Spies, R. A., Carlson, J. F., & Geisinger, K. F. (Eds.) (2010). *The eighteenth mental measurements yearbook.* Lincoln, NE: University of Nebraska Press.

CHAPTER 15

The Power of Assessment and You

As I wrote this book, I displayed the messages that I wanted to convey on the wall behind my desk where I could see them every time I sat down to work. In this chapter, these messages take center stage. They fall into two categories:

- the power of assessment
- how you can realize that power

The chapter concludes with some strategies for moving forward.

The Power of Assessment

As I talked with teachers about assessment, I soon realized that they frequently viewed assessment as a burden rather than an integral part of teaching that could enhance their instruction as well as their relationships with children and families. Throughout this book, I have discussed the benefits of assessment for children and families. In this last chapter, I will highlight the power of assessment for you, the early childhood teacher.

Assessment helps you teach better. Most of the teachers I talked with as I wrote this book said that systematically using assessment improved their teaching. They described how they gained a deeper understanding of child development and individual children by using assessment. Many said that studying children helped them relate to children and appreciate their struggles and accomplishments. Others explained that using assessment information to guide their teaching made them feel more professional.

I firmly believe that you cannot teach well without systematic assessment, and the teachers with whom I collaborated to write this book agree. You can create learning opportunities, present activities, and "cover" particular content. However, without consciously assessing children's learning, you will not know who benefited from the experiences you provided or whether you should change what you are doing in any way. As I said in chapter 1, learning is the centerpiece of this book because it is the axis around which all good teaching revolves.

Teachers are more effective when they are clear about *what* they are teaching and *why*. Good teachers always understand why they are doing what they are doing. When you assess children on an ongoing basis and use the information to guide your planning, you always know why you have made particular instructional choices.

Assessment can help you see children in new ways and enhance your relationships with them. For many of us, one of the most enjoyable parts of teaching is developing positive relationships with our students. Whether our students are 4 or 24 years old, it is exciting to get to know them and witness their learning. Our assessment efforts can illuminate our students' hidden qualities. We may find greater capabilities than we anticipated—such as the strengths of a child with a disability—and newly developing interests. Our knowledge influences our interactions with students and strengthens our relationships with them.

Teachers can help children take charge of their own learning by sharing assessment information with them. When teachers are open with children about their assessment findings, children have a context and strategies for thinking about their own learning. Assessment provides occasions and an arena for discussions of learning. Even very young children say they go to school "to learn." Early childhood teachers can support young children as they begin to recognize and understand their own accomplishments and direct their own learning.

Being effective assessors enhances teachers' professionalism.
As I mentioned above, many early childhood teachers have commented that they feel more professional as their assessment skills increase. Some attributed this increased self-confidence to their deepening knowledge of child development and educational standards. By using an assessment instrument over time, teachers internalize the developmental knowledge and standards underlying that tool. As one teacher of 4-year-olds said, "It helps ground me in realistic expectations for children at various stages in various areas, and it helps me align my planning with my state's early learning guidelines."

Other teachers talk about being able to contribute detailed information to discussions with families and other professionals. When teachers work as child study teams to help children who are struggling to learn, they are able to describe relevant behavior and pinpoint problems more accurately.

Assessment is intellectually satisfying. For other teachers and me, assessment is intellectually satisfying. Once I am clear about what I want college students to learn, I enjoy figuring out how I am going to collect data about their learning (i.e., how I am going to design assignments at the college level). When I read the work of a struggling student, it presents a puzzle for me to solve: What's going on, and what can I do to help that student learn?

Intellectual satisfaction is evident in the stories of the early childhood teachers who contributed to this book. William (chapter 11) found great satisfaction in figuring out how to assess Maria, a nonverbal child, because he was then able to create ways for her to participate non verbally in classroom activities. His actions opened the door to her use of expressive language. He wrote,

> As long as assessment is ongoing, authentic, and reflected upon, it is intellectually rewarding. The teacher and the family are researchers who study how the child learns and who identify patterns and relationships between that particular child and how children typically learn. Then we use the information to refine our approach, planning, and follow-through. There are many benefits to authentic assessment.

Realizing the Power of Assessment

If you are a new early childhood teacher or just beginning to use assessment systematically, you may be wondering how you can harness the power of assessment. Here are some strategies to enhance your ability to use assessment to benefit children and your teaching.

Commit to being an accurate and effective assessor. You can choose to devote time and effort to assessment so that it becomes an integrated and reflexive part of your teaching. Assessment is as much a part of teaching as lesson planning is a part. In fact, because teaching and assessing go hand-in-hand, your assessment tasks should be written into your plans. You will know that you have internalized the power of assessment when you realize that you cannot develop a new approach to teaching, say, the properties of shapes, without thinking about how you will also assess children's learning through those activities.

Realize that it takes time to learn new assessment methods. Many teachers report that it takes about a year to learn to use a new assessment tool. It is only after they have mastered the basics of an assessment system that they can integrate it smoothly into their teaching. You may try some strategies that do not work for you. Sometimes the methods that work for the teacher next door will not work for you. You have to select strategies on the basis of your work style and your classroom. You can expect a period of trial and error as you learn or modify ways to assess children's development and learning.

Monitor your development as an assessor. As you gain confidence about assessing young children, assess your own skills. One approach is to revisit the assessment cycle:

- **Ask questions** Are you using assessment information effectively? What are you doing well? Are you learning about all of your children? Are you gathering information about all areas? Are you sharing information clearly with families? Are you talking with children about what they are learning?

- **Collect data** At the end of the year, take some time to look at the information you collected and the reports you wrote about children. Did you have the information you needed?

- **Interpret data** While things are still fresh in your mind, make notes about what your assessment experiences during the past year tell you. Perhaps you stopped filing matrices and later found them in several spots around your classroom. Maybe children's portfolios became unorganized during the last 10 weeks. You might have learned that you are very good at collecting data on literacy but less thorough about math. What do you want to do differently next year?

- **Take action** Whatever you learn by thinking about your assessment experiences, plan for next year. Write some goals for ways in which you would like to improve. Note new strategies to try.

Keep reflecting on your methods and approach to assessment. Talk with colleagues about strategies that work for them. Just as most teachers are never perfectly satisfied with their teaching, most are never entirely satisfied with their assessment procedures. Let self-knowledge fuel your drive to continue to learn about assessment.

Use what you learn. The last—and most important—way to realize the power of assessment is to use what you learn about children. Unless you take action based on what you learn, assessment will just be paperwork. If you do not do anything with the results of your assessment, you may as well not do it. The power of assessment lies in what smart, sensitive, caring teachers do with assessment information to benefit children and families.

Where Do You Go From Here?

Like many other aspects of teaching, assessment takes time, awareness, and commitment. As a professional, you realize that your assessment skills will need to be updated over time if you are to continue to have a high level of assessment competence. By attending conferences, reading professional journals, collaborating with other early childhood educators, and otherwise furthering your education, you can remain current about assessment issues and approaches to early childhood assessment.

Most importantly, let your curiosity about children guide you. Talk with children! Teachers' conversations with children can help children think about their learning while helping teachers in their roles as assessors. Daily conversations help you get to know each child. They give you insights about how the child thinks and processes information, and they help you learn about the child's experiences. When they occur regularly, brief, spontaneous interactions are a cornerstone of our relationships with children. As we build our knowledge of each child over time, we learn what excites and motivates each, and we begin to get an idea of how the child views him- or herself. Teachers' interactions with children have a major impact on children's development and learning (Pianta, 2003).

Our knowledge about each child informs our teaching and assessment practices. When we learn that Alfonso's mother went to the hospital last night to deliver her baby, we know that today is probably not the best day to observe his social skills because he is tired and excited. However, it might be an especially good time to read a story about having a new baby in the family. The more we know about a child, the more we can tailor teaching and assessment to that child's current needs and interests.

Teachers of infants and toddlers also have conversations with children. Many of these exchanges are not entirely verbal; only the adult speaks. Any time adults take turns communicating verbally or non verbally with an infant or toddler, they are, in effect, conversing with the child. These conversations can help the teacher get to know the baby.

> Shelley, a toddler teacher, was sitting next to Madison (18 months), who threw a block and then looked at Shelley. When this happened a second time, Shelley brought out a basket of balls and said, "It looks as though you want to practice throwing." Then they took turns throwing balls for a while. Infant–toddler teachers often interpret children's actions and gestures as beginnings of conversations.

As teachers observe, they frequently get so caught up in what they are seeing and hearing that they forget that they can talk with children when they have questions about children's behavior. Of course, conversations with infants and some toddlers will not yield a great deal of information, but preschoolers and kindergarten children can show remarkable insight about their own activities. For example, when Sara has written in her journal lately, she has made strings of letters to accompany her very detailed drawings. Today, when you get to her table, you observe that she is scribbling in her journal with a variety of colored pencils. At that moment, you could do one of two things: You could simply observe for a while and not necessarily find out why she is scribbling, or you could ask her about what she is doing. In fact, when asked, Sara says, "I wrote a message to my mommy, but I had to cover it up so it would stay secret." Without this information—information that could only come from the child—you would only know that today Sara scribbled in her journal.

Regardless of the assessment tool or method you use, cultivate the attitude of persistent curiosity discussed in chapter 1. Work actively to learn about your children, how they learn, what motivates them, what they are interested in, and how they express their knowledge. Let your interest in children suggest questions. Let your appreciation of children guide your data collection and interpretation. Let your commitment to young children and their families spur you to act on the basis of evidence so that they benefit from your improved teaching.

Reference

Pianta, R. C. (2003). *Standardized classroom observation from pre-k to 3rd grade: A mechanism for improving access to consistently high quality classroom experiences and practices during the p-3 years.* Retrieved March, 12, 2010, from http://www.fcd-us.org/sites/default/files/StandardizedClassroomObservations.pdf